Oxford
International
Lower Secondary

Science

Teacher's Guide

Alyssa Fox-Charles

Anna Harris

Jo Locke

OXFORD

Contents

Working scientifically 6

Biology 20

Chemistry 80

Chemistry

Physics — 158

Introduction

The joy of learning science

We are living in an ever-changing world, where the way we work, live, learn, communicate, and relate to one another is constantly shifting. In this climate, we need to instil in our learners the skills to equip them for every eventuality so they are able to overcome challenges, adapt to change, and have the best chance of success. To do this, we need to evolve beyond traditional teaching approaches and foster an environment where students can start to build lifelong learning skills. Students need to learn how to learn, problem-solve, be agile, and work flexibly. Going hand in hand with this is the development of self-awareness and mindfulness through the promotion of wellbeing to ensure students learn the socio-emotional skills to succeed.

Teaching and learning with *Oxford International Lower Secondary Science*

This series is suitable for use alongside the Oxford International Curriculum and the English National Curriculum. The books for each year (or stage) follow the scheme and meet all the learning objectives for both curricula – including Working scientifically. Objectives are written in student-friendly language in the Student Book.

The teaching units in the series are flexible: they can be adapted to meet the needs of your students. Each unit stands alone and can be taught in any order.

This series is designed for students aged 11 to 14. Each year has a **Student Book** and a **Teacher's Guide**. There are also numerous digital resources and sources of support on www.kerboodle.com. Underpinning the rationale for the series is the strong belief that science provides a way of thinking and working. It helps us make sense of the world and provides intellectual skills that help us in all curriculum areas and in life.

This series has seven main aims:

1 to deliver scientific knowledge and facts

2 to deliver scientific understanding

3 to deliver scientific methods of enquiry

4 to deliver scientific thinking and reasoning

5 to help students understand the development of science and its uses in context in the world around them

6 to support the wellbeing of students

7 to give students a global outlook.

1 Scientific knowledge and facts

The Student Book introduces concepts in a logical sequence and ensures that new ideas are introduced sensitively and explained clearly. Students are then asked to discuss and apply their new knowledge.

2 Scientific understanding

Knowledge without understanding is only useful for recall. Understanding moves to a deeper intellectual level and enables students to think and apply that knowledge.

Effective learning requires students to develop appropriate attitudes, skills, and enthusiasm, and this can be encouraged by good teaching and exciting resources. Through effective learning, students can gain an understanding of the principles and practice of science.

It is important to consider underpinning ideas that have informed good practice in the classroom:

- Teaching approach
- Cognitive style
- Active learning

Teaching approach

The kind of teaching strategies used are key to achieving understanding. Telling and giving students information is important, but only improves their short-term memory of scientific facts. This is often called 'passive learning' as students are not intellectually engaged in the process.

Teaching and learning can either be teacher-centred (didactic) or student-centred (heuristic). Good teaching is a combination of these. The table on the opposite page summarizes the advantages and disadvantages of both approaches.

Cognitive style

Cognitive style is a student's personal and preferred way of organizing and representing information. Their chosen way of thinking determines how they see and make sense of the world.

There are four cognitive styles:

1 wholists like to see the 'big picture' when learning

2 analysts prefer to focus on one or two details

3 verbalizers welcome opportunities to talk through problems

4 imagers see mental pictures when processing information.

Advantages	Advantages
• Clear learning objectives • Teacher can demonstrate a professional approach (e.g. presentations) • Teacher is seen as 'expert' • Fewer problems with classroom management and behaviour	• Can be motivating and powerful • Develops a range of skills • Learning is relevant • Encourages creativity and problem-solving • Student has a say in the learning
Teacher-centred (didactic) ⟵⟶	**Student-centred (heuristic)**
Disadvantages	Disadvantages
• May build on inaccurate knowledge • May not be motivating • Does not develop skills • Does not give students responsibility • Limited by the teacher	• May not deal with underlying principles – too pragmatic • If only existing skills are learned, this approach may not encourage questioning of existing approaches • Lack of structure may confuse • Classroom management may be problematic

Advantages and disadvantages of teacher-centred and student-centred approaches (Cotton, J., 1995, *The theory of learning: an introduction*, Kogan Page, London) © Kogan Page 1995. Reproduced with permission of the Licensor through PLSclear.

Most people are a combination of all of these cognitive styles, but have a preference for one or two. We need to be aware of the possible cognitive styles of our students and ensure that our approach balances all four styles.

Benjamin Bloom proposed an 'educational taxonomy', identifying different learning 'domains':

- Cognitive (knowledge)
- Affective (attitudes)
- Psychomotor (skills)

The domain can be seen as a ladder that starts with remembering and proceeds to more complex tasks such as analysing, as follows:

1 Recall data

2 Understand

3 Apply (use)

4 Analyse

5 Synthesize

6 Evaluate

This ladder will help you devise tasks, sequences of tasks, and level-appropriate questions for your students. Considering this will help develop your students' ability to think and reason.

Active learning

Active learning is an approach in which students are encouraged to engage with material through activities that promote participation and interaction. Students are active participants in their learning rather than passively taking in information. They are encouraged to develop skills that they may not develop during teacher-centred (didactic) lessons.

As well as deepening students' understanding of key concepts and ideas, active learning methodologies often heighten class enthusiasm and bring the joy of learning to the forefront of lessons. When students are motivated to learn and facilitate activities themselves, they will learn better.

Active learning strategies include, but aren't limited to:

- group discussion (talking and listening)
- active reading
- active writing
- presentation
- role-play and drama
- information technology
- visits, visitors, and field trips
- data handling
- problem-solving
- video and audio tape recording
- games and simulations.

Whole-class instruction can be as effective as individual instruction, especially in terms of the time students spend on tasks. The table on the next page summarizes common teaching approaches to promote active learning. It does not indicate poor teaching on the left (teacher-centred) and good teaching on the right (student-centred).

The Student Book presents ideas in a range of ways: written, diagrams, charts, tables, and photographs. The lessons contain a rich variety of learning and teaching approaches, such as individual reading and writing, paired and small-group discussion work, whole-class discussion and activity, problem-solving, investigations, research activities, presentations, and review and reflection.

Teacher-centred learning	Student-centred learning
Teacher exposition	Group work
Accent on competition	Accent on cooperation
Whole-class teaching	Resource-based learning
Teacher responsible for learning	Students more responsible for learning
Teacher providing knowledge	Teacher as guide/facilitator
Students seen as empty vessels which need filling	Students have ownership of ideas and work
Subject knowledge valued	Process skills are valued
Teacher-imposed discipline	Self-discipline
Teacher and student roles emphasized	Students seen as source of knowledge and ideas
Teacher decides the curriculum	Students involved in curriculum planning
Passive student roles	Students actively involved in learning
Limited range of learning styles and activities	Wide range of learning styles employed

Select a variety of approaches to promote active learning.

3 Scientific methods of enquiry

This series promotes scientific enquiry and closely follows the Working scientifically objectives in the English National Curriculum. Students are encouraged to use and reflect on the different ways that scientists work and think, which have produced the knowledge, theories, and laws of science over the last 1000 years. It is based on 'empiricism' – arriving at knowledge and understanding through observation and experiment.

Scientists progress through observation and questioning what they see and already know. From this, they make hypotheses, which they test in experiments, and develop new knowledge. This will be further explored in the 'Being a scientist' pages in this Teacher's Guide and in the Student Books.

This series allows students to work scientifically by addressing each of the appropriate scientific enquiry processes at each stage. Students are encouraged to plan and carry out full-scale investigations in the later stages, applying the skills learned earlier.

4 Scientific thinking and reasoning

It is essential to encourage students to think and reason for themselves. Their ability to think, reason, and research will make them independent learners who can interpret and understand new ideas quickly. This aspect of education is often neglected.

In this series, the ability to think and reason will be encouraged, nurtured, practised, and assessed at each level. Scientists use logical thinking to make sound inferences, taking them from the known to discover the unknown. They use reason and argument based on fact and evidence to prove their case. By experiencing these processes through 'discovery learning', students will similarly experience the thrill of finding out.

Resist the temptation to provide answers, solutions, and too much support for your students. We hope that the learning activities within the Student Book, and the support provided in the Teacher's Guide, will help you create a learning environment where students can plan, find out, and learn new ideas themselves – with you as a guide and facilitator. Allow them time to think and discuss ideas before gently guiding those who need support.

5 Science in context

It is vital to link what students learn in the classroom to the real world. This makes their learning relevant and helps them relate new ideas to their own experience.

Stress that science involves an ongoing process of change and improvement in ideas. Explain that our ideas about science are built on earlier ideas, and that people in the past could only use what they knew at the time to make sense of the world. Sometimes this meant they put forward ideas that scientists now know are not correct. For example, many people thought that the world was flat, and the Sun orbited Earth.

Emphasize that some early thinkers created ideas that are still remarkably similar to our modern ideas. For example, over 2200 years ago, Aristarchus suggested Earth orbits the Sun. Democritus stated that matter is made up of smaller particles more than 2300 years ago. Even our understanding of forces, based on Isaac Newton's laws of motion, was proposed by Philoponus over 1500 years ago.

Explain that science theories develop when a person or a team puts forward new ideas. If other scientists test these ideas and agree, then the idea becomes a part of science theory. It could change later with new evidence. This is how ideas develop.

Explain that developing new technologies and materials also helps form new science ideas. For example, until the invention of the microscope 500 years ago, scientists could not see microorganisms and did not know they existed. Improvements in telescopes have resulted in changing ideas about the stars and even our nearest planets. Modern materials have allowed spacecraft and computers to be made.

The activities in each lesson provide you with many opportunities to relate the science content and processes to the real world.

6 Wellbeing

The series provides opportunities for you to consider the vital importance of wellbeing and to weave this into your teaching. The enquiry-based approach encourages curiosity and helps students explore the world around them. Wellbeing does not mean feeling happy all of the time. Making mistakes, feeling challenged, and even being confused at times can help to develop resilience.

This series supports wellbeing directly by:

- **Providing questions** This challenges and engages students. They can reflect on prior learning and apply new skills.
- **Promoting group work** This gives students the opportunity to develop their collaborative skills. Growth through practice builds confidence.
- **Presenting stretch zone challenges** This encourages students to develop thinking skills and welcome challenge. In each chapter of the Student Book, the 'stretch zone' icons in the 'Summary questions' sections signpost where students will be stretched and challenged to think more deeply and apply their understanding of the topic. This kind of practice will support students to move away from their comfort zone into the stretch zone without worrying.
- **Offering mindful moments** This provides opportunities for students to pause and re-focus their attention. In the Student Book, the 'What have I learned?' pages promote metacognition (students' ability to think about their own thought processes). These pages empower students to quietly reflect on their learning so far and how they learn best.

Teachers are encouraged to develop the following approaches:

- **Provide praise with a growth mindset** Praise students' process rather than their intelligence or marks. Giving positive feedback on how something is being done is highly effective. This includes praising effort, perseverance, resilience, teamwork, strategies, etc.
- **Discuss and evaluate mistakes** Learning always involves making mistakes. Students should not fear or worry about mistakes. They should see them as opportunities to learn.

7 A global outlook

This series is designed to address the idea that academic lifelong success is the result of both academic performance and emotional wellbeing. As educators, we want to prepare our students for a workplace that is unknown to us. Ideas and activities identify areas where students can develop real-world skills while feeling safe and confident enough to apply themselves to the content of the lessons.

Teaching techniques for this series

Science learning is made up of remembering science facts, gaining scientific knowledge, developing science skills, and developing science understanding.

Facts are important, but being told facts does not ensure knowledge and understanding. Working out science problems and engaging with scientific processes is much more likely to help students develop understanding. This is why applying scientific skills – *doing* science rather than *remembering* it – is vital.

This series aims to provide science facts and knowledge but also science understanding. Certain strategies are better at teaching understanding than others.

Effective questioning is the key

Research tells us that teachers ask up to 400 questions per day, which can amount to 30 per cent of teaching time. Improving questioning techniques will therefore have an important impact on learning.

Consider your own practice:

- why you are asking a question
- what type of questions you ask
- when you ask questions
- how you ask questions
- who you ask questions to
- how you expect questions to be answered
- how you respond if a student does not understand the question
- how you react to an inappropriate or wrong answer
- how you react to an appropriate answer
- how long you wait for an answer.

Teachers ask questions for a number of reasons:

- to get attention
- to check students are paying attention
- to check understanding
- to reinforce or revise a topic
- to increase understanding
- to encourage thinking
- to develop a discussion.

Bloom describes six levels of thought process:

1 Knowledge

2 Comprehension

3 Application

4 Analysis

5 Synthesis

6 Evaluation

We need to ask questions that encourage deeper thinking. If we only ask questions at the knowledge end of the spectrum, we will not encourage students to analyse or synthesize new ideas.

We also need to think about the nature and style of questions. Two major categories are closed and open.

Closed questions

These tend to have only one or a limited range of correct answers. They require factual recall. They are useful for whole-group question and answer sessions, to quickly check learning or refresh memory, or as a link to new work. For example:

Question: What is the boiling point of water?

Answer: 100 °C.

Closed questions are very good for knowledge recall but are generally non-productive regarding anything else.

Open questions

These may have several possible answers, making it difficult to decide which are correct. They are used to develop understanding and encourage students to think about issues and ideas. We are not looking for a single right answer; we are looking for what the student thinks may be the right answer. Once you get the student thinking, you can use this information to move the learning on towards the right answer, while promoting understanding at the same time. For example:

Question: Where do you think the water in rain clouds comes from?

Answer: Any answer will have a little 'rightness' in it that the teacher can use. The student may answer 'From the sea'.

You can then follow several lines of enquiry to extend the learning. For example, 'Do you know of any other places the water might have come from?' or 'How do you think that the water got into the clouds?'.

These follow-up 'how' and 'why' questions encourage students to think more deeply about key scientific ideas and principles.

Question sequence

In this series we promote an 'enquiring classroom' where closed questions are used, but also open questions which promote enquiring minds.

Closed and open questions can be linked together to form a question sequence. A question sequence must be well planned but can lead to much improved understanding. Start with a few easy factual closed questions and move towards more open questions. This is known as 'agenda building'. At the same time, you can move from individual to paired and then to small-group discussion as the questions become more open and demand higher-level thinking.

Differentiation

Differentiation is closely linked to inclusion: ensuring all students have access to the curriculum. This means that learning and teaching approaches must consider individual needs. Not all students will learn at the same pace or in the same ways.

This series supports the following approaches:

- **Differentiation by task** Content can be adjusted for some students to provide sufficient support or adequate challenge. Examples are activities and 'stretch zone' questions in the Student Book. The latter are designed to extend more confident students and challenge them to think more deeply. For less able students, prioritize the in-text questions after each section of text. They will be able to find the correct answers in the text they have just read.

- **Differentiation by outcome** This allows all students to tackle the same tasks, but with differentiated learning outcomes – usually in terms of 'All students should … ', 'Most students will … ', and 'Some students may … '. The differentiated outcomes are provided for each lesson in this Teacher's Guide.

- **Differentiating the process** This means providing more or less support as students are carrying out a task. Advice on this is provided for each lesson in this Teacher's Guide.

- **Questioning** This is a very effective way of differentiating work. Use questions to check progress and decide when extra support or challenge is needed. Summary questions are designed to progress from low on Bloom's taxonomy (remember and understand) towards higher levels (analyse and evaluate).

- **Varied approaches to assessment** The resources include a wide range of assessment methods. These include verbal, written, and drawn responses, as well as individual and collaborative assessments.

Assessment

Assessment is an essential part of learning. Without being able to check progress, teachers and students will not be able to identify areas of strength and areas in need of development.

Assessment can be classified as either formative or summative.

Formative assessment

This takes place during learning and is used to address issues as they arise. This means learning and teaching can be modified during lessons to better meet students' needs. Feedback is ongoing.

Each activity within the Student Book provides opportunities for formative assessment and feedback. You can do this by listening to discussions or presentations; observing the outputs of investigations; and assessing outcomes such as posters, reports, and leaflets. Individual questions in discussion tasks can be used to monitor understanding and identify misconceptions. These can be addressed as they are noted. Questions are suggested for each lesson in the 'Review and reflect' sections in this Teacher's Guide.

Summative assessment

This is used to measure or evaluate student progress at the end of a process – for example, when a unit is completed or at the end of a year. Summative assessment compares students' attainment against a standard or benchmark.

The 'What have I learned?' pages at the end of each chapter can be used for summative assessment. You can record which questions each student is answering correctly and use this to measure individual attainment. It can also indicate how well the class is progressing though the work. In this way, the assessment can inform individual interventions (extra support for a student) or whole-class interventions (reviewing work that is not well understood).

Each activity – group and individual – can be assessed through observation, questioning, and progress notes. Written or drawn responses for each activity can be assessed/marked using the school's marking policy; and unit, end-of-term, and end-of-year judgements made about individual and class progress.

Feedback is a crucial aspect of assessment. This should be as positive and encouraging as possible, in which clear targets are identified. Involve students in assessment and target setting – assessment is done *with* learners not done *to* learners.

How to support non-native English speakers

Ministries of Education at both local and national level are increasingly adopting the policy of English Medium Instruction (EMI), for either one or two subjects or across the whole curriculum. The rationale for doing so varies according to the local context, but improving the levels of achievement in English is usually an important factor.

In international schools, it is likely that students do not share a mother tongue with each other or perhaps the teacher. English is, therefore, chosen as the medium of instruction to level the playing field and to provide the opportunity to develop proficiency in an international language.

This does not mean that the science teacher is expected to replace the English teacher, or to have the same skills or knowledge of English. However, it does mean that the science teacher needs to become more language aware.

This raises significant challenges, including:
- the teacher's knowledge of English
- students' level of English (which may vary considerably in international schools)
- resources which provide language support
- assessment tools which ensure that it is the content and not the language which is being tested
- differentiation which acknowledges different levels of proficiency in both language and content.

Language in the classroom

Often non-native-speaker teachers are more concerned about their ability to run and manage the whole class in English than they are about the actual teaching of science. This series should help you with the latter. However, using English in the classroom is very important as it provides exposure to an additional language (often a student's second or third), which plays a valuable role in language acquisition. The 'teacher talk' for purposes such as checking attendance and collecting homework does not have to be totally accurate or accessible to students.

When teaching scientific concepts, however, it is essential that the 'teacher talk' is comprehensible. The following strategies can help to ensure this:
- simplify your language
- use short, simple sentences and project your voice
- paraphrase as necessary
- use visuals, the board, gestures, and body language to clarify meaning
- repeat as necessary
- plan before the lesson
- prepare clear, simple instructions and check understanding.

Creating a language-rich environment

Providing a colourful and visually stimulating environment for students becomes even more important in the EMI classroom. Posters, lists of key words and structures, displays of students' work, and signs and notices in English all maximize students' exposure to English and, in big or small ways, contribute to their language acquisition.

Planning

In your planning, identify what the Language Demands are. You will need to think about what language students will need to understand or produce, and decide how best to scaffold the learning to ensure that language does not become an obstacle to understanding the concept. This kind of Language Support goes beyond the familiar strategy of identifying key vocabulary.

Support for listening and reading

Listening and reading are receptive skills, requiring understanding rather than production of language.

If students need to listen to or read texts in English, ask yourself the following questions:

1. Do I need to teach any vocabulary before they listen/read?

2. How can I prepare them for the content of the text so that they are not listening 'cold'?

3. Can I provide visual support to help them understand the key content?

4. How many times should I ask them to listen/read?

5. What simple question can I set before they listen/read for the first time to focus their attention?

6. How can I check more detailed understanding of the text? Can I use a graphic organizer (e.g. tables, charts, or diagrams) or a gap-fill task?

7. Do I need to differentiate the task for less able and more able students?

8. Can I make the tasks interactive (e.g. jigsaw reading – when students access different information before coming together and sharing their learning with each other)?

9. How can I check their answers and give feedback?

Support for speaking and writing

Speaking and writing are productive skills and may need more language input from the teacher, who has to decide what language students will need to complete the task and how best to provide this. When you plan to use a task which requires students to produce English verbally or in writing, you will need to think about how to help them.

This means that you have to think in detail about what language the task requires (Language Demands) and what strategies you will use to help students use English to perform the task (Language Support).

Ask yourself the following questions:

1. What vocabulary does the task require? (LD)

2. Do I need to teach this before they start? How? (LS)

3. What phrases/sentences will they need?
   Think about the language for learning science (e.g. predicting and comparing). What structures do they need for these language functions? (LD)

4. While I am monitoring this task, is there any way I can provide further support for their use of English (especially for less confident students)? (LS)

5. What language will students need to use at the feedback stage (e.g. when they present their task)? Do I need to scaffold this? (LD, LS)

Teaching vocabulary and structures

Vocabulary

Learning key science vocabulary is central to EMI, and 'learning' means more than simply understanding the meaning. Knowing a word also involves being able to pronounce it accurately and use it appropriately. Aim to adopt the following strategies:

- Avoid writing a vocabulary list on the board at the start of the chapter and 'explaining' it. The vocabulary should be introduced as and when it arises. This helps students associate the word or phrase with the concept and context.

- Record the vocabulary clearly on the board. Check that you are confident with pronunciation and spelling.

- Give students a chance to say the word once they have understood it. The most efficient way to do this is through repetition drilling.

- Use visuals whenever possible to reinforce students' understanding of the word.

- Ensure students are recording the vocabulary systematically in their glossaries and, if possible, use a 'word wall' which lists key words under headings.

- Remember to recycle and revise the vocabulary.

Structures

Students will need to go beyond vocabulary to discuss or write about their learning in science. They will also need to use phrases and sentence frames that are relevant to a particular task. For example, they may need the following expressions in science:

I predict that X will happen.

If X happens, then Y happens.

The next step is …

You will need to build up these banks of common science phrases and encourage students to record them. This is an important part of identifying the Language Demands and providing the necessary support. You do not have to focus on grammar here as the language can be taught as 'chunks' rather than specific grammatical structures.

Language support in *Oxford International Lower Secondary Science*

The Student Book supports language development by clearly identifying and making bold the key words in each lesson. The combination of words and pictures or diagrams on these pages will also help students make connections between the two, and consolidate their understanding of the meaning of words and phrases. The glossary is also of vital importance in helping students understand new vocabulary.

Each section of the teaching notes linked to a particular activity or lesson also provides language support. Detailed and specific advice is provided for key words vital for scientific literacy. A range of strategies are suggested, including games and activities to define or explain words; using similar words to explain meaning; and exploring prefixes, suffixes, and word origin.

The following key principles underpin language support in this series:

- words should be introduced and explained carefully in context
- repetition is vital
- words should be linked to pictures or actions
- students should develop their own glossaries
- the learning of vocabulary should be fun
- language should not be a barrier to learning.

Not all students will understand ideas and concepts at the same rate and there is likely to be variation in language skills. The Student Book pages are set out to be easy to follow and use, but there are also suggestions for further work and activities in this Teacher's Guide. These will help you differentiate the learning and provide alternative learning opportunities. The advice about pair and group work will be particularly valuable in helping you to meet individual needs.

Component overview

Student Books

The Student Books are textbooks for students to read and use. They include everything you need to deliver the course to your students, guide their activities, and assess their progress.

Student Book	Typical student age range
Student Book 7	Age 11–12
Student Book 8	Age 12–13
Student Book 9	Age 13–14

Teacher's Guides

There are three Teacher's Guides, corresponding to the three Student Books. Each Teacher's Guide includes:

- an introduction with advice about delivering science and using the Student Books
- a brief lesson plan for every lesson in each Student Book
- model answers to the activities and investigations, and answers to the assessment activities.

Digital

Kerboodle Online Learning (www.kerboodle.co.uk) provides engaging Kerboodle Online Books, lesson resources, and a comprehensive assessment package.

- **For the teacher:** You can access the Student Books and Teacher's Guides online in eBook format. The Online Books show the course content on screen, making it easier for you to deliver engaging lessons. You can set homework and assessments through the Assessment system and track progress using the Markbook. A set of tools is available with the Online Book so you can make notes. You can choose to share your notes with students or hide them from view. You can also upload your own resources so that everything can be accessed from one location.
- **For the students:** Teachers can allocate the Online Books to the students for use at home. The Online Books include interactive activities and videos. A set of tools is available with the Online Book – student notes can only be accessed by the individual.

Resources

- Videos – on the topics in each chapter
- Interactive quick quizzes – formative assessment that can be taken individually or as a class, and can be taken multiple times
- Activity sheets, Practical sheets, Information sheets, and Support sheets
- Teacher and technician notes – provides further support on setting up activities and practicals, answer keys, and a list of resources required by technicians
- Glossaries and glossary quizzes
- Curriculum mapping to the English National Curriculum
- Guidance on how the series supports progression to further study at iGCSE
- Letters to parents to introduce the series and offer guidance on how to support their student at home

Assessment

You can import class registers and create user accounts for your students. Once your classes are set up, you can assign students assessments to do at home, independently, or as a group.

- Interactive end of chapter tests – one per chapter that can only be taken once
- End of chapter assessments – available as downloadable PDFs
- End of chapter assessment answers and mark schemes

Markbook

This provides reporting functionality that will help you keep track of your students' results. It includes both automatically marked assessments and work that needs to be marked by you. Results from the interactive end of chapter tests are saved to the student's Markbook.

Subscription options

There are whole-school or teacher-only subscriptions. Visit www.oxfordsecondary.com/international-science to find out more.

Tour of a Student Book

Unit opener

This asks some important questions that students will find the answers to in the unit, and shows students the key topics they will study.

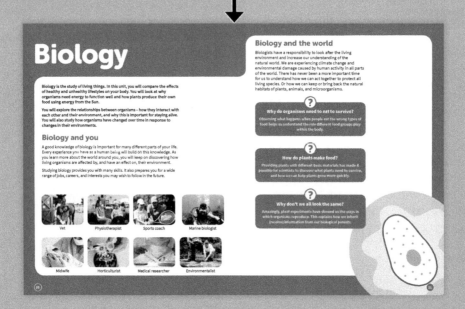

Chapter opener

This reminds students what they already know, and shows them what is coming up in the chapter. It also shows students the Working scientifically and Maths skills that they will learn. The 'Learning journey' map shows how far through the unit students have progressed.

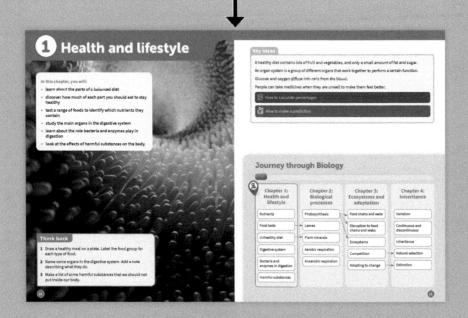

Lesson pages

These pages guide students through a particular topic in each chapter. Organized under headings, language is clear and accessible to ensure students' understanding of the key ideas. The key idea and key words in each lesson are presented clearly. Images, tables, and diagrams are included to complement the text and to support visual learners to grasp the scientific concepts. Skills boxes, in-text questions, and 'Summary questions' can then be used to check students' understanding of what they have just read and to stretch their thinking further.

Learning objectives for the lesson are clearly set out at the start and summarized in the Key idea box at the end.

Think back boxes remind students of prior learning.

Key words boxes show the main science vocabulary for the lesson.

The student-friendly text is accessible for English language learners. Simplified language guides students through scientific concepts without difficulty. Where complex scientific words are needed, a brief explanation or synonym is included in parentheses.

What have I learned? pages

These pages summarize the content that students have learned so far and show their progress through the unit. Each chapter concludes with exam-style questions to test how well students have learned and understood the topics.

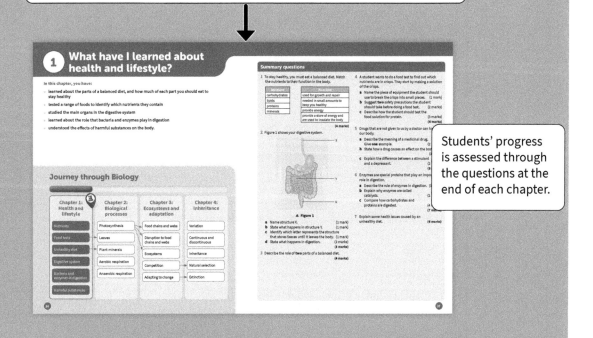

Students' progress is assessed through the questions at the end of each chapter.

Strategies for effective learning

Metacognition: A review

Metacognition refers to the understanding a student has about their own learning processes. This includes their knowledge of tasks that they may face and the strategies they have available to use, as well as knowledge of themselves as a learner.

The seven-step approach

The following seven-step approach helps teach metacognitive skills.

1. Activate prior knowledge
2. Explicit strategy instruction
3. Modelling of learned strategy
4. Memorization of strategy
5. Guided practice
6. Independent practice
7. Structured reflection

This approach allows students to learn about a strategy in relative isolation. If introducing students to the EVERY method outlined in the Student Book, you would do it in the context of a very simple calculation. You would also use an example that they are very familiar with. This removes the extra cognitive load of unfamiliar science content.

A key aspect of this approach is modelling. Metacognitive modelling is where the focus is on demonstrating how an expert learner would approach a task by verbalizing your inner thought processes. For example, you could answer a question 'live' in front of the class. This helps students because they are learning about how an expert learner plans, monitors, and evaluates their own learning.

A question tree (see Figure 1) is a tool that can complement the modelling process. For example, when completing circuit calculations, it is common for values to be placed on a circuit diagram. Then students need to choose which values are needed for a calculation. The question tree in Figure 1 summarizes how students should approach the task.

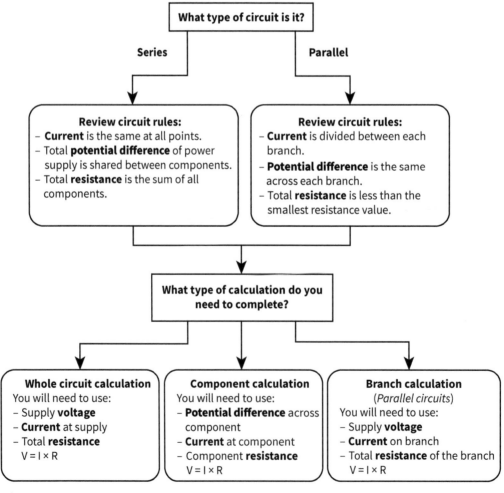

▲ **Figure 1** A question tree for completing circuit calculations.

Scenario: You would like to introduce some independent study strategies and think graphic organizers would be appropriate.

Task	Suggested graphic organizers	
grouping, classifying, or summarizing your ideas	spider diagram	concept map
sequencing events or ordering ideas	cycle circle	flowchart
making links between ideas	fishbone	bridge
making comparisons	Venn diagram	Is / Isn't T chart

▲ **Table 1** Different types of graphic organizer and when to use them.

Seven-step approach: Table 2 illustrates how the seven-step approach can be used to introduce independent study strategies.

1. **Activate prior knowledge**	The teacher reviews key content relating to the topic with the class, using low-stakes quizzes, topic maps, and some independent reading.
2. **Explicit strategy instruction**	The teacher explores the different types of graphic organizer and examples of when each would be used. They talk through the table in the Student Book and ask students what scientific content each one could be useful for. They explore why graphic organizers are useful in each case.
3. **Modelling of learned strategy**	The teacher identifies a topic to translate into a graphic organizer, and models how they approach condensing the information and selecting the key information. At all stages, the teacher is explicitly explaining why they are doing what they are doing.
4. **Memorization of strategy**	The students are given time to note down the strategy. The teacher moves around the room, questioning students to see if they understand how to use the strategy and why it is effective.
5. **Guided practice**	The teacher hands out a partially completed graphic organizer and some topic information to fill it with. When finished, the class compares it to a WAGOLL (what a good one looks like) on the board.
6. **Independent practice**	In the next lesson, students are given time to create a different type of graphic organizer. This will allow them to practise the skill of translating scientific content into the simplified structure.
7. **Structured reflection**	At the end of the lesson, the class reflects on whether the graphic organizers they have made are effective. They also reflect on their use of the graphic organizers and how they can use them for revision.

▲ **Table 2** A seven-step approach for introducing independent study strategies.

Using strategies effectively

Expert learners approach new and unfamiliar tasks in a structured way. Often they will start by studying the question or task, thinking carefully about what subject knowledge they are going to need or whether they have seen something similar before.

During a task, an expert learner will keep checking to make sure they are focusing on the right thing by regularly looking back at the question. Sometimes they may even decide to start the task again and choose a different approach. After they have finished, an expert learner will reflect on their work by thinking about any areas of improvement and what they would do differently next time.

The Plan, Monitor, Evaluate cycle is a structure you can follow to help you approach a new task like an expert learner. The cycle should be used every time you complete a task.

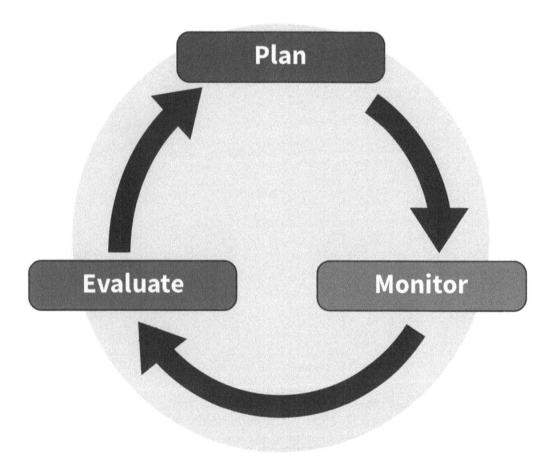

Talk about ...

Discuss with a partner your answers to these questions:

- When does the planning phase take place?
- How can you monitor your progress during the monitoring phase?
- Why is the evaluation phase important?

Supporting students to plan, monitor, and evaluate

Once students are familiar with the strategies they have available to them, this part of the Student Book aims to help them use these strategies effectively. It outlines what they should be doing when planning, monitoring, and evaluating their learning. But what does this look like in the classroom?

When introducing a new strategy using the seven-step approach, students will have an opportunity to complete independent practice. At this stage, they could use a checklist to help them regulate their learning. This is a series of questions that guide students through each of the plan, monitor, and evaluate phases. When first introducing the checklists, it may be more appropriate to focus on one of these phases rather than the whole checklist. Or it may be appropriate to have the whole class reflect on the questions as a group when completing their independent practice, rather than reflecting on the questions individually.

If we take the example of using the seven-step approach to teach the use of graphic organizers, here are some examples of the types of regulatory checklist that you could use with students:

Plan	Monitor	Evaluate
• How do you feel about completing this task? Confident or unsure? • Do you have a good understanding of the scientific content you are reviewing? If not, what can you do to change this? • Which type of graphic organizer suits the information you need to summarize? • Have you used a graphic organizer like this before? What did success look like? • Have you identified the key information that needs to be included in your graphic organizer?	• Are you doing well? • Do you still think the graphic organizer you have chosen is the correct one? • If not, which one would be more appropriate? • Do you need to make any changes to what you have done? Do you need to start again? • Is there any information you are unsure how to summarize? If so, what resources do you have to help you work it out?	• How do you feel now that you have completed the task? Confident or unsure? • Did you summarize all of the correct information? If not, what did you miss? • What were your strengths when completing this task? • What would you do differently next time?

Although this is just one example of how teachers can use a regulatory checklist to help students plan, monitor, and evaluate their learning, any of these questions can be adapted to suit any task that they complete. Over time, the need for a structured checklist will reduce and these types of question will naturally form the thoughts and discussions students will have when completing a new task.

Working scientifically

Introduction to unit

In this unit, students revisit the planning of investigations, focusing on collecting precise and reproducible data, and writing risk assessments to ensure their safety and the safety of those around them.

They will extend their focus on analysing data by looking at how to plot a pie chart and a histogram, along with how to identify the median and mode averages in a data set. They will identify linear and directly proportional relationships, and use lines of best fit to interpolate and extrapolate data. Students will also use secondary data to improve confidence in their conclusions.

Finally, students will study how our understanding of science develops over time, the importance of peer review, and how scientists communicate information to different audiences.

The Working scientifically skills have been sequenced to ensure effective development for learners and to accompany the course's scientific knowledge.

In addition to this unit, Working scientifically skills are embedded within lessons. Each lesson spread includes the relevant Working scientifically links.

Learning journey

Year 7 topics

Asking scientific questions
Developing questions, variables, predictions

Planning Investigations
Writing methods, choosing equipment, measurements

Recording data
Designing and completing results tables, calculating the mean

Working safely
Hazard symbols, hazards and risks

Presenting data
Types of data, plotting bar charts, line graphs, pie charts

Analysing data
Identifying patterns and trends, drawing conclusions

Evaluating data
The stages in evaluating data, suggesting improvements

This unit

Planning investigations
Hypotheses, precision, accuracy, risk assessments

Communicating scientific Information
Effective communication to different audiences

Presenting data
Selecting what graph to plot, pie charts, histograms, mean, median, mode

Analysing and evaluating
Linear and direct proportion, interpolation, confidence in conclusions

Development of scientific understanding
Scientific method, theories, laws, models, changes over time

Using evidence and sources
Peer review, assessing sources, bias

Later topics

Experimental skills and strategies

Vocabulary, units, symbols, and nomenclature

Development of scientific thinking

Analysis and evaluation

Working scientifically and you

Working scientifically skills are essential for a wide range of occupations, as well as wider interests. In the Student Book, a few careers that use these skills are listed:

- Microbiologist – being able to write and follow a risk assessment is essential when working with bacteria and viruses.
- Astronaut – being able carry out experiments independently is essential when doing research in space.

- Engineer – engineers need practical skills in the workplace and knowledge of how to analyse data.
- Meteorologist – communication skills are required when explaining scientific phenomena to the public about weather forecasts.
- Nutritionist – understanding possible bias in health claims about food is essential when advising on diet.
- Geologist – an understanding of staying safe is required when monitoring tectonic activity.

Working scientifically and the world

Regularly remind students that we are all responsible for protecting and enhancing the living world and the physical environment. The ability to think like a scientist is critical to ensure that we can listen to the evidence (e.g. about climate change), take account of what it says, and then act in a way that is the most beneficial to the planet.

Discuss with students that the collective actions of many people make an enormous difference, and are critical in ensuring a stable, sustainable future – not only for human beings, but for all species on Earth.

At the same time, explore with students the idea of misinformation and 'fake news', which is often shared via social media. Compare this with the rigorous process of peer review prior to scientific research being released. Reinforce to students that they should always interrogate information in the following way: Who does this information come from? Why was it published? What is the basis for any claims made?

Big questions

How do scientists stay safe?

Before carrying out a scientific investigation, a risk assessment is performed. This identifies the hazard (something that can cause harm), the risk (how likely it will harm you), and control measures to ensure no one is harmed. By thinking about risk before an activity is started, scientists ensure that their work is safe, even when working with hazardous substances and equipment.

How can you trust a scientific claim?

Scientists learn how to identify bias and check the reliability of a source. For a piece of research to be valid, it should be produced without bias. Students should be aware that scientific research is often funded by business, which may lead to an undue focus on the positive aspects of a product, potentially ignoring or sidelining any negative impacts.

Why do scientists change their minds about how things happen?

The development of new technology (including artificial intelligence), carrying out different experiments, and new ways of thinking can all provide new evidence. This can result in scientists amending a previous idea or changing their thinking entirely. Science is an ever-evolving subject. For example, some teachers may be teaching science to students that was not even known when they started their teaching career!

Working scientifically links

- pay attention to objectivity and concern for accuracy, precision, repeatability, and reproducibility
- make predictions using scientific knowledge and understanding

- select, plan, and carry out the most appropriate types of scientific enquiry to test predictions, including identifying independent, dependent, and control variables
- use appropriate techniques, apparatus, and materials during fieldwork and laboratory work, paying attention to health and safety

Learning objective	Learning outcomes		
	Developing	Secure	Extending
Write a hypothesis for a scientific investigation	Write a prediction for a scientific investigation	**Write a hypothesis for a scientific investigation**	Write a hypothesis using detailed scientific knowledge
Describe the difference between precise and accurate data	State the meaning of accurate data	**Describe the difference between precise and accurate data**	Categorize data into being accurate and/or precise
Write a risk assessment for a scientific investigation	State the meaning of hazard and risk	**Write a risk assessment for a scientific investigation**	Write a detailed risk assessment that identifies and controls all possible hazards

Tier 2 vocabulary	Tier 3 vocabulary
accurate, hazard, precise, prediction, risk, spread	control measure, dependent variable, hypothesis, independent variable, repeatable, reproducible

Digital resources

Practical: *Investigating bungee cords* (Practical sheet, Support sheet, Teacher and technician notes)
Video: *Planning investigations 2*

Student Book answers

Think back 1 what you think will happen in an investigation **2** risk assessment **3** data that is close to the true value

In-text questions A force applied/original length of elastic/material of elastic **B** burns/setting hair alight

Summary questions 1 accurate data – close to the true value; precise data – repeat measurements with a small spread; hazard – something that could hurt you or anybody else; risk – the chance someone could be hurt **2** repeatable – similar results/small spread/precise data when you repeat an investigation; reproducible – similar results when different people carry out the same investigation, or when you repeat an investigation using a different method or equipment **3** for example: hazard – boiling water, risk – scalding, control measure – leave to cool before moving; hazard – lit Bunsen burner, risk – hair catching fire, control measure – tie hair back

Getting started

Show students Figure 1 in the Student Book of the person bungee jumping. How do they think the person could be injured? What safety equipment can they see? What safety precautions may have been taken that they cannot see?

Use students' answers to introduce the three main parts of a risk assessment – hazard, risk, and control measure – using the example of broken glass in Figure 4. Ask students to create a risk assessment for using bleach (hazardous chemical, could damage skin/eyes, wear gloves/goggles).

Ask students to explain the meaning of *accurate* data (data that is close to the true value of what you are trying to measure). Then introduce *precise* data (getting similar results if you repeat a measurement). You may need to remind students that the spread of data refers to the difference between the smallest and largest results. Precise data therefore has a small spread. Illustrate the difference between accurate and precise data using the images of archery targets in Figure 3.

Explain that precise data is also referred to as repeatable. Discuss the difference between repeatable and reproducible data. (Reproducible data: when similar results are achieved by other people carrying out the same experiment, or through using different equipment.)

Main activity

Practical: Investigating bungee cords Students investigate the relationship between the thickness of an elastic band and how much it stretches.

Discuss with students the factors they think are important when choosing which bungee cord to use in a jump. Explain that in today's activity they are going to look at how the thickness of elastic affects how much it stretches. Ask them to predict what they think will happen. Then introduce the difference between a hypothesis and a prediction by asking them to explain their prediction. This can be repeated for a range of questions if required.

Before they complete the practical, students write a hypothesis and complete a risk assessment. Once they have collected their data, they need to decide if their data is repeatable, and whether it is reproducible by looking at other students' results. (Students need to keep their data for the activity in *1.5 Using evidence and sources* for further analysis. See page 17 in this Teacher's Guide.)

Review and reflect

State a number of different hazards, such as worn carpet, heating a test tube, or using a sharp knife. Students record the risk and control measures on their whiteboards and hold them up.

You can also watch the video on Kerboodle to consolidate students' learning.

Language support

Ask students what a risk is. Explain, using examples, that a risk is how likely it is that a hazard (e.g. a corrosive chemical) can cause harm or put you in danger.

Working scientifically links

- apply mathematical concepts and calculate results
- present observations and data using appropriate methods, including tables and graphs
- undertake basic data analysis, including simple statistical techniques

Learning objective	Learning outcomes		
	Developing	Secure	Extending
Select the appropriate graph to display data	Describe the difference between discrete, categorical, and continuous data	**Select the appropriate graph to display data**	Justify the graph chosen to display a set or sets of data
Present data as a pie chart or a histogram	Draw a pie chart when given section angles	**Present data as a pie chart or a histogram**	Draw a histogram using different class widths
Calculate the mean, mode, and median of a set of data	Calculate the mean	**Calculate the mean, mode, and median of a set of data**	Identify which is the most appropriate average to calculate for a set of data

Tier 2 vocabulary	Tier 3 vocabulary
bar chart, categorical, continuous, discrete, line graph, mean, median, mode, pie chart	histogram

Digital resources

Activity: *Pie charts and histograms* (Activity sheet, Support sheet, Teacher and technician notes)
Video: *Presenting data 2*

Student Book answers

Think back 1 data that can have any value within a range **2** data that can have only whole-number values **3** bar chart, line graph, pie chart

In-text questions A bar chart or pie chart **B** 60+

Maths skills: mean = 15, mode = 17, median = 16

Summary questions 1 mean – add up values, and divide by number of values; mode – identify the value that occurs most; median – place numbers from smallest to biggest, and find the middle one **2** blue 72°, brown 108°, green 126°, hazel 54° **3 a** mean = 146.8 cm, mode = 122 cm, median = 155 cm **b** The mean is affected by anomalies (the three shorter students). The mode finds the most common height, which is low in this example. The median is the best measure, as it ignores the anomalies.

Getting started

Show students Figure 1 in the Student Book. What charts do they recognize? How do they differ? Remind students that bar charts or pie charts are used to represent discrete or categorical data, and that line graphs are used to represent continuous data. To check understanding further, ask students to give some examples of continuous, discrete, and categorical data. This knowledge is essential when choosing which type of graph they should plot.

Show students the pie chart in Figure 2, which represents the age range of people. What are its main features? What can they remember about how to plot a pie chart? They should be familiar with how to use a protractor to plot given angles.

Main activity

Activity: Pie charts and histograms Introduce how to calculate the angle of each section of the pie chart by working through the steps on page 10 of the Student Book in combination with Figure 2. Students then complete Task 1 on their Activity sheet, which requires them to draw their own pie chart from raw data. Encourage students to check that their angles total 360° before starting to plot their pie chart.

Introduce students to a histogram using the example in the Student Book. Talk through its key features and how it differs from a bar chart. Introduce how the data the histogram was drawn from is recorded using a frequency table with grouped categories. Choose a couple of mass values and ask students to decide which category the data would fit into.

Explain that histograms are plotted against frequency density as it is the area of the bar that represents the number of people with a particular mass. Introduce the algebraic symbols '<' and '≤'. Then work through the example of how to calculate frequency density. Ask students to calculate one or two examples on the remainder of the chart. Students then complete Task 2 on their Activity sheet, which requires them to draw their histogram.

Discuss averages and ask students to explain how to calculate a mean. Introduce the mode and median averages, and demonstrate how to identify these using the worked example.

Review and reflect

Choose five students in the class and ask them for their shoe size. Ask students to calculate the mean, mode, and median values. For extension, students could be asked to explain which is the most appropriate average to use (unlikely to be the mean as this will usually result in a size that does not exist).

You can also watch the video on Kerboodle to consolidate students' learning.

Language support

Show students real-life examples of graphs, charts, and results tables online, in magazines, or in books. Ensure that they understand that the data presented is the evidence or measurements that scientists collect in an investigation.

Working scientifically links

- present observations and data using appropriate methods, including tables and graphs
- interpret observations and data, including identifying patterns and using observations, measurements, and data to draw conclusions

- present reasoned explanations, including explaining data in relation to predictions and hypotheses

Learning objective	Learning outcomes		
	Developing	Secure	Extending
Identify linear and directly proportional relationships	Describe a simple trend shown in data	**Identify linear and directly proportional relationships**	Describe inversely proportional relationships
Take readings from a graph using a line of best fit	Draw a line of best fit	**Take readings from a graph using a line of best fit**	Extrapolate data from a graph using a line of best fit
Describe how to improve confidence in a conclusion	Write a simple conclusion	**Describe how to improve confidence in a conclusion**	Describe the level of confidence in a set of data

Tier 2 vocabulary	Tier 3 vocabulary
	directly proportional relationship, line of best fit, linear relationship, secondary data

Digital resources

Activity: *Is the bungee safe?* (Activity sheet, Support sheet, Teacher and technician notes)
Video: *Analysing and evaluating 2*

Student Book answers

Think back 1 the pattern/trend in data **2** curved or straight (going through/close to as many points as possible) **3** median

In-text questions A 20 m **B** It will pass through the origin. **C** 4 cm

Summary questions 1 best fit, linear, directly proportional, secondary **2** repeat an experiment (several times), use a wider range, use secondary data **3** At 20 m bungee length, extension = 10 m; at 40 m bungee length, extension = 20 m (or equivalent data), showing that a doubling of the independent variable causes a doubling of the dependent variable; the line of best fit also passes through the origin.

Getting started

Show students Figure 1 in the Student Book of the man about to bungee jump. Ask them to make a list of all the data the organizers may need to collect/refer to when adjusting the bungee cord to ensure the jump is safe.

Explain that data the organizers refer to, which they have not collected themselves, is called secondary data.

Draw a graph on the board with a set of data that curves upwards, but draw a straight line of best fit. Ask students to spot the mistake (the line of best fit should be curved.) Remind them what a line of best fit shows and that, later in the lesson, they will use a line of best fit to predict values for which they have taken no data (interpolation).

Main activity

Introduce linear relationships using the graph in Figure 2 in the Student Book. The graph shows how the extension of the bungee rope is affected by its composition of artificial rubber. In this type of relationship, increasing the independent variable causes an increase in the dependent variable, so in this example the more artificial rubber the bungee rope contains, the more the rope extends. Students should be made aware that when plotted, these graphs are always straight (explain that this example shows a positive correlation, but linear relationships can also show a negative correlation).

Then introduce direct proportion using the graph in Figure 3. The graph shows how the extension of the bungee rope is affected by its starting length. Explain that this is a special type of linear relationship where doubling the independent variable causes a doubling of the dependent variable. It can be recognized on a graph by a straight line of best fit that goes through the origin.

Activity: Is the bungee safe? Students calculate the mean values of a set of data on the strengths of different bungee cords, before plotting a graph and adding a line of best fit. They then write a conclusion, using data from the graph to improve its validity.

Use the graph in Figure 4 to show how to take measurements using a line of best fit. Explain that this allows the extension of a cord to be determined without having to physically measure every thickness of elastic that may exist.

Explain that unless the relationship between two variables is linear, it is hard to predict with any confidence values for data above or below the graph's extremes. In the same way, Katie and Tom are only confident that their prediction is true for elastic that has a thickness of approximately 1–6 mm.

Introduce the role of secondary data in providing more evidence for a conclusion, and therefore increasing your confidence that you are correct.

Review and reflect

Show students a range of graphs. Students hold up a different coloured card to identify if they show a linear relationship, a directly proportional relationship, or a non-linear relationship.

You can also watch the video on Kerboodle to consolidate students' learning.

Language support

When students are carrying out the main activity, remind them that the numbers they are working with are the data. They are analysing (looking closely at) the data to make sense of it. Write the words 'analyse' and 'evaluate' on the board and invite a volunteer to explain the difference between them.

Working scientifically links

- develop use of scientific vocabulary, including the use of scientific nomenclature and units and mathematical representation
- present observations and data using appropriate methods

- present reasoned explanations, including explaining data in relation to predictions and hypotheses

Learning objective	Learning outcomes		
	Developing	Secure	Extending
Describe the key features of effective communication	State the meaning of concise and coherent writing	**Describe the key features of effective communication**	Identify places where writing is not clear, concise, or coherent and explain why
Describe how to adapt communication for different audiences	Name some examples of audiences	**Describe how to adapt communication for different audiences**	Explain the differences in writing for a scientific journal and a scientific magazine

Tier 2 vocabulary	Tier 3 vocabulary
audience, coherent, communication, concise, purpose	

Digital resources

Activity: *Same idea, different audience* (Activity sheet, Teacher and technician notes)
Video: *Communicating scientific information*

Student Book answers

Think back 1 using line graphs, pie charts, bar charts, and histograms **2** clear labels (and where relevant, magnification/scale) **3** any three from: hypothesis, method, results table, graph, conclusion

In-text questions A for example: peers, teacher, younger students, general public **B** real-life examples/ vivid words

Summary questions 1 make it clear, correct, coherent, and concise **2** Any four from: When you are writing for a journal, you need to use scientific vocabulary correctly, use formal language, and set out

evidence that supports any conclusions drawn. When you are writing for the public, you need to explain scientific vocabulary, write less formally, and use examples. **3** The leaflet should include appropriate vocabulary, explain scientific terms, use short words and sentences, and have illustrations or diagrams, with a separate description that explains the strategies used that reflects the content of the leaflet. These strategies will ensure that the child stays engaged, and is able to understand the information presented, since it is broken down into small, manageable chunks.

Getting started

Show students the photo of different types of literature in Figure 1 in the Student Book, or provide them with real-life examples to look through. Ask them, in small groups, to make a list of all the different audiences a scientist might need to share information with, and the different styles of writing that could be used. Discuss findings as a class.

Encourage students to think about writing scripts (e.g. for a TV advertising campaign for public health, for a media interview, or for digital forms of communication such as social media).

Ask students, in pairs, to think about features of effective communication (a list of features can be found in the Student Book for reference). What makes something easy to understand, especially when reading or hearing about a new topic for the first time? Use students' ideas to produce a class list, which can be added to throughout the lesson. If not identified by students from the Student Book, introduce them to the idea of 'the 4 Cs' – clear, concise, correct, and coherent.

Main activity

Ask students to write down key features that they think should be included in a report. For example, a method should be written in steps and contain a labelled diagram of the equipment needed.

Share ideas and then discuss how this may be reported for a different audience, such as a newspaper article: Is the method still needed? Or a results table? How will the article grab attention?

Activity: Same idea, different audience Students are provided with the outline of an experiment and data relating to it. They can use the genuine data on the Activity sheet, or use any other data you wish, even some from a novel situation, such as the discovery of organic material on Mars or the discovery of exoplanets.

Students produce a piece of writing about the experiment in a style of their choice, such as a newspaper article, a storyboard for a children's television programme, or a summary for a science journal. Students need to ensure their writing is clear, concise, correct, and coherent.

At the end of the activity, ask students to share their pieces of writing. Discuss the specific features of the style of writing chosen.

Review and reflect

Students work together to recall and describe four key features of effective communication.

You can also watch the video on Kerboodle to consolidate students' learning.

Language support

Ask students what an audience is. Have they ever experienced being in an audience? In everyday life, this word normally relates to watching or observing a show or performance. However, the audience in writing is the reader. In science, the reader observes what a scientist has written and, in doing so, learns about scientific investigations, evidence, and discoveries.

1.5 Using evidence and sources

Working scientifically links

- pay attention to objectivity and concern for accuracy, precision, repeatability, and reproducibility

- understand that scientific methods and theories develop as earlier explanations are modified to take account of new evidence and ideas, together with the importance of publishing results and peer review

Learning objective	Learning outcomes		
	Developing	Secure	Extending
Describe the peer review process	State where scientists publish their research	**Describe the peer review process**	Explain why peer review enables a finding to be accepted
Describe how to assess sources of evidence	Name some sources of scientific evidence	**Describe how to assess sources of evidence**	Assess a source of evidence for how reliable it is
Identify possible sources of bias	State what bias is	**Identify possible sources of bias**	Explain the effect of bias in unfamiliar situations

Tier 2 vocabulary	Tier 3 vocabulary
anecdotal, bias, evidence, journal, research	peer review

Digital resources

Activity: *Peer review* (Activity sheet, Support sheet, Teacher and technician notes)
Video: *Using evidence and sources*

Student Book answers

Think back 1 through measurements and observations **2** very similar measurements when repeated by the same person, using the same equipment and method **3** very similar measurements when repeated by a different person, using different equipment and/or methods

In-text question A journal **B** any three from: who wrote it, where was it published, is it up-to-date information, might the information be biased, is there enough data to form conclusions, is there other research that backs up these findings

Summary questions 1 peer reviewed, reliable, biased, funding **2 a** It was published in a journal, so peer reviewed before publication. **b** Any five from: the journalist may not personally believe in global warming; the journalist may believe climate change only has natural causes; the journalist may not want to reduce

their own use of fossil fuels; the journalist may see the claims as a threat to their existing lifestyle; the journalist may believe the claims are exaggerated; claims of climate change may harm the financial interests of their newspaper/employer; the claims challenged established scientific thinking, and so need further evidence to be collected before being fully accepted. **3** Any four from: if the funder of the research also produces the product being researched, they may ask the scientists to focus on possible positive effects; the company may risk losing money if the research does not produce positive effects; the scientists may worry about losing their jobs if they do not focus on the positive effects; any negative effects may be ignored or overlooked; named possible negative effect (e.g. high sugar content); the research has been published by the company, so has not been peer reviewed; these reasons make the research unreliable.

Getting started

Show students the quote from the Student Book on smoking and cancer. Ask them to discuss whether they think this is evidence. What different kinds of evidence can scientists collect to prove or disprove statements such as this? Explain that this statement is referred to as *anecdotal* evidence. You cannot reason from this one example that smoking does not cause cancer.

Explain that before a scientist can publish the results of an investigation, other scientists check the research to make sure that the results and conclusions are correct. This is called peer review. The investigation can then be published in a scientific journal.

Main activity

Hand out some examples of scientific journals and ask students to make a list of things that are common to the articles in the journal, such as an abstract, evidence/data/graphs, conclusion, and references (they can refer to this during the activity).

Explain that when you look for evidence to back up your own findings, you need to check if it is reliable. The more reliable it is, the more valid the information. Discuss ways that you can interrogate sources to check for reliability using the table in the Student Book for reference. Explain that it is best to look for more than one source, especially when looking at the internet, to check for consistency.

Lead the discussion on to the sources of funding for scientific research – government, companies, or charities – and how this may result in results being presented in a biased way.

Activity: Peer review Students use their data from the elastic band experiment in *1.1 Investigating bungee cords* (see page 9 in this Teacher's Guide) in conjunction with secondary data to write a paper for a scientific journal. Students then peer review each other's articles and decide if they should be published.

Review and reflect

Show students the statements on possible sources of bias. Students decide which examples may contain bias. Encourage them to explain how and why this may affect the results for their chosen statements.

You can also watch the video on Kerboodle to consolidate students' learning.

Language support

Talk about what a peer is. Explain to students that this is someone who is at the same level or stage (e.g. of learning, or in terms of age) as yourself. To check their understanding, encourage them to gesture to or stand next to one of their peers in class. Then ask: 'What is a peer review?'

Working scientifically link

- understand that scientific methods and theories develop as earlier explanations are modified to take account of new evidence and ideas, together with the importance of publishing results and peer review

Learning objective	Learning outcomes		
	Developing	Secure	Extending
Describe the scientific method	State the meaning of a hypothesis	**Describe the scientific method**	Explain how a theory is developed using the scientific method
Describe the difference between a theory, a law, and a model	State the meaning of a theory, a law, and a model	**Describe the difference between a theory, a law, and a model**	Use examples to describe the differences between a theory, a law, and a model
Describe how our understanding of science changes over time	State some ways new evidence can arise	**Describe how our understanding of science changes over time**	Use examples to describe how our understanding of science changes over time

Tier 2 vocabulary	Tier 3 vocabulary
law, model, observation, theory	scientific method

Digital resources

Activity: *What's the evidence?* (Activity sheet, Support sheet, Teacher and technician notes)
Video: *The scientific method* and *How scientific ideas develop*

Student Book answers

Think back 1 measurements, observations
2 a description of what you think will happen, backed up with scientific reasoning **3** scientific journals

In-text questions A A theory provides an explanation, whereas a law is a statement of fact. **B** other planets (except for Earth) in the correct order; planets have approximately circular orbits

Summary questions 1 explanation, evidence, method, law, model **2** if their experiment does not give the expected results/the conclusions disagree with

the hypothesis; if new evidence is discovered through new technology/different experiments **3** Any three from (accept other reasonable suggestions): Ptolemy was a respected scientist; the geocentric model had been in place for 1500 years; the model went against established scientific thinking; Copernicus was not a well-known scientist; Copernicus's work might have undermined the work of other eminent scientists; Copernicus's model did not always accurately predict planetary positions, so there might be a different explanation.

Getting started

Show students an image of the bacterium *Vibrio cholerae*. Tell them that people thought that infectious diseases were caused by a poisonous vapour that came from decaying matter. What do they think this is an image of? How do they think it was created? How does it support the idea that disease is not caused by vapour?

Explain that it is an image of the bacterium that causes cholera. Bacteria is spread through contaminated water sources. The image was developed using information gained through a microscope. This introduces the concept that scientific ideas are constantly revised when new evidence is gained.

Main activity

Talk through the main steps in the scientific method using the flowchart in Figure 1 in the Student Book. Focus on how the discovery of new evidence can lead to a scientific idea having to be changed, and that this is very much a part of science: not everything is yet known! Explain the difference between a model, a law, and a theory, discussing examples of each.

Recap that for a theory to be accepted, there has to be a lot of evidence to support it. Discuss how new evidence can arise through new technology, other scientists carrying out different investigations, and new ways of thinking. This can lead to a theory or model having to be revised.

Activity: What's the evidence? In small groups, students select a theory, law, or model, and research what it shows and the original evidence that led to its development. They also need to find out about at least one previous theory/model that was used to explain the same phenomenon and why this has since been discounted/amended.

Allow time at the end of the activity for groups to feed back on their findings, summarizing their theory and how it has changed from previous ideas as a result of new evidence.

Review and reflect

Students write one sentence to define each of the following key words: 'model', 'law', 'theory'.

You can also watch the two videos on Kerboodle to consolidate students' learning.

Language support

Ask students if they have ever heard the key word 'theory'. Use examples, such as: 'In *theory*, it will be sunny today because it was yesterday.' Explain that, in science, a theory is a carefully thought-out idea based on scientific understanding or observation. A theory helps scientists make sense of the world around them.

Biology

Introduction to unit

In this unit, students will compare the effects of healthy and unhealthy lifestyles. This involves looking at the structure and function of the digestive system and the role of enzymes in digestion. They will then combine their knowledge of biology and chemistry when studying the cellular processes of photosynthesis and respiration.

Building on their knowledge of food chains, students will study the interdependence of organisms and the adaptations that enable organisms to be successful competitors and survive in harsh and changing environments. They will then study the causes of variation and how characteristics are inherited through chromosomes, before learning about natural selection. Throughout this unit, students are introduced to a number of scientists who played a fundamental role in developing our understanding of biology.

Working scientifically

Each lesson lists the relevant Working scientifically links at the top of the spread.

Biology links

- Nutrition and digestion
- Health
- Photosynthesis
- Cellular respiration
- Relationships in an ecosystem
- Inheritance, chromosomes, DNA, and genes

Learning journey

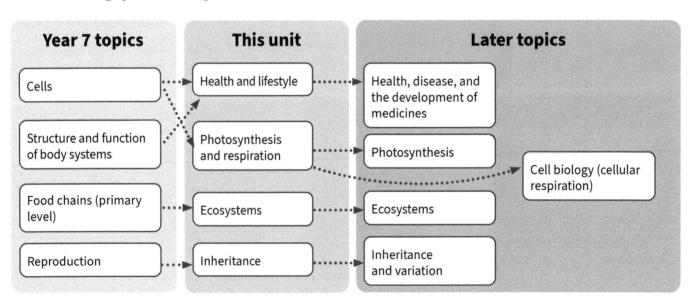

Year 7 topics	This unit	Later topics
Cells	Health and lifestyle	Health, disease, and the development of medicines
Structure and function of body systems	Photosynthesis and respiration	Photosynthesis
Food chains (primary level)	Ecosystems	Ecosystems
Reproduction	Inheritance	Inheritance and variation
		Cell biology (cellular respiration)

Biology and you

Studying biology equips students with many skills, and is essential for a wide range of occupations and interests. In the Student Book, a few careers that use biology are listed:

- Vet – knowledge of the anatomy and physiology of animals is required to diagnose what is wrong with an animal and provide the best level of care.

- Physiotherapist – an understanding of the muscular–skeletal system is essential to help patients recover full movement after illness or an accident.

- Sports coach – knowledge of healthy lifestyles and of the way the body moves enables sports coaches to get the best out of their teams.

- Midwife – understanding how a baby develops in the uterus and the process of birth is essential when caring for pregnant women and their babies.

- Marine biologist – understanding the differences in the way unicellular and multicellular organisms function is important when studying microscopic life in the oceans.

- Commercial flower grower – providing the best conditions for photosynthesis is essential for plants to produce the best quality flowers.

- Medical researcher – a detailed understanding of cell structure is essential when researching new treatments for diseases such as cancer.

- Environmentalist – knowledge of how organisms interact is crucial when studying the human impact on the environment, and identifying ways of minimizing potential damage.

Biology and the world

Make students aware that the lifestyle choices they make have a direct effect on their health. Learning about healthy eating, for example, enables them to make informed decisions about the way they wish to live their life and the lives of their families.

Instil in students a responsibility to conserve the living environment, and enhance their understanding of the natural world, particularly in terms of the interdependence of organisms. For example, we depend on bees to pollinate the crops for our survival. Negative human impacts mean there has never been a more important time for us to understand how we can act collectively to protect all living species.

Big questions

Why do organisms need to eat to survive?

Eating the right foods in the right amounts is fundamental for remaining healthy. Observing when people do not have enough food, or when they eat the wrong foods, provides clues to the roles different foods play in the body. As well as providing energy, which is needed even when an organism is asleep, the nutrients foods contain are required for the body to grow and repair itself.

How do plants make food?

Performing experiments where plants are given a range of raw materials has enabled scientists to discover what plants need to survive and how we can help them grow.

Conditions in industrial greenhouses are monitored to provide optimum conditions for photosynthesis, resulting in the highest crop yields. This is one way in which scientists are tackling food shortages.

Why don't we all look the same?

The way in which characteristics are passed on from parents to their offspring were discovered using the work of many scientists, including Mendel, who studied pea plants; and Watson, Crick, Franklin, and Wilkins, who developed the model of DNA replication. Detailed understanding of genetics can now calculate a person's risk of having a disease. It can also be used to modify plants to have a specific characteristic such as insect resistance.

Chapter 1: Health and lifestyle

Introduction to chapter

In this chapter, students are introduced to the different parts of a balanced diet and their importance in staying healthy. They will study the process of digestion, focusing on the role of enzymes, bacteria, and some of the main organs in the digestive system. In the final section of the chapter, students will look at the effects of harmful substances on the body.

Core concepts

- Food groups and food tests
- Structure and function of the digestive system
- The role of enzymes in digestion
- Absorption of food molecules by diffusion
- The effect of harmful substances on the body

What have students already learned?

- The impact of diet, exercise, harmful substances, and lifestyle on the way their bodies function
- The levels of organization of multicellular organisms: from cells to tissues, to organs, to systems, to organisms
- The role of diffusion in the movement of materials in and between cells

What will students learn next?

- Enzymes
- Factors affecting the rate of enzymatic reactions
- Carbohydrates, proteins, nucleic acids, and lipids as key biological molecules
- The relationship between health and disease
- The impact of lifestyle factors on the incidence of non-communicable diseases

Think back

1 Draw a healthy meal on a plate. Label the food group for each type of food.

2 Name some organs in the digestive system. Add a note describing what they do.

3 Make a list of some harmful substances that we should not put inside our body.

Teaching strategy

Percentage change In this chapter, there are several opportunities for students to practise calculating a percentage change (covering positive and negative changes). It is important for students to recognize that if their answer is negative, a percentage decrease has occurred; a positive answer represents a percentage increase. Encourage students to write out the formula in full each time so their working can be checked. If the student gets the final answer wrong, method marks can be awarded.

Model gut When introducing the digestive system, ask students to imagine their body as having a hosepipe running from the mouth to the anus. This tube carries food and fluids into and out of the body. However, the analogy is limited. Unlike a hose, the gut is permeable in parts. This allows nutients and waste products to pass into the body from the tube, or from the body back into the tube.

Evaluations When looking at models of the digestive system, encourage students to think about where the model represents the system well and where the model does not work as well. Link this to the skill of writing an evaluation. Explain to students that they should consider the negative aspects or failings of a model or practical in an evaluation and try to suggest improvements.

Energy in food practical If more time is available, you could carry out an investigation into the energy content of different foods before introducing dietary energy requirements to students. One approach is to burn a range of foods, and measure the temperature increase of a fixed volume of water. Challenge more confident students to calculate the energy transferred to the water using the specific heat capacity formula:

energy transferred (J) = mass of water (g) × 4.2 × temperature increase (°C)

Common learning misconceptions

- Vitamins and minerals are only found in fruits and vegetables.

- All fats are bad. (We need fats in our diet because the body cannot make them. Without fats, we would not be able to absorb essential vitamins like vitamin D.)

- Overweight people have 'big bones'. (Most skeletons are the same size. Some are slightly smaller and others are slightly bigger, but not enough to affect weight.)

- Males always have a higher energy requirement than females.

- Enzymes are living.

- All bacteria make us unwell and cause 'germs'. (Most bacteria do not harm us. They help us digest food, protect against infection, and keep our skin healthy.)

- All drugs are harmful. (Medicines are also drugs.)

- Caffeine (e.g. in coffee) is not a drug.

- Alcohol (and other legal drugs) are not harmful.

- Medical drugs do not have any negative medical effects.

Broader context

This chapter looks at the effects of an unhealthy diet on body mass. It is essential that this issue is introduced with sensitivity. Students may be undergoing significant body changes as a result of puberty, while some may be over- or underweight. Be aware of any students that have, or have experienced, eating disorders.

Scientists working in the food industry use a calorimeter to measure the amount of heat energy that is released when food is burned. This is how they calculate the calories, or energy, that will be transferred when we eat certain foods. These values are on most food labels. However, energy intake from food is now measured in joules (J), which is the correct scientific unit.

Biology link

- the content of a healthy human diet: carbohydrates, lipids (fats and oils), proteins, vitamins, minerals, dietary fibre, and water, and why each is needed

Learning objective	Learning outcomes		
	Developing	Secure	Extending
Define a balanced diet	Name some foods which are considered healthy or unhealthy	**Define a balanced diet**	Explain why eating a balanced diet is important for health
Name the seven parts of a balanced diet, giving examples	Name some parts of a balanced diet	**Name the seven parts of a balanced diet, giving examples**	Suggest a balanced diet for one day
Describe the role of each part of a balanced diet	Identify the functions of some parts of a balanced diet	**Describe the role of each part of a balanced diet**	Explain the role of each part of a balanced diet

Tier 2 vocabulary	Tier 3 vocabulary
balanced diet, carbohydrate, fibre, mineral, nutrient, protein, vitamin	lipid

Digital resources

Practical: *Healthy eating campaign* (Practical sheet, Support sheet, Teacher and technician notes)

Student Book answers

Think back 1 stomach **2** group of organs working together to perform a function **3** digestive system

In-text questions A carbohydrates and lipids **B** fish/ eggs/meat/milk **C** more water is lost through sweating

See p.36 for the answers to the **Summary questions** for this lesson.

Getting started

In pairs, ask students to produce a list of five foods they believe are 'good for you' and five foods they believe are 'bad for you'. Discuss what the 'good' foods have in common (vitamins and minerals) and do the same for the 'bad' foods (high sugar/fat content).

Use this to introduce the concept of a balanced diet – eating food containing the right nutrients in the correct amounts – and that not all fats/sugars are 'bad'.

Main activity

Practical: Healthy eating campaign This activity is divided into two main tasks.

Task 1: Explain that there are seven main parts of a balanced diet. Ask students to use the Student Book to identify the parts and their functions, and give examples of foods that contain them. Address the misconception that vitamins and minerals are only found in fruits and vegetables, using examples such as milk as a good source of calcium.

Task 2: Working in small groups, ask students to design and film a healthy-eating YouTube/TV advert on behalf of the government. The advert should aim to encourage young people to eat a balanced diet. It should introduce the seven parts of a balanced diet, giving examples. Students then share their films.

As an extension, students could compare the nutritional values of cuisines from different countries.

Review and reflect

Describe the function of a part of a balanced diet. Students record the name on their whiteboards and hold their answers up to share.

Language support

Give students time to discuss the word 'diet'. Bring the class back together and invite a few volunteers to share their ideas. Help students understand that a diet is the food that we eat, not just a method of losing weight.

Use the opportunity to inform students that no food is 'bad' – instead, we need to eat a variety of foods to make sure that we have a balanced diet. A balanced diet contains everything we need to stay healthy.

Biology link

- simple food tests for starch, simple (reducing) sugars, protein, and lipids

Working scientifically links

- use appropriate techniques, apparatus, and materials during fieldwork and laboratory work, paying attention to health and safety
- make and record observations and measurements using a range of methods for different investigations
- interpret observations to draw conclusions

Learning objective	Learning outcomes		
	Developing	Secure	Extending
Name the chemicals used to test foods for starch, lipids, sugar, and protein	Identify some of the chemicals used for food tests	**Name the chemicals used to test foods for starch, lipids, sugar, and protein**	Determine which chemical(s) would produce a positive test result for a named food sample
State the positive result for each food test	Identify the positive result for each food test	**State the positive result for each food test**	Identify the nutrients present in a food based on the outcome of the four food tests
Describe how to test foods for starch, lipids, sugar, and protein	State the meaning of a food test	**Describe how to test foods for starch, lipids, sugar, and protein**	Explain some safety precautions to be taken for the four food tests

Tier 2 vocabulary	Tier 3 vocabulary
protein, sugar	Benedict's solution, biuret solution, food test, iodine, lipid, starch

Digital resources

Practical: *Testing food solutions* (Practical sheet, Support sheet, Teacher and technician notes)

Student Book answers

Think back 1 protein **2** provide energy **3** eating food containing the right nutrients in the right amounts

In-text questions A blue-black **B** Rub some food onto a piece of filter paper. If the paper becomes translucent, the food contains fat. **C** boiled sweets **D** If you add biuret solution, it turns purple.

See p.36 for the answers to the **Summary questions** for this lesson.

Getting started

Show students a photo of some chips wrapped in paper. Ask them which food group the chips belong to, based on their observations.

Hopefully, they will recognize that fatty foods leave grease marks on paper. Demonstrate that there is a test for fats by rubbing some cheese/butter on a piece of filter paper and showing that the paper has gone translucent. Explain that scientists need clear results to tell us whether a food contains a chemical or not.

Main activity

Practical: Testing food solutions Demonstrate the food tests for starch, lipids, sugar, and protein. Discuss the safety precautions that must be followed, such as the use of eyewear and washing skin immediately upon contact, as some of the chemicals are irritants. Explain also how a food solution is required for three of the tests, and how this has been produced for them. Students should then complete the summary table on their Practical sheet, which states the chemical used for each test and how to determine a positive result.

Students then work in small groups to carry out a circus activity where they will test for themselves, during their allocated time at each station, the presence of starch, lipids, sugar, and protein in the foods provided. Give students the opportunity to test for all four chemicals during this practical.

Students should then answer the questions that follow on the Practical sheet.

Review and reflect

Hold up some test tubes of results from today's food tests. Ask students what each test result shows and what indicator has been used.

Language support

Ask students to try to define the following key words: 'starch', 'lipids', 'sugar', and 'protein'. Starch is a carbohydrate that we take from plant-based foods. Sugar is a sweet substance from plants, while lipids are oils and fats also from plants. Proteins are a main part of our body that we use to grow and repair tissues.

1.3 Unhealthy diet

Biology links

- calculations of energy requirements in a healthy daily diet
- the consequences of imbalances in the diet, including obesity, starvation, and deficiency diseases

Working scientifically links

- apply mathematical concepts and calculate results
- interpret observations and data, including identifying patterns and using observations, measurements, and data to draw conclusions

Learning objective	Learning outcomes		
	Developing	**Secure**	**Extending**
Describe some health issues caused by an unhealthy diet	List some health problems associated with an unhealthy diet	**Describe some health issues caused by an unhealthy diet**	Explain some health issues caused by an unhealthy diet
State the meaning of a vitamin or mineral deficiency	Name some examples of vitamins and minerals needed in a human diet	**State the meaning of a vitamin or mineral deficiency**	Describe examples of specific vitamin or mineral deficiencies
Compare the energy requirements of different people	Name some factors which affect a person's daily energy requirements	**Compare the energy requirements of different people**	Estimate and justify the energy requirements for different occupations

Tier 2 vocabulary	Tier 3 vocabulary
malnourishment, obese, starvation	deficiency

Digital resources

Activity: *Energy requirements* (Activity sheet, Support sheet, Teacher and technician notes)
Video: *Staying healthy*

Student Book answers

Think back 1 become overweight/lack energy/any other sensible suggestion **2** lipids and carbohydrates **3** fruits/vegetables

In-text questions A 2000 **B** any three from: suffer health problems, poor immune system, lack energy, likely to suffer from a lack of vitamins or minerals (accept named condition) **C** any three from: heart disease, stroke, diabetes, some cancers **D** farmer

See p.36 for the answers to the **Summary questions** for this lesson.

Getting started

Energy content of food Introduce the idea that all the energy we require for life comes from food. Demonstrate the energy provided in food by sprinkling fine custard powder into a Bunsen flame using a funnel with some tubing (the 'screaming jelly baby' experiment is also a classic option). This is a dramatic demonstration that creates a huge roaring flame. Keep students at a reasonable distance away from the experiment. Explain that energy is measured in joules (foods usually in kilojoules). The energy provided by a food source is listed on a food label.

Main activity

Underweight vs overweight Discuss what the body needs energy for – everything! Explain how eating foods with more energy than you use can result in weight gain. If the energy in the food you eat is less than the energy you use, you will lose body mass. This leads to you being underweight. These conditions both have associated medical issues. Using the Student Book for guidance, write a list on the board (in a random order) of common medical issues linked to being under- and overweight. In pairs, students classify them into issues linked to being underweight, and those linked to being overweight. (Throughout this lesson, be aware of students with a poor body image or those who have struggled/are struggling with an eating disorder.)

Explain the meaning of a deficiency disease using examples from the Student Book. Steer the discussion to explain that both extremes are caused by malnourishment – the people have eaten the wrong amounts or the wrong types of food.

Activity: Energy requirements Students compare the energy requirements of different people using the graph on the Activity sheet, then answer the questions that follow.

Before students complete the task, explain how to calculate a percentage change by working through the Maths skills box on page 29 of the Student Book with an example.

Review and reflect

Play the 'higher or lower' game. State a job/gender/age – if the person has a higher energy requirement, students stand up; if lower, students sit down. Ask a student who identifies the answer correctly why this is the case.

You can also watch the video on Kerboodle to consolidate students' learning.

Language support

Ask students if they know the word 'malnutrition'. To help them make a connection, you could give them the word in their L1. On the board, separate the word into 'mal' and 'nutrition'. Students might recognize nutrition as food or nutrients. Then explain or elicit that the prefix 'mal-' means bad. Therefore, malnutrition refers to 'bad nutrition'. This is a synonym for the key word 'malnourishment'.

Biology link

- the tissues and organs of the human digestive system, including adaptations to function and how the digestive system digests food (enzymes simply as biological catalysts)

Working scientifically links

- use models and analogies as a way of understanding things
- evaluate the effectiveness of a model

Learning objective	Learning outcomes		
	Developing	Secure	Extending
Describe the process of digestion	Give the definition of digestion	**Describe the process of digestion**	Explain the importance of digestion
Describe the function of the main structures in the digestive system	Label the main structures in the digestive system	**Describe the function of the main structures in the digestive system**	Explain the structural adaptations of the main structures in the digestive system

Tier 2 vocabulary	Tier 3 vocabulary
stomach	anus, digestion, digestive system, faeces, gullet, gut, large intestine, rectum, small intestine, villi

Digital resources

Activity: *Model of the digestive system* (Activity sheet, Support sheet, Teacher and technician notes)

Student Book answers

Think back 1 break down food **2** stomach/intestine/mouth **3** fibre

In-text questions A smaller after digestion **B** mouth → gullet → stomach → small intestine → large intestine → rectum → anus **C** Muscles in the wall of the gut squeeze food along it.

See p.37 for the answers to the **Summary questions** for this lesson.

Getting started

Look at the labelled diagram of the digestive system in Figure 2 in the Student Book. Ask students to identify as many organs as possible.

Share students' answers. Use these to label a class diagram. Point out the main structural difference between the small and large intestines – the opening of the tube being wider. Add that if you unravelled your small intestine, it would be roughly four times taller than you – it is not very small!

Define the process of digestion and its purpose using Figure 2 to visually represent the process. Discuss the misconception that all digestion occurs in the stomach – digestion starts in the mouth, when the action of the teeth and the tongue break down food, then continues in the small intestine.

Using an anatomical model of the human torso or Figure 2, talk through each organ in the digestive system in turn and its role in digestion. Then use Figure 4 to introduce the role of the villi in the small intestine (increasing the surface area of the small intestine, thus maximizing absorption). Enzymes should not be introduced at this point – refer to 'digestive juices' instead.

Main activity

Model the movement of food through the digestive system by squeezing a nearly empty tube of toothpaste, or squeezing a pair of socks moving along a pair of tights.

Activity: Model of the digestive system Working in small groups, students produce a simple model of the digestive system using plastic tubing and a range of modelling materials to form the digestive organs. Students should label each key structure with a sticky note describing its function. Encourage them to include any structural adaptations. When complete, get students to pour coloured liquid through their model to show the movement of food through the digestive system. The coloured liquid may stain, so perform this testing in bowls or near a sink.

Ask students to evaluate how well their model represents the digestive system. Allow time for them to share their thoughts and discuss any improvements.

Review and reflect

Put the following structures in the order that food will pass through on its journey through the digestive system:

mouth   rectum   small intestine   stomach
large intestine   gullet   anus

Language support

Write the key words 'digest', 'digestion', and 'digestive' on the board or hand them out as flashcards. Give students a few minutes to work out which word categories the words belong to. Elicit or explain that 'digest' is a verb (e.g. to digest food), 'digestion' is an abstract noun for the process of digesting food, and 'digestive' is an adjective that describes the type of organ system. The digestive system is separated from the rest of the body. It is like a tube that runs through the body with an opening at each end.

Biology links

- enzymes simply as biological catalysts
- the importance of bacteria in the human digestive system

Working scientifically links

- make predictions using scientific knowledge and understanding
- use appropriate techniques, apparatus, and materials during fieldwork and laboratory work, paying attention to health and safety
- make and record observations and measurements using a range of methods for different investigations

Learning objective	Learning outcomes		
	Developing	Secure	Extending
Describe the role of bacteria in digestion	List some facts about bacteria	**Describe the role of bacteria in digestion**	Explain the importance of bacteria in digestion
Describe the role of an enzyme	Identify the role of an enzyme in digestion	**Describe the role of an enzyme**	Explain the role of enzymes in digestion
Describe the role of enzymes in carbohydrate, protein, and lipid digestion	Identify the enzymes used to digest carbohydrates, proteins, and lipids	**Describe the role of enzymes in carbohydrate, protein, and lipid digestion**	Explain how bile supports the digestion of lipids

Tier 2 vocabulary	Tier 3 vocabulary
bacteria	bile, carbohydrase, catalyst, enzyme, lipase, protease

Digital resources

Practical: *Investigating enzyme action* (Practical sheet, Support sheet, Teacher and technician notes)
Video: *Digestion*

Student Book answers

Think back 1 organism made of only one cell **2** breakdown of large food molecules into small molecules **3** carbohydrates

In-text questions A Bacteria in the digestive system make vitamins. **B** They speed up the reaction where large molecules are broken down.

See p.37 for the answers to the **Summary questions** for this lesson.

Getting started

Provide students with packaging from probiotic foods. Ask them to try to find out from the labelling what they are, what they contain, and why they are good for you.

Share students' ideas to determine that probiotic foods contain a range of bacteria that help digestion inside the human body. The bacteria live naturally in the large intestine on the fibre in your diet. They make important vitamins, such as vitamin K, which is needed for blood clotting and helping wounds to heal. These vitamins are then absorbed into your body and help keep you healthy. This is a good opportunity to address the misconception that all bacteria are bad for you.

Introduce the role of enzymes in the body by showing the video *Digestion*. Then use Figures 3–5 in the Student Book to reinforce the reactions catalysed by carbohydrase, protease, and lipase. Reinforce that enzymes are not living (they are proteins) and do not get 'used up'.

Main activity

Practical: Investigating enzyme action Students carry out a practical to observe the action of carbohydrase on the breakdown of starch, then answer the questions that follow.

Take time before the practical to discuss how enzyme action is being studied in this practical, so that students can complete their prediction.

You may wish to demonstrate the importance of timing in this practical and explain what results students are looking for – that is, for the colour change to stop occurring, showing that all the starch has been broken down.

Wash anything that comes into contact with skin under a running tap, since iodine will stain skin and clothing. The pipettes should be labelled to prevent cross-contamination.

Review and reflect

Create sets of sort cards (one per group) with three arrow cards and the following key words: 'carbohydrates', 'carbohydrase', 'sugar', 'proteins', 'proteases', 'amino acids', 'lipids', 'lipase', 'fatty acids', and 'glycerol'.

Give each group of students a set of cards for them to explain enzymatic digestion. Students should then write the resulting word equations in their books. (For support, have sets of cards where different colours are used to distinguish between substrates, enzymes, and products.)

carbohydrates → sugar (using carbohydrase)

proteins → amino acids (using proteases)

lipids → fatty acids and glycerol (using lipase)

You can also watch the video on Kerboodle to consolidate students' learning.

Language support

When introducing enzyme names, explain that the suffix '-ase' is used in biology to form the names of enzymes. The most common way to name enzymes is to add this suffix onto the end of the substrate, for example, an enzyme that breaks down carbohydrates is called carbohydra*se*. You could ask students to predict the names of other enzymes, for example, peroxides are broken down by peroxida*se*.

1.6 Harmful substances

Biology link

- the effects of drugs and harmful substances on behaviour, health, and life processes

Learning objective	Learning outcomes		
	Developing	**Secure**	**Extending**
Describe what a drug does, and the difference between medicinal and illegal drugs	List some medicinal drugs	**Describe what a drug does, and the difference between medicinal and illegal drugs**	Describe some effects of drugs on the human body, identifying their health benefits and potential to cause harm
Describe the dangers of smoking tobacco	Identify some dangers of smoking tobacco	**Describe the dangers of smoking tobacco**	Describe what passive smoking is and how it can affect us
Explain why alcohol is a harmful substance	Identify some risks related to alcohol consumption	**Explain why alcohol is a harmful substance**	Describe some effects of alcohol on the human body, and the associated health risks

Tier 2 vocabulary	Tier 3 vocabulary
alcohol, drug	carbon monoxide, depressant, ethanol, medicinal drug, nicotine, passive smoking, stimulant, tar, tobacco

Digital resources

Practical: *Investigating harmful substances* (Practical sheet, Support sheet, Teacher and technician notes)
Video: *Harmful substances*

Student Book answers

Think back 1 eat a balanced diet/exercise regularly/ sleep well **2** for example: cough medicine, aspirin, paracetamol **3** nervous system

In-text questions A a chemical substance that affects the way the body works **B** treat symptoms of a condition/cure an illness **C** any three from: stomach ulcers, heart disease, brain damage, liver damage, harm to a fetus **D** breathing in other people's smoke

See p.37 for the answers to the **Summary questions** for this lesson.

Getting started

Guide conversations in this lesson sensitively, based on what is appropriate in your cultural context.

Write the term 'harmful substance' on the board and give students time to discuss in pairs or in a group the question: *What is a harmful substance?* Elicit ideas and add them to the board.

Then turn to pages 34–35 in the Student Book to check students' answers. Go through each harmful substance in turn and talk about how each one can severely damage health, including the negative effects of passive smoking.

As new vocabulary is introduced, such as 'stimulant' or 'depressant', write it on the board. Understanding these key words will help students complete the main activity.

Main activity

Practical: Investigating harmful substances The main activity is divided into three separate tasks to choose from. Depending on what is appropriate in your cultural context and the amount of time you wish to dedicate to teaching harmful substances, students can participate in just one task or all three.

The harmful effects of smoking Task 1 focuses on the harmful effects of smoking. Students observe the effects of tobacco smoke on the human body by watching a teacher-led smoking machine demonstration. Students record the results of the demonstration as they watch, then answer the questions that follow on the Practical sheet.

The dangers of drinking alcohol Task 2 focuses on alcohol consumption, and why it is dangerous. Students summarize the information in the Student Book to complete a diagram of the human body. They describe how alcohol harms different organs in the body, before answering the questions that follow on the Practical sheet.

Medicinal or illegal drugs? For Task 3, students make a presentation about the difference between medicinal and illegal drugs in their country, and the effects these drugs have on the body. The aim of the presentation is to educate other teenagers on the harmful effects of drugs. They could perform their presentation to their peers in the classroom and/or to other year groups, if appropriate.

Ensure that students understand that even if a drug is prescribed or legal, it can have side-effects or negative effects on health.

Review and reflect

Ask students to write definitions of the key words. They then share their definitions with a partner, and then in a group, to see if they can improve their definitions.

You can also watch the video on Kerboodle to consolidate students' learning.

Language support

Check that students are familiar with the words 'harm' and 'harmful'. These are useful to know in science, and they have probably come across them already in their lessons on hazards and risk assessments. Encourage students to write two sentences, using one of the words in each, to check their understanding.

Getting started

Encourage students to review their learning in this chapter. The 'Summary questions' in the Student Book can be used formatively during lessons. For the 'What have I learned?' pages, students can answer the questions one at a time after each topic, or as a single summative activity. This could be done as a whole-class or group activity, or set as an independent task.

Whichever approach is adopted, the questions are designed to give you and students feedback about progress and identify targets for development.

Student reflection

Allow students time to reflect on how confident they feel about each topic. Remind them to use the learning objectives provided in their Student Book for guidance. They should focus on whether there were any questions they found difficult or easy, and on how well they prepared for the summative assessment at the end of the chapter. Listen to and deal with students' reflections sensitively so that they feel comfortable to report areas they are not confident with.

Learning objectives and learning outcomes

Each lesson is guided by the learning *objectives*. The learning objectives are provided at the beginning of each topic in the Student Book. They outline what students are going to learn in each topic.

In contrast, the learning *outcomes* in this Teacher's Guide are statements that describe the knowledge or skills that students should acquire by the end of each topic. They are linked to the learning objectives, but are *not* often seen by students. The learning outcomes are used by teachers to assess and measure if or how each learning objective has been achieved.

Answer key

Chapter 1: Health and lifestyle

1 diagram should show and label foods containing sources of protein (e.g. meat, fish, nuts, cheese), carbohydrate (e.g. potato, rice, bread), fat (e.g. meat, cheese), fibre (e.g. vegetables, bread), and vitamins and minerals (e.g. fruit, vegetables)
2 for example: stomach – breaks down/digests food, small intestine – absorbs nutrients, large intestine – absorbs water
3 for example: alcohol, illegal drugs, tobacco, poisons

1.1 Nutrients

Maths skills: 1 500/100 = 5 servings **2** 55 g/5 servings = 11 g sugar
1 carbohydrates – provide energy; vitamins and minerals – remain healthy; lipids – energy store and insulation; water – needed in cells and bodily fluids; protein – growth and repair; fibre – provide bulk to food

2 any two from: provide you with a store of energy/keep you warm by providing a layer of insulation under your skin/protect your organs from damage
3 **a** Carbohydrates provide energy through the process of respiration in cells.
 b adds bulk to food so food is pushed along the gut/out of the body more easily

1.2 Food tests

Working scientifically: wearing safety gloves and glasses, wearing a lab coat, washing hands after using chemical
1 starch – turns blue-black; lipids – makes paper translucent; sugar – turns orange-red; protein – turns purple
2 **a** crush cereal with a pestle and mortar, add a few drops of water
 b Benedict's solution
3 Benedict's solution as cakes contain sugar, ethanol as cakes contain butter/margarine/oil.

1.3 Unhealthy diet

Maths skills: (11000 kJ – 9000 kJ)/9000 kJ = 2000 kJ/9000 kJ = 0.2222 kJ
0.2222 kJ × 100 = 22%

1 energy, joules, overweight, diabetes, tired
2 a 11000 kJ – 9000 kJ = 2000 kJ
   b difference in energy requirement = 15000 kJ – 10000 kJ
     = 5000 kJ
     percentage increase from original job
     = 5000 kJ ÷ 10000 kJ × 100 = 50%
3 estimate within the range 9000–13000 J
   reasoning: teacher will be on their feet for much of
   the day so will use more energy than an office worker
   but is not doing manual work so will use less than a
   construction worker

1.4 Digestive systems

1 stomach – food is mixed with acid and digestive juices
   small intestine – small molecules of nutrients are
   absorbed into the blood
   large intestine – water is absorbed back into the body
   rectum – faeces are stored here until they pass out of
   the body
   mouth – food is chewed and mixed with saliva
2 large food molecules like carbohydrates/proteins/fats
   are broken down into smaller molecules like sugar/
   amino acids/fatty acids and glycerol
3 any four from: walls covered with villi, increasing the
   surface area for more nutrients to be absorbed; lots of
   blood capillaries to transport absorbed nutrient molecules

1.5 Bacteria and enzymes in digestion

Literacy skills: The simple flowchart will begin with
bread mixing with saliva containing carbohydrase in the
mouth, which breaks down the starch in the bread, to
form sugar molecules.

1 carbohydrates, carbohydrase, amino acids, protease,
   fatty acids and glycerol, lipase
2 a large intestine
   b fibre
   c produce vitamins/named vitamin which we use
3 Any four from: they speed up digestion, breaking down
   large molecules into small molecules so they can be
   absorbed into the bloodstream; enzymes do not get
   used up, as they are catalysts.

1.6 Harmful substances

1 chemicals, illegal, medicinal, antibiotic, paracetamol
2 any one from: breathing problems, cancer, heart attacks,
   strokes
3 Alcohol slows down the body's reactions. As a result, it
   would be dangerous to drive or cycle, use machinery,
   cross roads, etc. It could cause an accident.

What have I learned about health and lifestyle?

1 proteins – used for growth and repair [1 mark]
   vitamins and minerals – needed in small amounts to
   keep you healthy [1 mark]

carbohydrates – provide energy [1 mark]
lipids – provide a store of energy and are used to insulate
the body [1 mark]
2 a gullet/oesophagus [1 mark]
   b Nutrients are absorbed into the blood. [1 mark]
   c U [1 mark]
   d Large food molecules are broken down [1 mark] into
     smaller food molecules (which can be absorbed).
     [1 mark]
3 carbohydrates – for energy, lipids – for energy/
   insulation/organ protection, proteins – for growth/repair,
   vitamins and minerals – needed in small amounts to
   maintain health, water – needed in cells/body fluids,
   fibre – to add bulk to food/prevent constipation [Award
   up to 2 marks for naming relevant functions, and up to
   2 marks for linked descriptions]
4 a pestle and mortar [1 mark]
   b any two from: wear eye protection, wash hands
     immediately if chemicals come into contact with skin,
     wear gloves, keep alcohol away from naked flame
     [1 mark each, maximum 2 marks]
   c Add copper sulfate solution and sodium hydroxide
     solution (biuret) to the food solution. [1 mark] If the
     solution turns purple [1 mark], protein is present.
     [1 mark]
5 a Medicinal drugs have a medical benefit to health.
     [1 mark] For example, paracetamol reduces pain and
     helps us feel better when taken correctly and sensibly.
     [any correct example, 1 mark]
   b Drugs alter chemical reactions in the body. [1 mark]
   c Stimulants speed up the nervous system. [1 mark]
     Depressants slow down the nervous system. [1 mark]
6 a Enzymes break large molecules down into smaller
     molecules. [1 mark]
   b Enzymes speed up reactions [1 mark] without being
     used up. [1 mark]
   c Any four from: Both are broken down from large
     molecules into smaller ones. Both are broken down by
     enzymes. Both are broken down in the stomach and
     small intestine. Carbohydrates are broken down by
     carbohydrase whereas proteins are broken down by
     protease. Carbohydrates are broken down into sugar
     molecules whereas proteins are broken down into
     amino acids. Carbohydrates are also broken down/
     digested in the mouth while proteins are not. [1 mark
     each, maximum 4 marks]
7 If you eat too much/more energy than you need, you
   will become overweight [1 mark] as the body stores
   additional fat over the skin. [1 mark] Overweight/obese
   people have an increased risk of heart disease/strokes/
   diabetes/some cancers/arthritis; [1 mark] explanation of
   disease (e.g. as blood vessels become blocked/increased
   body mass damages joints). [1 mark]
   If you eat too little/less energy than you need, you will
   become underweight. [1 mark] Underweight people
   often suffer from a poor immune system/lack energy to
   do things, [1 mark] and may suffer from a lack of vitamins
   or minerals. [1 mark; alternatively, award 1 mark for a
   correctly named deficiency]

Introduction to chapter

In this chapter, students will study the process of photosynthesis, how leaves are adapted to maximize this process, and its importance for all life on Earth. They will then look at the effects of minerals on plant growth. The focus of the second half of the chapter is on the process of respiration, beginning with aerobic respiration. Students will then compare this with anaerobic respiration in animals and fermentation in plants.

Core concepts

- The process and importance of photosynthesis
- The adaptation of leaves for photosynthesis
- The process of aerobic respiration in living organisms
- The process of anaerobic respiration in humans and microorganisms

What have students already learned?

- The difference between producers and consumers
- The functions of the cell wall, cell membrane, cytoplasm, nucleus, vacuole, mitochondria, and chloroplasts
- The role of diffusion in the movement of materials in and between cells

What will students learn next?

- Photosynthesis as the key process for food production and therefore biomass for life
- Factors affecting the rate of photosynthesis
- The importance of cellular respiration

Think back

1 Draw and label a diagram of a leaf cell or a root hair cell.

2 Draw an animal cell. Label the parts and describe their function (job).

3 Use a table to compare the different parts of inhaled and exhaled air.

Teaching strategy

Word equations Remind students that, in word equations, the reactants are always written on the left of the arrow, and the products on the right. In photosynthesis, light is part of the process, but is neither a reactant nor a product. Therefore, 'light' is written above the arrow. Likewise, in respiration, we write 'energy transferred' in brackets within the word equation to differentiate it from the physical products formed.

Photosynthesis practicals If more time is available, students could investigate the effect of light intensity on photosynthesis by counting the number of bubbles produced by pondweed such as *Elodea,* or testing leaves kept in the dark for the presence of starch

by covering up parts of leaves on a tree. However, photosynthesis practicals are often season-dependent in terms of success.

Fermentation Students could investigate the effect of different factors (e.g. temperature and glucose concentration) on yeast fermentation by measuring the volume of carbon dioxide gas given off, or counting the number of bubbles produced. This would provide a good opportunity for students to calculate a mean and then plot their results as a line graph, adding a line of best fit. Divide the class into groups, with each group responsible for collating the data for one temperature. Then work through the process of plotting and analysing the data as a whole class.

Common learning misconceptions

- Breathing and respiration are the same thing. (Air enters and leaves the lungs during breathing. Respiration produces energy in the cells.)

- Animals respire, plants do not. (Plants also have to respire to transfer the energy from the glucose produced in photosynthesis to the plant cells. This is then used for growth.)

- Only organisms with lungs can respire. (All living things respire. Plants respire all the time and photosynthesize in sunlight.)

- Plants obtain water through their leaves when it rains. (The roots of a plant absorb water from their surroundings.)

- Anaerobic respiration only takes place when there is no air. (It takes place when energy is needed quickly.)

Broader context

All living things on Earth depend on plants to absorb energy from the Sun. Remind students that this is why we always show the Sun at the start of all food chains and food webs. It is important that scientists continue to study how plants grow and photosynthesize to

make sure that they grow well. We rely on plants for food and materials to make useful products. They are also used to make medicines and to recycle the carbon dioxide in the atmosphere.

Biology links

- the reactants in, and products of, photosynthesis; and a word summary for photosynthesis
- the dependence of almost all life on Earth on the ability of photosynthetic organisms, such as plants and algae, to use sunlight in photosynthesis to build organic molecules that are an essential energy store and to maintain levels of oxygen and carbon dioxide in the atmosphere
- plants making carbohydrates in their leaves by photosynthesis

Working scientifically links

- use appropriate techniques, apparatus, and materials during laboratory work, paying attention to health and safety
- evaluate risks
- interpret observations to draw conclusions

Learning objective	Learning outcomes		
	Developing	Secure	Extending
Describe the process of photosynthesis	Describe the difference between a producer and a consumer	**Describe the process of photosynthesis**	Explain the importance of photosynthesis to all organisms on Earth
Give the word equation for photosynthesis	Identify the substances that a plant uses for photosynthesis and the substances that it makes	**Give the word equation for photosynthesis**	Explain why plants require light to photosynthesize
Describe how to test a leaf for starch	Give the chemical test used to show the presence of starch	**Describe how to test a leaf for starch**	Predict the outcome of a starch test on a variegated leaf

Tier 2 vocabulary	Tier 3 vocabulary
	algae, chlorophyll, consumer, glucose, photosynthesis, producer

Digital resources

Practical: *Testing a leaf for starch* (Practical sheet, Support sheet, Teacher and technician notes)

Student Book answers

Think back 1 water, sunlight, carbon dioxide, minerals
2 contain chlorophyll **3** cell wall, vacuole, chloroplast

In-text question A consumer **B** glucose
C chloroplast

See p.50 for the answers to the **Summary questions** for this lesson.

Getting started

Before the lesson, set up some pondweed photosynthesizing under a light with a test tube to collect the gas given off. Ask students which gas it is.

Show that it is oxygen by relighting a glowing splint.

Discuss the difference between consumers and producers. Then, building on students' previous knowledge, discuss the process of photosynthesis and introduce the word equation that summarizes this process.

Explain that it is not just plants that photosynthesize by showing Figure 1 in the Student Book (some bacteria photosynthesize as well). Using the information provided, explain the differences between algae and plants.

Main activity

Practical: Testing a leaf for starch Before introducing the practical, explain that plants store the glucose they make through photosynthesis as starch.

Ask students to follow the instructions on the Practical sheet to carry out an experiment to test a leaf for starch. They should write a risk assessment for the experiment and answer the questions that follow.

If time is available, students can compare observations from different types of leaf (variegated or coloured).

Review and reflect

Working on their own, ask students to write a description of photosynthesis. Ask them to then share their definition with a partner to see if they can improve it.

Language support

Elicit from students the meaning of the word 'reaction'. Use examples, such as making a loud noise and then discussing their reaction to it. Highlight that a reaction is a response to something. In a chemical reaction, the chemicals or reactants change or *react* with each other to make a new product. Photosynthesis is an example of a chemical reaction.

Biology links

- the reactants in, and products of, photosynthesis
- the adaptations of leaves for photosynthesis

Working scientifically links

- use appropriate techniques, apparatus, and materials during laboratory work, paying attention to health and safety
- make and record observations

Learning objective	Learning outcomes		
	Developing	Secure	Extending
Describe the main adaptations of a leaf	List some features of a leaf	**Describe the main adaptations of a leaf**	Explain the main adaptations of a leaf
Describe the role of stomata	Give the definition of stomata	**Describe the role of stomata**	Explain how stomata allow gas exchange in a leaf
Describe how water travels through a plant	Name the organs through which water passes within a plant	**Describe how water travels through a plant**	Explain how plants obtain the reactants for photosynthesis

Tier 2 vocabulary	Tier 3 vocabulary
	chlorophyll, chloroplasts, guard cells, photosynthesis, stomata

Digital resources

Practical: *Observing stomata* (Practical sheet, Support sheet, Teacher and technician notes)

Student Book answers

Think back 1 root, leaf, flower, stem
2 They make their own food (photosynthesis).
3 chlorophyll in leaves and stems, carbon dioxide, water, and sunlight

In-text question A green/contain chlorophyll and large surface area **B** upper layer **C** to prevent water loss **D** Carbon dioxide diffuses in and oxygen diffuses out.

See p.51 for the answers to the **Summary questions** for this lesson.

Getting started

Provide students with a range of leaves from common plants. Ask them to make a list of the common features of the leaves. Can they explain why they have these features?

(Include at least one non-green leaf to address the misconception that all leaves are green. Red leaves, such as maple, contain anthocyanin, which provides the characteristic colour. The leaves also contain chlorophyll, but the anthocyanin levels are much greater.)

Through discussion, draw out the four main adaptations of a leaf as explained in the Student Book: green, thin, large surface area, and presence of veins.

Ask students to turn their leaves upside down. What do they notice? Explain that most sunlight hits the top of the leaf, so this is where the chloroplasts need to be to absorb as much sunlight as possible, so the upper surface is a darker green.

Provide students with waxy leaves to feel, such as privet. Explain that this layer prevents water loss by evaporation. Then introduce the movement of water through a plant to reach the leaves. Demonstrate, by sucking through a straw, that water being lost from the leaves draws water up the vessels. Take care to ensure students do not gain the misconception that plants 'suck' water in through their roots.

Main activity

Show students the images of stomata in Figure 2 in the Student Book. Explain their function in gas exchange and the role of guard cells.

Practical: Observing stomata Ask students to produce an imprint of the underside of a leaf using

nail varnish. They then observe stomata under the microscope (or a magnifying glass if it is easier) and answer the questions that follow.

Review and reflect

Ask students, in pairs, to sketch a diagram to show the movement of water through a plant, adding arrows

and simple descriptions such as 'diffuses into the roots from the soil'.

Language support

Remind students of the meaning of the scientific word 'photosynthesis'. This is an unusual and long word. On the board, break it down into two parts: 'photo' and 'synthesis'. Can students now make better sense of the word? The prefix 'photo-' means light

(e.g. photograph) and 'synthesis' refers to the combination of different parts to make a whole. In photosynthesis, plants use *sunlight*, water, and carbon dioxide to *make* oxygen and energy in the form of sugar.

2.3 Plant minerals

Learning objective	Learning outcomes		
	Developing	**Secure**	**Extending**
Describe how a plant uses minerals for healthy growth	List some minerals required by plants	**Describe how a plant uses minerals for healthy growth**	Explain how minerals enable healthy growth in a plant
Describe the symptoms of plant mineral deficiencies	List some symptoms of unhealthy plants	**Describe the symptoms of plant mineral deficiencies**	Suggest and justify a mineral deficiency based on a plant's appearance
Explain why farmers use fertilizers	List some ways farmers can add minerals to the soil	**Explain why farmers use fertilizers**	Explain why using fertilizers enable land to be used for crop growth year after year

Tier 2 vocabulary	Tier 3 vocabulary
fertilizer	chlorophyll, deficiency, magnesium, nitrate, phosphate

Digital resources

Practical: *Investigating fertilizers* (Practical sheet, Support sheet, Teacher and technician notes)
Video: *Photosynthesis and plant growth*

Student Book answers

Think back 1 through the roots (by diffusing into the root hairs) **2** to allow gases to diffuse into and out of the plant **3** any three from: green, thin, large surface area, have stomata, have veins, waxy layer

In-text question A nitrates, phosphates, magnesium **B** absorbed through root hair cells from soil (water) **C** phosphorus **D** manure/animal dung and fertilizers

See p.51 for the answers to the **Summary questions** for this lesson.

Getting started

Provide the class with packaging from garden fertilizers, or project an image of the contents of some fertilizers onto the board. Ask students to identify what chemicals are found in the fertilizer and explain why fertilizers are used.

Introduce the three minerals needed for plant growth described in the Student Book – nitrates, phosphates, and magnesium – and their specific functions. Use the photos to explain what can happen if the plant is deficient in each mineral (link this to the concept of vitamin and mineral deficiencies in a human diet). Discuss why fertilizers or manure are not needed for plants to flourish in natural areas, but are required in large quantities on farmland.

Main activity

Practical: Investigating fertilizers Give students two trays of seedlings (one treated with fertilizer, the other untreated) to compare. They should choose an appropriate variable for comparison, record results in a suitable table, calculate a mean, and answer the questions that follow.

Allow a few minutes at the end of this practical to discuss conclusions and the importance of calculating means in an experiment like this one.

Review and reflect

Provide students with three cards: nitrates, phosphates, and magnesium. Read out a series of statements such as *'needed to make chlorophyll'* or *'What might a plant be deficient in if its leaves are yellow?'*. Students hold up the appropriate card.

You can also watch the video on Kerboodle to consolidate students' learning.

Language support

Demonstrate a sponge soaking up water. Explain that the sponge is *absorbing* the water. The verb 'absorb' means to take in or soak up, and it is used a lot in science. For example, the roots of a plant absorb nutrients from the soil.

Biology links

- aerobic respiration in living organisms, including the breakdown of organic molecules to enable all the other chemical processes necessary for life
- a word summary for aerobic respiration

Learning objective	Learning outcomes		
	Developing	Secure	Extending
Describe the process of aerobic respiration	Name the chemical reaction where energy is transferred to cells	**Describe the process of aerobic respiration**	Explain why respiration is performed by all living organisms
Give the word equation for aerobic respiration	Identify the substances used for aerobic respiration and the substances produced	**Give the word equation for aerobic respiration**	Compare the processes of aerobic respiration and photosynthesis
Describe how the reactants and products of respiration move to and from cells	Identify the substances which move into and out of cells during respiration	**Describe how the reactants and products of respiration move to and from cells**	Explain how the reactants and products of respiration move to and from cells

Tier 2 vocabulary	Tier 3 vocabulary
	aerobic respiration, glucose, haemoglobin, mitochondria, plasma

Digital resources

Activity: *Investigating aerobic respiration* (Activity sheet, Support sheet, Teacher and technician notes)

Student Book answers

Think back 1 mitochondria **2** alveoli **3** transport oxygen

In-text question A glucose and oxygen **B** carbon dioxide **C** diffusion **D** carbon dioxide and glucose

See p.51 for the answers to the **Summary questions** for this lesson.

Getting started

Give students two minutes to produce a list of everything you need energy for (everything!).

Ask students where this energy comes from (food) and how it is released to the body (respiration).

This is another opportunity to address the misconception that respiration is breathing (ventilation).

Explain that, like photosynthesis, the process of respiration can be summarized in a word equation.

Main activity

Activity: Investigating aerobic respiration This activity is divided into two tasks. For Task 1, put the blank word equation for aerobic respiration on the board. Then, as a class, deduce the word equation. Fill in the answers on the board and ask students to fill in the Activity sheet as each step is discussed/demonstrated.

1. What sugar is produced after food is broken down during digestion? (glucose)

2. What gas do people breathe in? (oxygen)

3. Give students a test tube of limewater. Using a straw, ask them to repeatedly breathe out into the water for 1 minute. What happens? Why? (The limewater turns cloudy as respiration produces carbon dioxide.)

4. Give students a strip of cobalt chloride paper. Demonstrate that the paper, when placed in a test tube of water, turns from blue to pink. Ask students to repeatedly breathe on the strip. What happens? Why? (The cobalt chloride paper turns pink as respiration produces water.) Note that cobalt chloride paper should not be handled without using tweezers.

5. Demonstrate burning food by sprinkling sugar or custard powder over a Bunsen burner. (This is dramatic! Even if used to introduce energy content of foods, students like to see it again. Alternatively, burn a crisp.) Discuss what happens in the reaction. (When glucose reacts with oxygen, energy is transferred thermally, representing energy being transferred to the cell. In the human body, the reaction is less energetic, but does release small quantities of thermal energy – generating warmth.) Explain that energy is written in brackets as it is not a physical substance.

6. Students should complete Task 1 on the Activity sheet as each step is demonstrated.

For Task 2, ask students to produce a visual summary of how the reactants of aerobic respiration enter the body and travel to the cell, and how the waste products of aerobic respiration leave the body. They can use information from the Student Book to help them.

Students then answer the questions that follow.

Review and reflect

Ask students to write down the ending of the following sentences and hold them up:

Aerobic respiration occurs in ... (mitochondria)

The purpose of respiration is to transfer ... (energy to the cell)

The products of aerobic respiration are carbon dioxide and ... (water)

The reactants of respiration are glucose and ... (oxygen)

Language support

Write the words 'inhale' and 'exhale' where all students can see. Elicit or explain that these are verbs (action words). First, say 'inhale' out loud as you breathe in, then 'exhale' when you breathe out. Encourage students to practise this with you to help them remember the meaning. (Check that they do not have any breathing problems or conditions first.) During the course of the lesson, help students understand that the key word 'aerobic' means involving oxygen. Therefore, aerobic respiration involves oxygen.

2.5 Anaerobic respiration

Biology links

- the process of anaerobic respiration in humans and micro-organisms, including fermentation, and a word summary for anaerobic respiration
- the differences between aerobic and anaerobic respiration in terms of the reactants, the products formed, and the implications for the organism

Learning objective	Learning outcomes		
	Developing	Secure	Extending
Compare the processes of aerobic and anaerobic respiration	Give the definition of anaerobic respiration	**Compare the processes of aerobic and anaerobic respiration**	Explain why the body normally respires aerobically
Give the word equation for anaerobic respiration	Identify the substances used for anaerobic respiration and the substances produced	**Give the word equation for anaerobic respiration**	Explain the meaning of oxygen debt
Give the word equation for fermentation	Name some food products made using fermentation	**Give the word equation for fermentation**	Explain how the fermentation reaction is used to manufacture some food products

Tier 2 vocabulary	Tier 3 vocabulary
	anaerobic respiration, fermentation, microorganism, oxygen debt

Digital resources

Activity: *Fermentation and food production* (Activity sheet, Support sheet, Teacher and technician notes)
Video: *Respiration*

Student Book answers

Think back 1 glucose + oxygen → carbon dioxide + water (+ energy) **2** plasma **3** to contract (to cause movement)

In-text question A in the absence of oxygen **B** aerobic respiration **C** Lactic acid is produced in humans, whereas ethanol and carbon dioxide are produced in fermentation.

See p.51 for the answers to the **Summary questions** for this lesson.

Getting started

Show a video clip of a runner who becomes exhausted and pulls up in pain, or show images of, for example, athletes/footballers who have cramp. Ask students to suggest what has happened to these sportspeople's bodies.

Introduce the idea of anaerobic respiration in short bursts to supply energy without the need for oxygen, making lactic acid as a by-product, which causes cramp. Explain that when you have finished exercising, you keep on breathing heavily. The extra oxygen you inhale breaks down the lactic acid. The oxygen needed for this process is called the oxygen debt.

Introduce the word equation for anaerobic respiration. Write this next to the word equation for aerobic respiration. Then, working in pairs, ask students to write down a similarity and a difference between aerobic and anaerobic respiration. Share answers.

Ask students to give a reason why the body normally respires aerobically (to avoid cramp through lactic acid build-up). Go on to explain that aerobic respiration transfers more energy per glucose molecule than anaerobic respiration. Therefore, it is a preferable process for the body.

Main activity

Activity: Fermentation and food production

Introduce the microorganism yeast using Figure 2 in the Student Book. Explain that when microorganisms respire anaerobically, the process is called fermentation and different products are produced.

Show students a conical flask of yeast fermenting sugar, with a tube passing through limewater, to demonstrate that carbon dioxide is produced. Represent fermentation using its word equation. Students then complete the activity by researching a useful food or drink product made using fermentation, and producing a leaflet to explain how it is made.

Students then answer the questions on anaerobic respiration that follow.

Review and reflect

Issue cards with all the words and arrows necessary for the three equations for respiration (aerobic, anaerobic, and fermentation). Ask students to make the three equations by arranging the cards.

You can also watch the video on Kerboodle to consolidate students' learning.

Language support

Ask students to recall what the key word 'aerobic' means from their lesson on aerobic respiration. They should say that it means involving oxygen. Based on this understanding, ask them to predict what the key word 'anaerobic' means. The prefix 'an-' means without. Therefore, anaerobic respiration is respiration *without* oxygen.

Getting started

Encourage students to review their learning in this chapter. The 'Summary questions' in the Student Book can be used formatively during lessons. For the 'What have I learned?' pages, students can answer the questions one at a time after each topic, or as a single summative activity. This could be done as a whole-class or group activity, or set as an independent task.

Whichever approach is adopted, the questions are designed to give you and students feedback about progress and identify targets for development.

Student reflection

Allow students time to reflect on how confident they feel about each topic. Remind them to use the learning objectives provided in their Student Book for guidance. They should focus on whether there were any questions they found difficult or easy, and on how well they prepared for the summative assessment at the end of the chapter. Listen to and deal with students' reflections sensitively so that they feel comfortable to report areas they are not confident with.

Learning objectives and learning outcomes

Each lesson is guided by the learning *objectives*. The learning objectives are provided at the beginning of each topic in the Student Book. They outline what students are going to learn in each topic.

In contrast, the learning *outcomes* in this Teacher's Guide are statements that describe the knowledge or skills that students should acquire by the end of each topic. They are linked to the learning objectives, but are *not* often seen by students. The learning outcomes are used by teachers to assess and measure if or how each learning objective has been achieved.

Answer key

Chapter 2: Biological processes

1 correct drawing and labels of a leaf cell (including nucleus, cell membrane, cell wall, cytoplasm, vacuole, chloroplasts, mitochondria) or a root hair cell (including nucleus, cell membrane, cell wall, cytoplasm, vacuole, mitochondria, root hair, large surface area, *no* chloroplasts)
2 correct drawing and labels of an animal cell (including nucleus – controls the cell and contains genetic material; cell membrane – controls the movement of substances into and out of the cell; cytoplasm – where chemical reactions take place; mitochondria – where respiration takes place)
3 inhaled air: nitrogen (79%), oxygen (21%), carbon dioxide (0.04%); exhaled air: nitrogen (79%), oxygen (16%), carbon dioxide (4%), water vapour

2.1 Photosynthesis

Working scientifically: A plant placed in a dark cupboard would be unable to photosynthesize due to a lack of light, and would eventually die.
1 algae, producers, photosynthesis, carbon dioxide, glucose, light
2 a Yes because sunlight is available.
  b No because no sunlight is available.
  c No because there is no sunlight. There are no chloroplasts in the root hair cells.
3 Producers/plants use the process of photosynthesis to produces glucose. This provides energy for plants to grow. Animals cannot make their own food. Animals therefore eat plants/producers to gain energy.

2.2 Leaves

Maths skills: 9200 × 10 = 92 000 stomata
1 stomata – allow gases to diffuse into and out of the leaf
waxy layer – reduces amount of water evaporating
guard cells – open and close stomata
veins – transport water to cells in leaf
2 Water diffuses into the root/root hair cells, is transported through the plant in the water vessels, and evaporates out of leaves.
3 thin – to allow carbon dioxide to diffuse into the leaf; large surface area – to absorb as much (sun)light as possible; both factors allow the plant to maximize the rate of photosynthesis

2.3 Plant minerals

1 minerals, nitrates, root hair cells, vessels
2 to replace missing minerals from the soil/provide additional minerals to ensure a crop does not have a mineral deficiency/has all the minerals it needs for healthy growth
3 nitrates make amino acids; amino acids join together to make proteins; proteins are needed to grow new leaves/shoots/for repair

2.4 Aerobic respiration

1 food, respiration, glucose, energy, water
2 Aerobic respiration occurs in the mitochondria. Mitochondria are found in cells. Oxygen reacts with glucose. It releases carbon dioxide and water, together with energy.
3 Inhaling fills alveoli (in the lungs) with oxygen; the oxygen diffuses into the bloodstream. Oxygen is carried by red blood cells/binds to haemoglobin and is transported in the bloodstream to cells. Glucose is taken in through food; the food is digested and glucose absorbed through the wall of the small intestine. Glucose is carried to cells in the blood (plasma).

2.5 Anaerobic respiration

1 anaerobic, oxygen, energy, lactic acid, muscles,
2 Anaerobic respiration occurs without oxygen, aerobic respiration requires oxygen.
Anaerobic respiration produces lactic acid, aerobic respiration does not.
Anaerobic respiration produces less energy per glucose molecule.
Aerobic respiration produces water, anaerobic respiration does not.
3 Aerobic respiration transfers more energy per glucose molecule, so is more efficient/requires less food to be eaten; anaerobic respiration produces lactic acid, which causes painful cramps/makes moving difficult.

What have I learned about biological processes?

1 a (aerobic) respiration [1 mark]
  b mitochondria [1 mark]
  c oxygen [1 mark] carbon dioxide [1 mark]

2 a producers [1 mark]
  b chloroplasts [1 mark]
  c oxygen [1 mark]
  d add iodine, [1 mark] turns blue-black [1 mark]
3 a nitrates/phosphates [1 mark]
  b manure/fertilizer [1 mark]
  c to make chlorophyll [1 mark] which absorbs light [1 mark] for photosynthesis [1 mark]
4 a B, D, A, C [3 marks for all correct, 2 marks for 2 correct, 1 mark for one correct]
  b yellow-brown [1 mark] → blue/black [1 mark]
  c for example: for respiration/to build cell walls [1 mark]
5 a oxygen [1 mark]
  b carbon dioxide and water [2 marks]
  c allow carbon dioxide into the leaf [1 mark] and allow oxygen out of the leaf [1 mark]
  d Bubbles would stop [1 mark] as photosynthesis would stop [1 mark], because there is no light. [1 mark]
6 Students should be marked on the use of good English, organization of information, spelling and grammar, and correct use of specialist scientific terms. The best answers will provide a full explanation of the adaptations for photosynthesis. [maximum 6 marks]

Examples of correct scientific points:
Fermentation is a type of anaerobic respiration.
Fermentation occurs in some microorganisms/yeast.
These microorganisms respire in the absence of oxygen.
Energy is transferred from glucose.
glucose → ethanol + carbon dioxide (+ energy)
The ethanol product can be used in alcoholic drink production.
The carbon dioxide product is used in bread production/to make dough rise.
7 Students should be marked on the use of good English, organization of information, spelling and grammar, and correct use of specialist scientific terms. The best answers will provide a full explanation of fermentation, with the process explained in a logical order. [6 marks maximum]

Examples of correct scientific points:
Leaves contain chlorophyll, which traps light.
Leaves are thin, which allows gases to diffuse in and out of the leaf easily.
Leaves have a large surface area to absorb as much light as possible.
Leaves have veins/xylem to transport water to cells.
Leaves have a palisade layer/cells with more chloroplasts near the top of the leaf, to maximize the absorption of sunlight.
Leaves have stomata to allow carbon dioxide into (and oxygen out of) the leaf.

Introduction to chapter

In this chapter, students will begin by looking at the feeding relationships within food chains and webs, and how this can result in bioaccumulation. They will then study the interdependence of organisms by looking at what happens to the population of one organism when the population of another is changed. Students will then look in detail at the adaptations of a number of organisms that enable them to be successful competitors and survive in harsh and changing environments.

Core concepts

- Interdependence
- Plant and animal adaptations

What have students already learned?

- How to construct and interpret a variety of food chains, identifying producers, predators, and prey
- Environments can change, sometimes posing dangers to living things
- How animals and plants are adapted to suit their environment in different ways
- The structural adaptations of some unicellular organisms
- The dependence of almost all life on Earth on the ability of photosynthetic organisms, such as plants and algae, to use sunlight in photosynthesis to build organic molecules (an essential energy store) and to maintain levels of oxygen and carbon dioxide in the atmosphere

What will students learn next?

- Levels of organization within an ecosystem
- Some abiotic and biotic factors that affect communities; the importance of interactions between organisms in a community
- The role of microorganisms (decomposers) in the cycling of materials through an ecosystem
- Organisms are interdependent and adapted to their environment
- Methods of identifying species and measuring distribution, frequency, and abundance of species within a habitat

Think back

1 Write an example of a food chain with at least three links.

2 Write down a list of 10 animals. Sort the animals into predators (they eat other animals) and prey (they are eaten). Identify any features they have in common.

3 Choose an animal or plant. List three ways it is adapted to its habitat (where it lives).

Teaching strategy

Predator–prey graphs If working with a less mathematically able class, introduce predator–prey graphs by sketching a coloured line on a blank graph showing a trend of increasing and decreasing in a repeating pattern. Discuss what this shows (over time, a population increases then decreases). Then add a second line in a different colour showing the same pattern with a time lag. Explain that the first line shows the prey population, the second line shows the predator population, and that one is dependent on the other. Break the graph down into sections, ensuring that students understand what is happening to both populations at each stage and how the populations are interdependent. Then repeat this by looking at graphs with data.

This might also be the first time that students have met graphs with different scales on the y-axis, so ask students to read relevant prey and predator numbers from a range of graphs. This will help them appreciate that prey numbers are always bigger than predator numbers.

Arrows in food webs At every opportunity when talking about feeding relationships between organisms, represent the relationships as food chains or webs (or parts of food chains or webs). This will give students plenty of practice drawing arrows to show where the energy/biomass is being transferred to.

Sampling ecosystems If more time is available, there are a number of simple practical activities that could be included for students to measure the abundance and distribution of organisms within an ecosystem. For example, using pooters and pitfall traps to investigate invertebrates. Students can then be introduced to the use of keys in identifying organisms. Sampling bias could also be introduced at this stage – teach students how to compensate for it by using a random number generator to select a sample area. The data collected can be used to estimate population sizes.

Common learning misconceptions

- In food chains, the arrows show what an organism eats. (The arrows show the movement of *energy* from one organism to another.)

- Organisms that are higher in a food web eat all organisms that are lower in the food web.

- Animals choose to adapt to suit their surroundings. (The adaptation of a species is a slow change over time, by chance, where useful adaptations give an advantage. These organisms survive and reproduce.)

- Adult animals do not change their appearance.

- Camouflaged animals are brown or green.

- Only predators can run fast.

- Plants are prey organisms.

- Predator and prey populations are similar in size.

Broader context

Scientists study ecosystems and how animals adapt to their surroundings to protect them. Some species are becoming extinct as their surroundings change quickly. This is often a result of human actions.

Being better informed about ecosystems can help save some species from extinction. Some species can also be bred in captivity to support their survival.

3.1 Food chains and webs

Biology link

- the interdependence of organisms in an ecosystem, including food webs and insect-pollinated crops

Learning objective	Learning outcomes		
	Developing	Secure	Extending
Use relevant information to create a food chain	Describe a food chain	**Use relevant information to create a food chain**	Explain why the Sun is the ultimate source of energy in food chains
Describe the feeding relationships between organisms in a food chain	Identify the producer and a consumer in a food chain	**Describe the feeding relationships between organisms in a food chain**	Explain why food chains rarely have more than four links
Describe the feeding relationships between organisms in a food web	Describe a food web	**Describe the feeding relationships between organisms in a food web**	Explain why food webs describe feeding relationships more realistically than food chains

Tier 2 vocabulary	Tier 3 vocabulary
predator, prey	decomposer, food chain, food web, producer

Digital resources
Activity: *A woodland food web* (Activity sheet, Support sheet, Teacher and technician notes)   Video: *Feeding relationships*

Student Book answers

Think back 1 an organism that makes its own food by photosynthesis **2** an organism that eats plants or animals to gain energy
3 carbon dioxide + water $\xrightarrow{\text{light}}$ glucose + oxygen

In-text questions A grain → mouse → owl
B predator **C** impala

See p.64 for the answers to the **Summary questions** for this lesson.

Getting started

Ask students, in pairs, to arrange the following organisms into a food chain: lion, acacia tree, giraffe. Ask them to add as many key feeding relationship words as possible (e.g. 'producer', 'carnivore').

Food chains are covered in primary school. This activity will allow you to determine prior understanding. Check that all students have added arrows pointing in the correct direction. Explain that these represent the transfer of energy (through food). Discuss all the key words: 'producer', 'consumer', 'herbivore', 'carnivore', 'prey', 'predator' (and 'top predator').

Introduce the concept that most food chains do not have more than four or five links, due to less energy being transferred at each level. Ask students to come up with ways energy is **not** passed on. For example, leaves shed in winter/not all parts of an organism are eaten/energy is transferred to the environment as heat. (Reinforce the concept that energy is transferred to the environment; it is not 'lost'.)

Show this mathematically. First, look at the food chain example in Figure 1 in the Student Book. Then answer the question in the Maths skills box, calculating a 10% transfer each time.

Main activity

Look at the food web in Figure 3 in the Student Book. Discuss how different food chains can link together to create a food web like this one. This diagram is therefore a more realistic representation of the feeding relationships present in an African grassland. Discuss various feeding relationships shown in the food web.

Activity: A woodland food web Students make their own food webs using the organisms provided on the cards. They answer the questions that follow.

Review and reflect

Show students a food web. Ask them a series of questions about the web, including identifying a food chain. Students record their answers on their whiteboards and hold them up.

You can also watch the video on Kerboodle to consolidate students' learning.

Language support

Ask students to suggest the meaning of the word 'compose'. Take answers and explain that it means to make or create something. For example, a composer or musician *composes* (makes) music. Since the prefix

'de-' means the opposite of, the word 'decompose' means the opposite of making or creating something. In science, this means to break down. Decomposers break down matter into smaller particles.

Biology links

- the interdependence of organisms in an ecosystem, including food webs and insect-pollinated crops
- how organisms affect, and are affected by, their environment, including the accumulation of toxic materials

Learning objective	Learning outcomes		
	Developing	Secure	Extending
Describe the meaning of interdependence of organisms	Name some ways in which organisms depend on each other to survive	**Describe the meaning of interdependence of organisms**	Use specific examples to explain why organisms are interdependent on each other
Suggest and give reasons for how the change in population of one organism affects the population of another in a food web	List the food chains within a food web	**Suggest and give reasons for how the change in population of one organism affects the population of another in a food web**	Suggest and explain the effect of a population change of one organism on a range of other organisms in a food web
Describe how toxic materials can build up in a food chain	Describe how the number of animals changes as you move through a food chain	**Describe how toxic materials can build up in a food chain**	Explain how bioaccumulation can lead to human health problems

Tier 2 vocabulary	Tier 3 vocabulary
population	bioaccumulation, insecticides, interdependence

Digital resources

Activity: *Factors affecting food chains and webs* (Activity sheet, Support sheet, Teacher and technician notes)
Video: *Interdependence in ecosystems*

Student Book answers

Think back 1 a series of linked food chains **2** producer **3** Pollen is transferred from the anther to the stigma.

In-text questions A bees and flowers/crops/named plant **B** increase in populations of consumers **C** build-up of chemicals inside organisms in a food chain

See p.64 for the answers to the **Summary questions** for this lesson.

Getting started

Ask students to think about how a bee and a flower depend on each other to survive (flower for pollination, bee for nectar). Then ask students to produce a list of other factors that organisms depend on each other for (e.g. shelter, food, mates). Use these discussions to introduce the concept of interdependence.

Introduce the key word 'population'. Ask students to think about a population of rabbits in a field. State a number of situations such as disease, a bumper crop, fire, foxes, new fencing. Ask students to raise their hands if the population increases and to point to the floor if the population decreases.

Show students the food web in Figure 2 in the Student Book. Start by naming a few animals and ask what they eat. Then discuss what would happen to the numbers of different consumers if the grass died. Do the same for vole and thrush numbers if the caterpillar population decreased. Repeat this activity for other organisms until students have a good grasp of the concept. For each scenario, ask students to suggest what will happen to the population numbers, and to explain their reasoning for this.

Main activity

Activity: Factors affecting food chains and webs
Ask students to complete Task 1 on their Activity sheet. They answer questions about the interdependence of organisms in a food web.

In Task 2, students rearrange a series of statements to describe the process of bioaccumulation of insecticides in otters. They then write a definition of bioaccumulation.

Review and reflect

Show students the food chain in Figure 3 in the Student Book, which illustrates the bioaccumulation of insecticides in polar bears. In pairs, ask students to write a description of bioaccumulation using this example.

You can also watch the video on Kerboodle to consolidate students' learning.

Language support

Display the key word 'bioaccumulation'. Ask students to break the word down into two parts: 'bio' and 'accumulation'. They will already be familiar with the word 'biology' from prior learning. Biology means the study of living organisms. Then challenge students to think about the word 'accumulate' by placing it in context. It means to gather or collect something. Therefore, bioaccumulation is when substances gather, or slowly build up, in a living organism.

Biology link

- the interdependence of organisms in an ecosystem, including food webs and insect-pollinated crops

Working scientifically links

- apply sampling techniques
- interpret observations and data, including identifying patterns

Learning objective	Learning outcomes		
	Developing	Secure	Extending
Define a habitat, a community, and an ecosystem	Give an example of a habitat, and the plants and animals that live there	**Define a habitat, a community, and an ecosystem**	Describe the levels of organization within a named ecosystem
Describe how different organisms co-exist within an ecosystem	Name some organisms that co-exist within a familiar ecosystem	**Describe how different organisms co-exist within an ecosystem**	Explain why different organisms within an ecosystem have different niches

Tier 2 vocabulary	Tier 3 vocabulary
community, environment, habitat, niche	ecosystem

Digital resources

Practical: *Investigating plant distribution* (Practical sheet, Support sheet, Teacher and technician notes)

Student Book answers

Think back 1 the number of a particular type of plant/animal in an area **2** food/shelter/mates/pollination **3** They break down dead plant and animal material.

In-text questions A forest **B** any three named animals found in or around an oak tree, for example: bees, sparrows, earthworms **C** They have different food sources.

See p.65 for the answers to the **Summary questions** for this lesson.

Getting started

Show students the image of the coral reef ecosystem in Figure 1 in the Student Book. Ask them to list the organisms present (explain that this is the *community*) and to describe the *habitat* (this is a key word with which they should be familiar from primary school). Then explain that the key word 'ecosystem' refers to both the community and the habitat found in an area.

Use the image of the oak tree ecosystem in Figure 3. Ask students to describe the habitat and name some organisms present in the community.

Discuss how organisms can co-exist, because they fulfil different niches, by using the information in the Student Book. Look at the organisms present in different layers of the tree, and also within a layer.

Main activity

Show students a quadrat. Ask: *What do you think it is?* Talk about how sampling techniques are used to estimate the number of plants in a field because the number within a whole field could not be easily counted. Explain to students that they only need to count plants that lie completely within the quadrat.

Practical: Investigating plant distribution Students use sampling techniques to measure the abundance of a named plant on the school field (e.g. dandelions), and record their observations. Students then return to the classroom to answer the questions on their Practical sheet.

Review and reflect

Ask students to write definitions of the key words 'habitat', 'community', and 'ecosystem' on their whiteboards, and then to hold them up.

Language support

Talk about the key word 'ecosystem'. It refers to a community of living things, including plants and animals as well as much smaller living things, that live, feed, reproduce, and interact with each other.

3.4 Competition

Biology link

- the variation between species and between individuals of the same species, meaning some organisms compete more successfully

Working scientifically link

- interpret observations and data, including identifying patterns and using observations and data to draw conclusions

Learning objective	Learning outcomes		
	Developing	Secure	Extending
Explain the resources that plants and animals compete for	Name some resources that plants and animals compete for	**Explain the resources that plants and animals compete for**	Compare the resources that plants and animals compete for
Describe how predator and prey populations interact	State the meaning of predator and prey organisms	**Describe how predator and prey populations interact**	Explain the interaction between predator and prey populations

Tier 2 vocabulary	Tier 3 vocabulary
competition, population, predator, prey	

Digital resources

Activity: *Predator–prey relationships* (Activity sheet, Support sheet, Teacher and technician notes)

Student Book answers

Think back 1 an animal that eats another animal **2** an animal that gets eaten by another animal **3** when two or more organisms depend on one another to survive

In-text questions A food, water, space, and mates **B** light, water, space, and minerals **C** food

See p.65 for the answers to the **Summary questions** for this lesson.

Getting started

Show students the photo in Figure 1 in the Student Book of birds fighting over food. Ask: *What are the birds competing for? What else do animals compete for?*

Ask students to make a list of what plants compete for. Share students' ideas to compose a class list. Discuss how this differs to what animals compete for.

Discuss the interdependence of predator and prey populations. Then use the graph in Figure 2, showing the relationship between lynx and hare populations, to introduce the patterns shown on predator–prey graphs. Break the graph down into sections and ensure students understand what is happening to both populations at each stage. They should realize that the trendlines follow the same pattern, but with a time lag.

Main activity

Activity: Predator–prey relationships Students plot a graph to show the number of Canadian wolves in Quebec between 2001 and 2009. This graph is drawn on top of an existing graph, showing the number of caribou in the same period. Students then interpret the graphs to answer the questions that follow.

Review and reflect

On a whiteboard, ask students to sketch a predator–prey graph to show the interdependence between populations of zebra and cheetah. Encourage students to use different colours to represent the populations (or represent one population as a dashed line).

Describe certain situations – for example, a rise in the predator population. Ask students to point to where this is being represented on the graph.

Language support

Elicit from students examples of competitions. They might mention a sports event, a poetry competition, a spelling bee, or playing a board game. The idea is that people *compete* or play against each other to win a prize. Likewise, organisms compete against each other for important resources (the prize). Living things often need the same things to survive in their environment.

Biology link

- changes in the environment may leave individuals within a species, and some entire species, less well adapted to compete successfully and reproduce, which in turn may lead to extinction

Learning objective	Learning outcomes		
	Developing	Secure	Extending
Describe how organisms are adapted to their environment	Identify some adaptations of organisms that help them survive	**Describe how organisms are adapted to their environment**	Explain how organisms are adapted to their environment
Describe how organisms adapt to environmental changes	Describe some seasonal changes that take place throughout the year	**Describe how organisms adapt to environmental changes**	Use examples to explain how organisms adapt to environmental changes

Tier 2 vocabulary	Tier 3 vocabulary
camouflage, competition, hibernation, migration	adaptation

Digital resources

Activity: *On thin ice* (Activity sheet, Support sheet, Teacher and technician notes)
Video: *Adaptation and competition*

Student Book answers

Think back 1 food, water, space, mates **2** light, water, space, minerals **3** A special feature that allows a cell to perform its function or an organism to survive. Explain that the word 'adaptation' refers to any special characteristics a cell or organism may have.

In-text questions A any two from: large body heats up slowly, does not sweat, moves around at night (when cooler) to feed, produces concentrated urine, produces dry faeces **B** widespread root systems **C** hibernation, migration, grow thicker fur

See p.65 for the answers to the **Summary questions** for this lesson.

Getting started

Ask students to work in small groups to design the best-adapted predator or prey organism. This predator/prey can be real or imaginary, but a drawing of the organism must be accompanied by annotations of its adaptations. Students should then compare their organisms. Some adaptations are likely to be features of all organisms, such as good eyesight, being fast, and camouflage. This task will allow you to assess the level of knowledge students already have on adaptations from the work they covered in primary school.

If further explanation/examples are needed, discuss with students how the cactus and oryx are adapted using Figure 2, Figure 3, and information in the Student Book.

Introduce the concept that some plant species are adapted to changes in the seasons. Ask students to produce a timeline of the changes that take place in deciduous trees throughout the year, and how this is linked to seasonal changes.

Ask students to produce a list of ways animals are adapted to changing seasons using named examples of organisms. If needed, prompt students by giving them a list of organisms to discuss such as bears (hibernate), swallows (migrate), or squirrels (hide acorns). Then share students' ideas.

Main activity

Activity: On thin ice Students read an article about environmental changes in the Arctic, and the effects of these changes on polar bears and their population. They then answer the questions that follow.

Review and reflect

Show students the two photos of the snowshoe hare in Figure 4 in the Student Book. Ask them to explain how it is adapted to seasonal changes.

You can also watch the video on Kerboodle to consolidate students' learning.

Language support

Ask students to discuss in groups what the phrase 'adapt to something' means, and to think of examples. For example, some people adapt to hearing less well by reading other people's lips in conversation.

They must change their behaviour according to their needs. Likewise, plant and animal species must adapt, or change, to survive in changing environments.

Getting started

Encourage students to review their learning in this chapter. The 'Summary questions' in the Student Book can be used formatively during lessons. For the 'What have I learned?' pages, students can answer the questions one at a time after each topic, or as a single summative activity. This could be done as a whole-class or group activity, or set as an independent task.

Whichever approach is adopted, the questions are designed to give you and students feedback about progress and identify targets for development.

Student reflection

Allow students time to reflect on how confident they feel about each topic. Remind them to use the learning objectives provided in their Student Book for guidance. They should focus on whether there were any questions they found difficult or easy, and on how well they prepared for the summative assessment at the end of the chapter. Listen to and deal with students' reflections sensitively so that they feel comfortable to report areas they are not confident with.

Learning objectives and learning outcomes

Each lesson is guided by the learning *objectives*. The learning objectives are provided at the beginning of each topic in the Student Book. They outline what students are going to learn in each topic.

In contrast, the learning *outcomes* in this Teacher's Guide are statements that describe the knowledge or skills that students should acquire by the end of each topic. They are linked to the learning objectives, but are *not* often seen by students. The learning outcomes are used by teachers to assess and measure if or how each learning objective has been achieved.

Answer key

Chapter 3: Ecosystems and adaptation

1 should include a producer, a herbivore, and at least one carnivore (e.g. grass → rabbit → fox)
2 answers depend on animals chosen; features in common may include having fur, ability to run fast, etc.
3 answers depend on species chosen

3.1 Food chains and webs

Maths skills: level 1: 10% of 1000 = 100 kJ; level 2: 10% of 100 = 10 kJ; level 3: 10% of 10 = 1 kJ energy transferred to top predator

1 food chain – diagram showing the transfer of energy between organisms
food web – diagram showing linked food chains
predator – animal that eats another animal
prey – animal that is eaten

2 a giraffe/impala/zebra
  b acacia tree/grass
  c acacia tree
  d credit any suitable answer, for example:
    grass → impala → leopard → lion
3 As energy is transferred along a chain, some is transferred to the surroundings/by heating, some energy is lost in waste products, and not all of an organism is eaten; therefore, at each level of the food chain, less energy is transferred to the organism in the next level; this means there is not enough energy available to support higher levels within a food chain.

3.2 Disruption to food chains and webs

1 survive, growth, interdependence, bioaccumulation
2 the way in which organisms depend on each other to survive/grow/reproduce
3 a Rabbit population would increase as it has no predators/it will not get eaten.

b The hawk/fox populations may decrease as they have reduced food supplies.
The caterpillar population may increase as they have fewer predators.

3.3 Ecosystems

Working scientifically: 400 × 3 = 1200 daisies approximately

1 ecosystem – living organisms in a particular area, and the habitat they live in
community – plants and animals found in a particular habitat
habitat – place where a plant or animal lives

2 Bees and birds have different niches/they eat different things. Bees require nectar from flowers, whereas birds live off insects living on the leaves.

3 A niche is the place or role that an organism has in a habitat.
Examples with associated explanations, for example: Not every organism lives in the same part of the tree.
Microorganisms at the base of the tree break down old leaves. This gives the tree further nutrients to absorb for growth.
Insects live in the tree trunk. The insect larvae are food for birds that may live in the canopy.
Squirrels and bees live in the canopy. The activities of each organism do not conflict each other, and so different organisms can co-exist.
Bees gather pollen and nectar when the tree is in blossom, while squirrels gather acorns as food.

3.4 Competition

Maths skills: sketch similar to Figure 2, with red line as fox (predator) and blue line as rabbit (prey), clearly showing interdependence

1 compete, resources, mates, minerals

2 A, E, D, B, C

3 Initially, the population of European ladybirds will increase significantly because they can feed on aphids and other ladybird species. Eventually their food supply will decrease so the seven-spotted ladybird population will decrease; this allows the population of aphids to increase as less are eaten. The cycle then starts again.

3.5 Adapting to change

1 characteristics, camouflaged, staying alive

2 any three from: waxy layer, spines instead of leaves, large root system, stems that can store water

3 grow leaves in the spring when light/temperature is high to enable/maximize photosynthesis; lose leaves in the winter to save energy; leaves provide a layer of warmth/protection at the base of the tree; nutrients can be reused

What have I learned about ecosystems and adaptation?

1 **a** Arctic [1 mark]
b white fur – camouflage [1 mark]
thick fur – insulation [1 mark]
large feet – to stop the bear sinking into snow [1 mark]
sharp claws and teeth – to catch and eat prey [1 mark]

2 **a** shelter/food [1 mark]
b different from (a), for example: food/shelter/mates [1 mark]
c light [1 mark]

3 **a** grass → antelope → lion [1 mark]
b grass [1 mark]
c Producers have energy transferred from glucose they make. [1 mark] Consumers have energy transferred from the organisms they eat. [1 mark]
d The antelope population would increase [1 mark] as there are no lions to eat them. [1 mark]

4 **a** The spider population would increase [1 mark] as there are no predators/nothing would eat them. [1 mark]
b The grasshopper population would decrease [1 mark] as shrews and spiders would need to eat more of them to survive. [1 mark]
c Mice and shrews eat some different foods. [1 mark] Mice eat dandelions (a producer) and shrews do not. Shrews eat beetles and mice do not. There is enough food for them both to survive. [1 mark]
d Due to the lack of a producer (the dandelions), the entire food web collapses. [1 mark] For example [any example from the food web in Figure 2], dandelions are food for grasshoppers, grasshoppers are food for spiders, and spiders are food for owls. [1 mark] Without shrews, spiders, and mice, owls will no longer have a source of food and could die if they do not find a new food source. [1 mark]

5 Students should be marked on the use of good English, organization of information, spelling and grammar, and correct use of specialist scientific terms. The best answers will provide a correct food chain and a complete explanation of the insecticide's effects laid out in a logical order. [6 marks maximum]
Examples of correct scientific points:
plankton → fish → fish-eating birds
insecticide runs into river
taken up by plankton
DDT accumulates in fish when they eat the plankton.
One fish eats lots of plankton, but not enough to cause death.
DDT accumulates in birds when they eat the fish.
One bird eats many fish.
DDT level is now so high/concentrated that it causes the death of the bird.

6 Students should be marked on the use of good English, organization of information, spelling and grammar, and correct use of specialist scientific terms. The best answers will provide at least two named examples with relevant adaptations. [6 marks maximum; award 1 mark for each named example and up to 2 marks for explaining relevant adaptations]
Examples of correct named organisms and adaptations:
Snowshoe hair changes fur colour; [1 mark] it grows white fur in winter to blend in with the snow; [1 mark] it grows red/brown fur in summer for camouflage against the earth. [1 mark]
Birds/named bird (e.g. swallows) [1 mark] migrate and fly to warmer places in the winter [1 mark] for a better food supply/less harsh environmental conditions. [1 mark]

Introduction to chapter

In this chapter, students will look at the variation in characteristics in organisms within a species and determine whether these are a result of inherited variation, environmental variation, or both. They will categorize characteristics as showing discontinuous or continuous variation, and will plot this on appropriate graphs. Students will then study how characteristics are inherited through chromosomes. The final section in the chapter looks at the process of natural selection, why some organisms become extinct, and the role gene banks can play in trying to prevent extinction.

Core concepts

- Variation (genetic and environmental)

- Natural selection

What have students already learned?

- How living things have changed over time; and how fossils provide information about living things that inhabited Earth millions of years ago

- How living things produce offspring of the same kind, but normally offspring vary and are not identical to their parents

- The functions of the cell wall, cell membrane, cytoplasm, nucleus, vacuole, mitochondria and chloroplasts

- The role of the male and female gametes in the process of fertilization in humans

- Organisms are adapted to their environment

What will students learn next?

- The genome, and how its interaction with the environment influences the development of the phenotype of an organism

- Single gene inheritance and single gene crosses with dominant and recessive phenotypes

- Sex determination in humans

- Genetic variation in populations of a species

- The process of natural selection

- The importance of selective breeding and modern biotechnology of plants and animals in agriculture

Think back

1 Look around your class. Think about the features you and your classmates have inherited (received) from a parent.

2 Draw a diagram to explain the process of fertilization.

3 Describe one way in which a fossil can form.

Teaching strategy

Differences between a histogram and a bar chart
This is likely to be the first time that students have met histograms in context. Introduce this skill by showing a bar chart and a histogram next to each other, and then discuss how they differ. In a histogram, there are no gaps between the bars, the bars must be arranged on a continuous scale along the axis, the bars are plotted against frequency density, and the bars represent a range of values (the bars may also be different widths if the selected class widths are not equal). In a bar chart, there are gaps between the bars, the bars can be in any order, the bars are plotted against frequency, the bars are always the same width, and the bars usually represent single values.

Plotting continuous variation This description uses height as an example, but you could use any continuous variable, for example, foot length (which could then be compared with shoe size, showing discontinuous variation).

Ask students to organize themselves from smallest to tallest. How do they think they could plot these data? Prompt them to think about organizing people into groups of different heights. Measure the smallest and the tallest person, then use these as a guide to produce groups. (As this is the first time students have met this skill, it is best to keep class widths the same.) If you have a large whiteboard, mark the top of each class boundary on the board from left to right, so the width of the board represents the x-axis and the height of the board the y-axis. If the sample is large enough, you should find more students standing in the middle groups. This can be compared with the graph in the Student Book.

Represent the class data using the following data table:

Height in cm	Tally	Frequency	Class width	Frequency density
$120 \leq h < 124$				
$125 \leq h < 129$				

Record students' height as a tally, then a total frequency. Explain how to calculate class width (largest value – smallest value). Then introduce how to calculate frequency density using the formula:

$$\text{Frequency density} = \frac{\text{Frequency}}{\text{Class width}}$$

Finally, plot the class width against frequency density to produce a histogram.

Common learning misconceptions

- Characteristics are all caused by genetics.

- When organisms are no longer found in one area of the world, they have become extinct. (Extinction means that the species does not exist anywhere on Earth.)

- Species are organisms that can reproduce, for example, a donkey and a horse are the same species. (Different species can have similar characteristics but do not produce fertile offspring if they mate.)

- 'Survival of the fittest' relates to strength and dominance between individual organisms. (It refers to how the characteristics of certain species are better suited to their environment, so they survive and breed more successfully.)

Biology link

- differences between species

Learning objective	Learning outcomes		
	Developing	Secure	Extending
Describe variation	Give some ways that organisms of the same species are different from each other	**Describe variation**	Suggest why identical twins look very similar, but not exactly the same
Use examples to describe the difference between inherited and environmental variation	Name some human characteristics that are inherited, and some that are affected by the environment	**Use examples to describe the difference between inherited and environmental variation**	Explain why many characteristics are affected both by the environment and through inheritance

Tier 2 vocabulary	Tier 3 vocabulary
	environmental variation, inherited variation, species, variation

Digital resources

Activity: *Types of variation* (Activity sheet, Support sheet, Teacher and technician notes)

Student Book answers

Think back 1 reproduction **2** sperm cells **3** egg cells

In-text questions A a group of organisms that can reproduce to produce fertile offspring **B** any three relevant examples of variation, for example: size, colour of feathers, whether they can fly, beak shape, frequency of egg laying **C** eye colour, blood group, lobed or lobeless ears **D** any three from: piercings, scars, dyed hair, language spoken, hair length, hair colour

See p.78 for the answers to the **Summary questions** for this lesson.

Getting started

Allow two minutes for students to make a list of the differences between birds.

Introduce the fact that differences in characteristics between organisms are known as variation.

Variation within and between species Show students images of a goldfish and a lizard. Ask: *How do they differ in characteristics?* Then show them an image of several goldfish. Ask: *How do these differ in characteristics?* Students should find it easy to identify variation between different species, but harder to identify variation within a species because they share many of the same characteristics.

Introduce students to the definition of a species: organisms that can reproduce to produce fertile offspring. You may wish to use the example of a donkey being crossed with a horse to produce an infertile mule to address this. Donkeys and horses look similar but they are entirely different species.

Main activity

Use Figure 1 in the Student Book to discuss some variations in human characteristics. Students should be aware that some characteristics are passed on from their parents, but may have thought less about the effect of the environment. Can they pick out examples from the diagram of characteristics that show inherited variation? They may select height. Explain that this is a characteristic that is affected by both the genetic material they inherit from their parents and their environment in terms of their diet. Encourage students to think of other examples of environmental variation (e.g. language spoken).

Activity: Types of variation In pairs, students perform a card sort to identify whether a characteristic shows variation as a result of inheritance, the environment, or both. They then record their answers in a Venn diagram, before answering the questions that follow.

Review and reflect

Provide students with three colours of card (e.g. red for inherited, green for the environment, and blue for both). Read out a list of characteristics.

Students hold up the appropriate card to describe the type of variation the characteristic shows.

Language support

Provide students with a small set of coloured pencils or pens. Ask them to make a list of how they are different and how they are the same. Ask if there are any that are identical, and how they vary if they are different. Students might talk about colour, length of pencil, or how sharp they are. Link this to characteristics. Explain that the sharpness of the pencil can vary depending on external factors (e.g. the person who sharpened or used it). Use this analogy to explain environmental variation and contrast it with the colour of the pencil, which is an innate characteristic (link this to genetic variation).

Biology link

- the variation between individuals within a species being continuous or discontinuous, to include measurement and graphical representation of variation

Working scientifically link

- present observations and data using appropriate methods, including tables and graphs

Learning objective	Learning outcomes		
	Developing	**Secure**	**Extending**
Use examples to describe the difference between continuous and discontinuous variation	State the meaning of continuous and discontinuous data	**Use examples to describe the difference between continuous and discontinuous variation**	Explain why some characteristics that are measured numerically (e.g. shoe size) show discontinuous variation
Choose and give reasons for the most appropriate graph to display examples of variation data	Name the type of graph used to display continuous and discontinuous data	**Choose and give reasons for the most appropriate graph to display examples of variation data**	Explain why variation in characteristics caused only as a result of inheritance is usually plotted on a bar chart

Tier 2 vocabulary	Tier 3 vocabulary
	continuous variation, discontinuous variation

Digital resources

Practical: *Investigating arm span* (Practical sheet, Support sheet, Teacher and technician notes)
Video: *Classification systems and variation*

Student Book answers

Think back 1 differences in characteristics within a species **2** variation due to the characteristics/genetic material inherited from an organism's parents **3** variation caused by an organism's surroundings and lifestyle

In-text questions A sex, blood group, eye colour **B** height, body mass, arm span **C** bar chart

See p.78 for the answers to the **Summary questions** for this lesson.

Getting started

Ask students to organize themselves into groups depending on different types of variation (e.g. sex, whether they can roll their tongue, eye colour). Then ask students to organize themselves by height.

Discuss that some characteristics, such as sex, result in certain values. This is discontinuous variation. Other characteristics, such as height, can take any value within a range. This is continuous variation.

Plotting discontinuous variation Use the blood group bar chart in Figure 1 in the Student Book to explain that discontinuous data are always plotted on a bar chart because the data always result in certain values. Parallels can be drawn to discrete data in maths if students are familiar with this. Discuss that 'inherited only' characteristics tend to show discontinuous variation.

Plotting continuous variation Use height as an example for how they can display continuous data. Ask: *How could you plot the heights in your class?* Prompt students to think about organizing people into groups of different heights (this could be done practically if time allows). Show them the tally chart. Point out key features, such as organizing heights into

class widths and writing them in order from smallest to largest. Note that as this is the first time histograms have been met in science, the class widths are the same size in the Student Book and in the practical.

Show how the data are represented within the tally chart: a height h of any value between x (lowest value) and y (highest value) is written: $x \leq h < y$. The class width can then be calculated from $y - x$.

Pick some height values and ask students to decide in which category the data would fit. Work through the example of how to calculate frequency density. Ask students to calculate one or two examples on the remainder of the chart.

Show students the height histogram in Figure 2 in the Student Book. Point out the key ways a histogram differs from a bar chart (e.g. no gaps between the bars, bars need to be in a specific order). Point out the trends shown in the graph (e.g. few very tall/short people, most people being of 'average' height). Discuss that characteristics that occur as a result of inheritance and the environment tend to show continuous variation.

Main activity

Practical: Investigating arm span Students work in small groups to measure the arm spans of students within their own group. The class results are collated on

a tally chart (using group sizes of fixed width). Students then plot a histogram to show the class results for arm span, and answer the questions that follow.

Review and reflect

Call out different types of continuous variation (e.g. hair length) and discontinuous variation (e.g. tongue-rolling) for students to decide on the correct type of variation using whiteboards. Students should also

identify the type of graph needed to display the results.

You can also watch the video on Kerboodle to consolidate students' learning.

Language support

Ask students to discuss the word 'continuous'. What does it mean if something *continues*? They might suggest that they continue to learn or grow. Support students to understand that continuous variation is explained by the scale on which you are measuring

the feature or characteristic. It *continues* between one value and the next (e.g. height). On the other hand, discontinuous variation has a limited number of possible values (e.g. eye colour).

Biology links

- heredity as the process by which genetic information is transmitted from one generation to the next
- a simple model of chromosomes, genes, and DNA in heredity, including the part played by Watson, Crick, Wilkins, and Franklin in the development of the DNA model

Working scientifically links

- use models and analogies as a way of understanding things
- evaluate the effectiveness of a model

Learning objective	Learning outcomes		
	Developing	Secure	Extending
Define DNA, a chromosome, and a gene	State where genetic material is found within a cell	**Define DNA, a chromosome, and a gene**	Describe the relationship between DNA, chromosomes, and genes (e.g. genes are sections of DNA on a chromosome)
Describe how characteristics are inherited	Describe the role of sperm and egg cells in fertilization	**Describe how characteristics are inherited**	Explain why siblings appear similar, but not the same
Describe how scientists worked together to develop the DNA model	Identify some of the scientists involved in the development of the DNA model	**Describe how scientists worked together to develop the DNA model**	Explain the importance of collaborative working in scientific discoveries

Tier 2 vocabulary	Tier 3 vocabulary
	chromosome, DNA, gene, nucleus

Digital resources

Activity: *Building a model nucleus* (Activity sheet, Support sheet, Teacher and technician notes)
Video: *Inheritance and DNA structure*

Student Book answers

Think back 1 nucleus **2** egg and sperm nuclei join together **3** inherited variation

In-text questions A chemical that contains all the information needed to make an organism **B** a long strand of DNA **C** a section of DNA that contains the information to produce a characteristic **D** 46

See p.79 for the answers to the **Summary questions** for this lesson.

Getting started

Show students an image of a family. Ask them to list what features each child inherited from which parent. What features do the children share?

Use this to explain that the children have inherited some characteristics from each of their parents. Brothers and sisters do not look completely the same because they each inherit a different mixture of characteristics.

Watch the video *Inheritance and DNA structure*, which introduces students to how characteristics are passed on from parents to their offspring through chromosomes.

Use the diagrams in Figure 1 in the Student Book to recap what DNA, genes, and chromosomes are, and how genetic material is passed on from a parent to its offspring.

Use the information in the Student Book to introduce how Watson, Crick, Franklin, and Wilkins worked together to develop the model of DNA. Students should then complete the task in the Working scientifically box.

Main activity

Activity: Building a model nucleus Students use the materials provided to create representations of a nucleus containing chromosomes and genes. Each structure in the model should be labelled using the cocktail sticks. Students then evaluate their finished models, before answering the questions that follow.

Review and reflect

Show students the statements on DNA. Ask them to identify whether the statements are true or false. They should then correct the statements that are false.

Ask students to watch the video on Kerboodle again to consolidate their learning.

Language support

There are lots of unfamiliar key words in this topic. To help students learn and remember them, ask them to draw a flowchart to show where these words are in sequence. It should begin with 'sperm cell' and 'egg cell' with an arrow pointing to 'nucleus' to show that the cells contain the nucleus. Next an arrow should point to 'DNA', which is mostly located in the nucleus of each cell, and then to 'chromosome', which is made up of twisted strands (threads) of DNA. Finally, the last arrow should point to 'gene', which is a section of the chromosome. A gene holds the information needed to produce a characteristic.

Biology links

- the variation between species and between individuals of the same species, meaning some organisms compete more successfully, which can drive natural selection
- changes in the environment that may leave individuals within a species, and some entire species, less well adapted to compete successfully and reproduce, which in turn may lead to extinction

Learning objective	Learning outcomes		
	Developing	Secure	Extending
Describe the process of natural selection	State the meaning of an adaptation	**Describe the process of natural selection**	Use a named species to illustrate the process of natural selection (e.g. peppered moths)
Describe how species change and develop through the process of natural selection	State the meaning of a species	**Describe how species change and develop through the process of natural selection**	Explain how environmental change can lead to changes in species

Tier 2 vocabulary	Tier 3 vocabulary
	adaptation, fossil, gene, natural selection, species

Digital resources

Activity: *The limpet game* (Activity sheet, Support sheet, Teacher and technician notes)
Video: *Natural selection*

Student Book answers

Think back 1 through fossils **2** characteristics that enable an organism to survive **3** to blend in with their environment so they cannot be seen

In-text questions A Organisms with the characteristics that are most suited to the environment survive and reproduce; less well adapted organisms die. **B** the remains of plants or animals that lived a long time ago, which have changed to stone

See p.79 for the answers to the **Summary questions** for this lesson.

Getting started

Show images of how a mobile phone has changed over time. Ask students to discuss how and why it has changed (to suit our lifestyle and demands).

Use this analogy when you talk about how species have changed and developed over time. Address the misconception that an individual organism itself adapts.

Fossils Show the class fossils or images of fossils from the Internet. Ideally, include images of gradual changes in fossil records. Ask students to state what is being shown, to describe what they are made from, and to explain what scientists can deduce from the fossil record.

Natural selection Use the flowchart in Figure 2 in the Student Book to introduce the process of natural selection. Then illustrate the process using the example of the peppered moth as described in the Student Book.

Note that a new species is not created, since the moths can still reproduce to produce fertile offspring. However, the frequency of the different forms of the moth in the species dramatically changes through natural selection.

Main activity

Activity: The limpet game In pairs, students play the 'limpet game', which represents the process of natural selection in action. They then answer the questions that follow.

Review and reflect

Students hold up whiteboards with 'True' and 'False' written on them in response to a statement on the board. For example: *Natural selection is when an individual organism adapts to suit its environment* (false).

Invite students to justify their answers.

You can also watch the video on Kerboodle to consolidate students' learning.

Language support

To build on their learning from the inheritance topic, ask students to write the key word 'gene' at the centre of a circle or square. They should then write notes and draw diagrams to show that the gene is contained in the nucleus of egg cells and sperm cells. The gene is a sequence of DNA that is stored on a specific part of a

chromosome. Explain that using unfamiliar language regularly and adding images supports students' understanding of new vocabulary. You can do this at the beginning of the lesson before moving on to natural selection.

Biology links

- changes in the environment that may leave individuals within a species, and some entire species, less well adapted to compete successfully and reproduce, which in turn may lead to extinction
- the importance of maintaining biodiversity and the use of gene banks to preserve hereditary material

Working scientifically link

- understand that scientific methods and theories develop as earlier explanations are modified to take account of new evidence and ideas, together with the importance of publishing results and peer review

Learning objective	Learning outcomes		
	Developing	Secure	Extending
Describe some factors that may cause extinction	State the meaning of endangered and extinct	**Describe some factors that may cause extinction**	Explain how changes to an environment can lead to extinction of a species
Describe how gene banks can prevent the extinction of a species	State the meaning of biodiversity	**Describe how gene banks can prevent the extinction of a species**	Justify the importance of gene banks in maintaining biodiversity

Tier 2 vocabulary	Tier 3 vocabulary
endangered, extinct	biodiversity, fossil, gene bank, species

Digital resources

Activity: *Extinction of the dinosaurs* (Activity sheet, Support sheet, Information sheet, Teacher and technician notes)
Video: *Biodiversity and extinction*

Student Book answers

Think back 1 remains, or traces, of plants or animals **2** Organisms with the best adaptations will most likely survive and reproduce; organisms that are not well adapted will die. **3** space/shelter/mates/food/water

In-text questions A one that has completely died out; no new organism can be created **B** any three from: changes to the organism's environment, destruction of habitat, outbreak of a new disease, introduction of new predators and competitors **C** dinosaur, dodo **D** any three from: seeds, buds, pollen, embryo, sperm cells, egg cells

See p.79 for the answers to the **Summary questions** for this lesson.

Getting started

Show students images on the board of extinct and endangered animals (e.g. Siberian tigers, giant pandas, dinosaurs, and dodos). Ask students to suggest ways to separate these animals into two groups.

Then ask students to suggest definitions of the key words 'endangered' and 'extinct'. Make sure students' definitions of extinct refer to organisms of the species being found nowhere in the world. This key word is often used incorrectly in everyday conversation.

Extinction Watch the video *Biodiversity and extinction*, which introduces the difference between endangered and extinct organisms, some of the causes of extinction, and how scientists and conservationists are working to protect endangered species. Ask students to make a list of some causes of extinction as they watch the video.

Discuss the factors that lead to extinction, and how the loss of a species leads to the reduction of biodiversity in an area. This is directly through the loss of the species itself, and indirectly through the loss of shelter/a food source for another species.

Gene banks Using the information gained from the video, ask students to explain what the term 'gene bank' means. Ask them to give examples of the gene banks available, using the information in the Student Book.

Main activity

Activity: Extinction of the dinosaurs Students work in groups of three and use a 'home and expert' group format. They read three possible theories to explain the extinction of dinosaurs. They must teach each other about the different theories suggested, decide on the theory that seems most credible, and then answer the questions.

Review and reflect

Ask students to stand up. Read out a series of situations (e.g. the arrival of a disease, an abundance of food). Students sit down each time a scenario that increases the risk of extinction is mentioned.

Ask students to watch the video on Kerboodle again to consolidate their learning.

Language support

Elicit from students what a bank is. They should all be familiar with financial banks. Explain that a bank could be described as a safe store of money. Based on this idea, encourage students to think about what a gene bank could be (a safe store of genetic information of species that have or could become extinct).

Getting started

Encourage students to review their learning in this chapter. The 'Summary questions' in the Student Book can be used formatively during lessons. For the 'What have I learned?' pages, students can answer the questions one at a time after each topic, or as a single summative activity. This could be done as a whole-class or group activity, or set as an independent task.

Whichever approach is adopted, the questions are designed to give you and students feedback about progress and identify targets for development.

Student reflection

Allow students time to reflect on how confident they feel about each topic. Remind them to use the learning objectives provided in their Student Book for guidance. They should focus on whether there were any questions they found difficult or easy, and on how well they prepared for the summative assessment at the end of the chapter. Listen to and deal with students' reflections sensitively so that they feel comfortable to report areas they are not confident with.

Learning objectives and learning outcomes

Each lesson is guided by the learning *objectives*. The learning objectives are provided at the beginning of each topic in the Student Book. They outline what students are going to learn in each topic.

In contrast, the learning *outcomes* in this Teacher's Guide are statements that describe the knowledge or skills that students should acquire by the end of each topic. They are linked to the learning objectives, but are *not* often seen by students. The learning outcomes are used by teachers to assess and measure if or how each learning objective has been achieved.

Answer key

Chapter 4: Inheritance

1 for example: hair colour, eye colour, skin colour, height, blood group

2

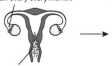

One egg is released from an ovary every month.

If a sperm meets an egg in the oviduct, fertilization occurs.

Sperm swim from the vagina, through the cervix, and into the uterus.

Many sperm die before they reach the oviduct.

The fertilized egg travels down the oviduct and attaches to the lining of the uterus.

3 Dead animals or plants are buried and preserved in mud, and gradually get replaced with stone over 10 000 years approximately. This retains the shape of the organism.

4.1 Variation

1 species, characteristics, variation, environmental, inherited
2 a environmental: tattoo, scar; inherited: blood group, eye colour; both: body mass, intelligence

b A person chooses to style their hair in a particular way; it is not determined by the genetic material they inherit.
3 Identical twins have the same genetic material so they have the inherited characteristics. Any differences between the twins must therefore be caused by environmental factors.

4.2 Continuous and discontinuous

Maths skills: data set **a** plotted as bar chart (discontinuous); data sets **b–d** plotted as histogram (continuous)
1 discontinuous, continuous, bar chart, histogram
2 continuous:, maximum running speed, average leaf size; discontinuous: hair colour, shoe size
3 a Most people are of an average height, around 150 cm. Few people are very short, below 135 cm. Few people are very tall, above 170 cm.
b Height is affected by both inherited and environmental factors. If your parents are tall, you are also likely to be tall (inherited). However, growth can be affected by environmental factors, (e.g. malnourishment).

4.3 Inheritance

1 DNA, chromosome, gene
2 **a** gene, chromosome, nucleus, cell
  b sperm contains chromosomes from the father; the egg cell contains chromosomes from the mother; the nuclei join during fertilization so the embryo/baby produced has genetic material from both parents
3 Chromosomes occur in pairs; one of the chromosomes in the pair is inherited from the mother and one from the father. During every fertilization, a different combination of chromosomes is inherited, so some characteristics will be the same if the same chromosome is inherited, but others may be different if a different characteristic is inherited.

4.4 Natural selection

1 changed, millions, fossils, remains
2 Organisms that have adaptations suited to their habitat survive for longer. This means they produce more offspring. Offspring are likely to inherit their parents' advantageous characteristics. Therefore more offspring with the advantageous characteristics survive, continuing the process.
3 Before the Industrial Revolution, pale moths were more successful as they were camouflaged from predators on pale tree bark. Therefore most of the peppered moth population was pale. The Industrial Revolution caused trees to become blackened. Pale moths became less camouflaged/successful. Dark moths became more camouflaged/successful. Therefore dark moths reproduced more than pale moths/the population of dark moths increased rapidly. Therefore a greater proportion of peppered moths were dark in colour.

4.5 Extinction

1 extinct, world, environment, predators, research
2 Gene banks store genetic samples from many different species. These samples can be used for research. These samples can be used to create new individuals.
3 A change to an organism's habitat (e.g. climate change/ introduction of disease) can cause individuals to die if they are less well adapted This could lead to more competition for food, food sources becoming more scarce, or disease killing organisms. Fewer or no offspring are produced as a result. The population of the species decreases. Extinction occurs when all individuals of a species, throughout the world, have died.

What have I learned about inheritance?

1 **a** nucleus [1 mark]
  b Watson, [1 mark] Franklin [1 mark]
2 **a** differences in a characteristic within a species [1 mark]
  b bathroom/newton scales [1 mark]
  c a characteristic/value that can take any value within a range [1 mark]
  d histogram [1 mark]
3 **a** DNA [1 mark]
  b A chromosome is a long strand of DNA. A gene is a (short) section of DNA. [1 mark] Chromosomes contain many genes and each gene codes for a single characteristic. [1 mark]

c Half of the chromosomes come from the mother and half from the father. [1 mark] Genetic material is transferred from the mother via the egg and from the father via the sperm. [1 mark] The sperm and egg's genetic material combines during fertilization. [1 mark] The embryo/fertilized egg contains pairs of chromosomes/46 chromosomes. [1 mark]
4 **a** fossils (of dinosaur skeletons) [1 mark]
  b The introduction of new predators [1 mark] can mean more organisms in a species are eaten than number of offspring produced. [1 mark] Destruction of habitat can mean loss of shelter for organisms, [1 mark] which leads to the death of individuals through exposure. [1 mark] Credit any other sensible suggestions of causes of extinction with a relevant explanation.
  c Gene banks store genetic samples (e.g. seeds/eggs/ sperm/tissue). [1 mark] Samples from gene bank can be used to create new organisms in the future. [1 mark] Samples can also be used for research. [1 mark]
5 **a** 70% [1 mark]
  b discontinuous; [1 mark] the characteristic can only take one of two values [1 mark]
  c for example: tattoo/body piercing/scar [1 mark]
6 Students should be marked on the use of good English, organization of information, spelling and grammar, and correct use of specialist scientific terms. The best answers will provide a full overview of the process of natural selection in a logical order. [6 marks maximum]
Examples of correct scientific points:
Organisms evolve through natural selection slowly over time.
Organisms in a species show variation – this is caused by differences in their genes.
The organisms with the characteristics that are best adapted to the environment survive and reproduce. Less well adapted organisms die.
This process is known as 'survival of the fittest'.
Genes from successful organisms are passed to the offspring in the next generation.
This means the offspring are likely to possess the characteristics that made their parents successful.
This process is then repeated many times.
Over a long period of time this can lead to the development of a new species.
7 Students should be marked on the use of good English, organization of information, spelling and grammar, and correct use of specialist scientific terms. The best answers will provide a full overview of the process of inheritance and the environment in a logical order. [6 marks maximum]
Examples of correct scientific points:
Variation is the difference in characteristics within a species.
Inherited variation depends on the genetic material/ characteristics inherited from parents.
This is passed on when the egg and sperm cell combine/ during fertilization.
Environmental variation is caused by the effects of a person's surroundings and/or lifestyle.
Many inherited characteristics can be altered through environmental factors.
named examples: hair colour, body mass, height, or leaf size
Explained example: you may inherit the genetic characteristics to be tall but if you eat a poor diet your growth may be reduced.

Chemistry

Introduction to unit

In order to be good global citizens, it is important to be aware of our place in the world and our interaction with it. We can do this by exploring what Earth is made from, how we can extract useful substances from it, how we can change these substances into more useful ones, and our impact on the environment when we do this. Following on from our introduction to the particle model, this unit develops on the knowledge of how some materials and substances are used and behave. Students will learn about the differences between metal and non-metal elements and their reactions, different separation techniques, and how patterns in behaviours can be used to make useful predictions about substances. They will delve into the study of Earth and rocks, understanding our impact and effect on the environment, and how we can best protect and look after our fascinating world.

Working scientifically links

Each lesson lists the relevant Working scientifically links at the top of the spread.

Chemistry links

- The particulate nature of matter
- Pure and impure substances
- Chemical reactions
- The Periodic Table
- Materials
- Earth and atmosphere

Learning journey

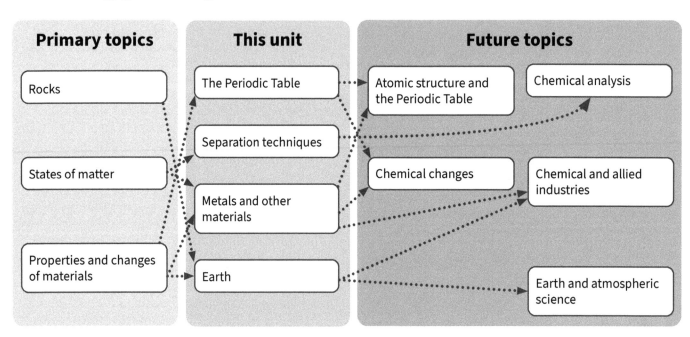

Chemistry and you

Students often think that chemistry is only useful for people who want to become chemists or work in drug companies, but the skills and knowledge from studying chemistry provide a strong basis for many jobs.

Ask students to suggest why chemistry is useful, what skills they can gain from studying it, and which careers might use chemistry. Discuss that the skills and content learned in chemistry, such as observation, analysis, evaluation, and problem solving, will help prepare them for many jobs. Discuss how everyone needs these skills, as well as a secure understanding of the environment we live in, how matter behaves, and how substances react, to make the most of our world.

Chemistry and the world

Ask students to explain what they know about vaccines, who uses toothpaste, and who has played with paints. Explain that these substances are all mixtures that were made using chemistry. Ask why water is important and whether we can just drink any water. Explain that we need to use chemistry to *make* some mixtures; and we also use chemistry to separate mixtures, such as clean water, metals from rocks, salt from the sea, and life-saving gases from the air.

As global citizens, we need to understand our impact on, and look after, Earth, in particular tackling the climate crisis. Explain that chemistry can help us understand climate change and global heating, and therefore how best to solve it and its challenges.

Big questions

How do we get the materials we need?

Although many of us are used to going to the shops or buying anything we want online, the reality is that the new substances that we need and use have to come from somewhere. They are extracted from the ground, air, or oceans before we can use them.

Ask students where we get the metals used in their smartphones, the building materials for their houses, the fabric used in their clothes, or the rubber for their shoes. Discuss that chemists separate out these materials and often perform chemical reactions to make them useful. Explain that eventually we will run out of some materials, so chemists need to devise new ways to recycle substances into new materials.

Can you drink seawater?

Ask students to vote – if they were stranded on a desert island with no drinking water, should they drink the seawater directly from the ocean? Hopefully, most would say no or explain that you would need to separate the salt from the seawater. Discuss that by using simple separation techniques, such as evaporation and condensation, you can separate and collect the drinking water.

How can we deal with climate change?

Students are probably well-versed in the climate crisis, but ask them if they know exactly what we need to do to combat it. They may suggest actions that people can take, such as using less energy, recycling, or car sharing, but why do these help tackle climate change? Explain that we need to add less carbon dioxide to the atmosphere (from burning fuels, cattle rearing, respiration, and decomposition) than plants and the oceans remove from it. This would reduce global heating and our climate crisis would end. You could discuss whether the climate crisis is the only environmental issue; we are also facing challenges surrounding the scarcity of resources, including rare earth metals, potable water, and arable land.

Introduction to chapter

In this chapter, students will develop their knowledge of elements, learning how to distinguish between metal and non-metal elements. Chemical and physical properties are introduced, and the chemical and physical properties and uses of some typical metals and non-metals. They will also explore elements in Groups 1, 7, and 0 in the Periodic Table.

Core concepts

- The difference between chemical and physical properties

- The uses and physical and chemical properties of typical metals and non-metals

- Groups and periods in the Periodic Table, and trends in the properties of elements in Groups or Periods

- Group 1 elements, their physical properties (including melting and boiling points), and trends in the reactivity of Group 1 elements with water

- Group 7 elements, their states and colours at room temperature, their physical properties (including melting and boiling points), and trends in the reactivity of Group 7 elements with iron

- Group 0 elements, their physical properties (including trends in boiling points), and how the properties of Group 0 elements make them suitable for their uses

What have students already learned?

- The definitions of an atom, an element, a molecule, and a compound

- Names and chemical symbols of common elements

- How to name simple compounds such as oxides and sulfates

- How to write chemical formulae, showing the ratio of atoms of each element in a molecule or compound

- The definition of boiling and melting points

What will students learn next?

- Atomic structure and its link to the reactivity and trends in properties of groups and periods in the Periodic Table

- Further reactions of Groups 1, 7, and 0 in the Periodic Table

- The transition metals; comparing their reactions and properties with the reactions and properties of typical metals

Think back

1 Gold is a metal element. Describe its properties.

2 Write a list of 10 elements.

3 Predict which has the higher melting point – oxygen or gold.

4 Four solutions have these pH values:

   A pH 3 **B** pH 6 **C** pH 7 **D** pH 10

   Write the letters of the two acids.

Teaching strategy

This chapter uses the concept of 'typical metals' and 'typical non-metals' by looking at the properties of Group 1 and Group 7/0 elements. These properties are considered to be the properties of the typical metal and non-metal elements, although there are some elements that do not follow these patterns of chemical and physical properties. It is important to use the word 'typical' so students understand that this is a model for most, but not all, metals and non-metals. This will help their awareness of the differing properties later on in the course.

Common learning misconceptions

- You cannot have a molecule of an element. (A molecule can be two or more atoms of the same element.)

- All molecules are examples of compounds. (A compound is where two or more atoms of different elements join together. This means that all compounds are molecules, but not all molecules are compounds.)

- Compounds cannot be broken down into their elements.

- Compounds display the properties of the elements they contain. (Chemical properties differ from the properties of the individual elements that form the compound.)

- Compounds are mixtures of elements. (A compound comprises of more than one element *chemically* bonded together. However, mixtures are formed by *physically* combining two or more substances.)

- The numbers in chemical formulae are written as superscripts (e.g. H^2O).

- Every compound has its own symbol. (Only elements have their own symbols.)

- The majority of chemical elements are non-metals. (In fact, there are more metals than non-metals.)

- The Periodic Table lists elements in order of their mass/weight/density/date of discovery. (The Periodic Table is organized into elements of increasing atomic number – the number of protons in the nucleus.)

- All metals are magnetic. (The only magnetic metals are iron, cobalt, and nickel.)

- Lithium is black and sodium is white.

- There are no non-metallic elements that are conductors of electricity.

- All metals behave the same.

- All non-metals are gases.

Broader context

The uses of substances rely on their properties, so it is important that students get used to identifying how the properties of substances make them suitable for their uses. In order to do this, students need to understand the difference between the chemical and physical properties of a substance.

Lots of industries rely on the use of trends in data to predict and make decisions about stocks, products, content, and other vital aspects of business, so regularly encourage students to identify and use patterns in data.

Chemistry links

- the varying physical and chemical properties of different elements
- the properties of metals and non-metals

Working scientifically links

- ask questions and develop a line of enquiry based on observations of the real world, alongside prior knowledge and experience
- present reasoned explanations, including explaining data in relation to predictions and hypotheses

Learning objective	Learning outcomes		
	Developing	Secure	Extending
Describe the properties of three elements	Identify the properties of three elements	**Describe the properties of three elements**	Compare the properties of three elements
Explain how the uses of three elements are determined by their properties	Identify the uses of three elements	**Explain how the uses of three elements are determined by their properties**	Justify how the properties of an unfamiliar element make it suitable for its use

Tier 2 vocabulary	Tier 3 vocabulary
metal, non-metal	

Digital resources

Activity: *Uses of elements* (Activity sheet, Support sheet, Teacher and technician notes)

Student Book answers

Think back 1 a substance that cannot be broken down into other substances – one type of atom **2** about 100 **3** a quality of a substance or material that describes its appearance or how it behaves

In-text questions A it is a good conductor of electricity **B** Copper is shiny but sulfur is not; copper is a good conductor of electricity but sulfur does not conduct electricity; copper can be hammered into thin sheets but sulfur is brittle. **C** Germanium is shiny but sulfur is not shiny.

See p.98 for the answers to the **Summary questions** for this lesson.

Getting started

Show students images of useless objects. Ask why they are not suitable for their uses.

Possible examples could be: a chocolate teapot, a glass hammer, a waterproof teabag, a cement parachute, an inflatable dartboard, or a lead balloon.

Ask students to recall the definition of an element as a substance that cannot be broken down into other substances, and discuss that elements are found in the Periodic Table. Recall the factors in the particle model that determine the properties of a material:

- what its particles are like (e.g. their shape and size)
- how its particles are arranged and separated
- how its particles move
- how strongly its particles hold together.

Main activity

Introduce copper, sulfur, and germanium and show samples of them to students. Pass the samples around the class and ask students to suggest words they might use to describe the different elements. Write these on the board. Discuss what the word 'property' means in science (properties describe what a substance looks like and how it behaves) and ask students to identify which words on the board are properties of substances. Discuss the properties of copper, sulfur, and germanium, and their uses.

Using the Student Book, create a knowledge organizer to summarize the information about the properties and uses of the three elements copper, sulfur, and germanium.

Activity: Uses of elements Answer questions on the elements copper, sulfur, and germanium, and explain why their properties make them suitable for these uses.

Review and reflect

Call out a property of copper, sulfur, or germanium and ask students to write on their whiteboard which element(s) it belongs to, and then ask students to explain why that property makes the element suitable for its use.

Language support

Show students a range of images or real samples of metals. Ask them to describe them. They are often shiny, strong, solid, ductile, and are conductors of heat and electricity. Then show them some common non-metals (e.g. carbon, nitrogen, phosphorus, and oxygen). They should notice that some are gases, and the solids are dull, brittle, and poor conductors of heat and electricity. They could make a mind map to show the comparisons they observed to act as a reminder.

Chemistry links

- the Periodic Table: periods and groups; metals and non-metals
- the properties of metals and non-metals
- the varying physical and chemical properties of different elements

Working scientifically links

- use appropriate techniques, apparatus, and materials during fieldwork and laboratory work, paying attention to health and safety
- make and record observations and measurements using a range of methods for different investigations; and evaluate the reliability of methods and suggest possible improvements
- interpret observations and data, including identifying patterns and using observations, measurements, and data to draw conclusions

Learning objective	Learning outcomes		
	Developing	Secure	Extending
Use the Periodic Table to find out whether a given element is a metal or non-metal	Identify metals and non-metals in the Periodic Table	**Use the Periodic Table to find out whether a given element is a metal or non-metal**	Suggest why it is useful to be able to determine which elements are metals or non-metals using the Periodic Table
Define physical properties	Identify the definition of physical properties	**Define physical properties**	Define physical properties, giving some examples
Describe the physical properties of typical metal and non-metal elements	From data presented in tables or bar charts, describe patterns in the properties of elements in groups or periods	**Describe the physical properties of typical metal and non-metal elements**	Compare the physical properties of typical metal and non-metal elements

Tier 2 vocabulary	Tier 3 vocabulary
physical property	metalloid

Digital resources

Practical: *Classifying metals and non-metals* (Practical sheet, Support sheet, Teacher and technician notes)

Student Book answers

Think back 1 for example: metals – copper, silver, gold; non-metal – sulfur **2** temperature at which a substance changes from the solid to the liquid state **3** the one- or two-letter code for an element

In-text questions A (no written answer required) **B** metal **C** poor conductor of electricity, poor conductor of thermal energy, dull, low density, brittle, not sonorous

See p.98 for the answers to the **Summary questions** for this lesson.

Getting started

Ask students how they know the horse sculpture in Figure 1 in the Student Book is made out of metal. Discuss any observations they could make to show it is metal.

Grouping materials Show students some materials in the room, and on the board, and ask them to come up with as many ways as possible to group the materials. Examples could be by colour, state, metal/non-metal, use, etc.

Periodic Table Display a Periodic Table. Ask students to suggest names of elements that they know are metals, and elements that they know are not metals. Highlight these on the board. Ask students to suggest if there is a pattern showing which elements are metals and which are non-metals. Introduce the stepped line on the Periodic Table as a way of determining which is which.

Main activity

Practical: Classifying metals and non-metals Discuss the meaning of physical properties in chemistry (properties you can observe and measure without changing the material), and make a list of common physical properties used to classify materials (e.g. electrical conductivity, density, ductility).

Students then investigate the properties of metals and non-metals to determine typical properties of each, and answer the questions that follow. After the practical, discuss the typical properties of metals and non-metals that the class have determined.

Review and reflect

Recalling properties Call out some physical properties of materials. Ask students to write on their whiteboards whether it is a property of a typical metal or a typical non-metal.

Then display the Periodic Table on the board again and call out the names of elements. Students should find the element on the Periodic Table and identify if it is a metal or non-metal.

Language support

Display the key word 'metalloid'. Can students break it down into familiar parts? They should recognize 'metal' but perhaps not 'oid'. Write the words 'humanoid', 'meteoroid', and 'cuboid' on the board. Encourage students to identify the root word in each case ('human', 'meteor', 'cube'). Elicit the meanings

of each word, and the similarity between them: they are all things that *look like* the root word, but are not the same. In the same way, a metalloid has some properties *similar* to those of metals, but they are not truly metals.

Chemistry links

- the varying physical and chemical properties of different elements
- the properties of metals and non-metals
- the chemical properties of metal and non-metal oxides with respect to acidity

Working scientifically links

- ask questions and develop a line of enquiry based on observations of the real world, alongside prior knowledge and experience
- make and record observations and measurements using a range of methods for different investigations; and evaluate the reliability of methods and suggest possible improvements
- interpret observations and data, including identifying patterns and using observations, measurements, and data to draw conclusions

Learning objective	Learning outcomes		
	Developing	Secure	Extending
Define chemical properties	Identify the definition of chemical properties	**Define chemical properties**	Explain the difference between physical properties and chemical properties, giving examples
Describe the chemical properties of metals and non-metals	Identify the chemical properties of metals and non-metals	**Describe the chemical properties of metals and non-metals**	Compare the products of the chemical reaction between a metal and oxygen, and a non-metal and oxygen

Tier 2 vocabulary	Tier 3 vocabulary
acid rain, chemical property	

Digital resources

Practical: *Reacting metals and non-metals* (Practical sheet, Support sheet, Teacher and technician notes)
Video: *Metals and non-metals*

Student Book answers

Think back 1 a substance made up of atoms of two or more elements, chemically joined together **2** sulfur, oxygen **3** 7

In-text questions A Less than 7 because nitrogen is a non-metal and most non-metal oxides are acidic. **B** non-metal **C** chemical – metals react with oxygen to make basic oxides; physical – for example: shiny, malleable, ductile, sonorous

See p.99 for the answers to the **Summary questions** for this lesson.

Getting started

Show an image of coal burning in air – ask students what they can observe in the image that suggests a chemical reaction is occurring (light being given off, a smell being given off, new substances being made, crackling, heat being given off) and to suggest the reactants (carbon and oxygen) and products (carbon dioxide) of this reaction. This might be a good time to discuss some of the advantages and disadvantages of using coal as a fuel.

Introducing the chemical properties of metals and non-metals Ask students to suggest the meaning of the term 'chemical properties' in chemistry. The chemical properties of a substance describe its chemical reactions. Ask students to recall where to find metals (on the left) and non-metals (on the right) on the Periodic Table. Recall the colours that litmus/universal indicator paper will turn in acidic (red/pink) and alkaline (blue/purple) solutions.

Main activity

Practical: Reacting metals and non-metals
Demonstrate burning magnesium in oxygen and write the word equation (magnesium + oxygen $\rightarrow$ magnesium oxide) for this reaction on the board. Demonstrate or show a video of the reaction of sulfur with oxygen, write the equation (sulfur + oxygen $\rightarrow$ sulfur dioxide) for this reaction on the board, and discuss the reactions of metals and non-metals with oxygen.

Then students blow through a straw into a mixture of limewater and universal indicator (showing non-metal oxides and water make an acidic solution), dissolve magnesium oxide powder in water and add universal indicator/litmus (showing many metal oxides in water make an alkaline solution), and make a note of their observations.

Students then answer the questions that follow.

Review and reflect

Call out chemical properties of metals and non-metals. Ask students to hold up their left or right hands depending on whether the chemical property belongs to a typical metal or a typical non-metal.

You can also watch the video on Kerboodle to consolidate students' learning.

Language support

Ask students to describe the meaning of a property in their own words. What are the properties of a material? They are the characteristics that describe what the material looks like (e.g. size and colour), feels like, and how it behaves. It can also refer to its state of matter. These characteristics can be observed and measured. Chemical properties are the observable characteristics of a substance in a chemical reaction.

1.4 Groups and periods

Chemistry links

- the principles underpinning the Mendeleev Periodic Table
- the Periodic Table: periods and groups; metals and non-metals.
- how patterns in reactions can be predicted with reference to the Periodic Table

Working scientifically links

- interpret observations and data, including identifying patterns and using observations, measurements, and data to draw conclusions
- make predictions using scientific knowledge and understanding

Learning objective	Learning outcomes		
	Developing	Secure	Extending
Give the group and period numbers of elements	Give the names of the columns and rows in the Periodic Table	**Give the group and period numbers of elements**	Compare the positions of two given elements in the Periodic Table
Use data from tables or bar charts to describe patterns in the properties of elements in groups or periods	Identify patterns in properties of elements in groups or periods	**Use data from tables or bar charts to describe patterns in the properties of elements in groups or periods**	Use data from tables or bar charts to compare patterns in the properties of elements in groups or periods
Use data to predict the properties of another element in a group or period	Use data to describe a pattern in the properties of elements in a group or period	**Use data to predict the properties of another element in a group or period**	Use data to justify errors in predictions of the properties of another element in a group or period

Tier 2 vocabulary	Tier 3 vocabulary
	group, period

Digital resources

Activity: *Patterns, groups, and periods in the Periodic Table* (Activity sheet, Teacher and technician notes)

Student Book answers

Think back 1 right of the stepped line **2** for example: copper, gold **3** the temperature at which a substance changes state from the solid state to the liquid state

In-text questions A 4 **B** The melting point increases from top to bottom of the group. **C** 5

See p.99 for the answers to the **Summary questions** for this lesson.

Getting started

Show Figure 1 in the Student Book of the metal palladium and ask students to predict its physical and chemical properties. Discuss how the position of palladium in the Periodic Table can give us more information about its properties.

Layout of the Periodic Table Display the modern Periodic Table on the board and discuss the layout. Introduce groups and periods. Explain how, a long time ago, scientists, including one called Mendeleev, built up a wealth of data on elements as they were discovered. When Mendeleev arranged them in order of increasing atomic mass, he noticed they had similar chemical properties. This grouping of elements with others showing similar chemical and physical properties led to the layout of the modern Periodic Table.

Patterns in the Periodic Table Discuss how the elements in the groups in the Periodic Table have similar properties: for example, Group 1 elements all have similar chemical properties, and Group 7 elements all have similar properties (to be covered in more detail in later lessons). Show Figures 4 and 5 in the Student Book of the bar charts of melting points going across periods. Discuss the trend in melting points across Period 2 and Period 3. Highlight that they follow similar patterns.

Main activity

Activity: Patterns, groups, and periods in the Periodic Table Students group together elements based on things they have in common. Highlight that they are practising finding similarities and patterns in groups of elements, not trying to reproduce or rewrite the Periodic Table. Students then identify groups and periods in the Periodic Table, describe the trends in the Periodic Table, and predict properties of elements using given data.

Review and reflect

Call out a group and a period and ask students to identify the element in that position, and vice versa.

Then ask students to recall as much as they can about the patterns and trends in the Periodic Table.

Language support

Ask students what makes a group. Can they group, or categorize, anything in the classroom? Explain that a group in the Periodic Table is a set of elements organized in columns. They all have similar electronic structures and, as a result, similar physical and chemical properties. A period is a row of elements with the same number of electron shells. This means there are patterns in the properties of the elements (e.g. in melting points).

1.5 The elements of Group 1

Chemistry links

- the varying physical and chemical properties of different elements
- how patterns in reactions can be predicted with reference to the Periodic Table
- the properties of metals and non-metals

Working scientifically links

- make predictions using scientific knowledge and understanding
- make and record observations and measurements using a range of methods for different investigations; and evaluate the reliability of methods and suggest possible improvements
- interpret observations and data, including identifying patterns and using observations, measurements, and data to draw conclusions

Learning objective	Learning outcomes		
	Developing	Secure	Extending
Describe the physical properties of the Group 1 elements	Identify the physical properties of the Group 1 elements	**Describe the physical properties of the Group 1 elements**	Compare the physical properties of Group 1 elements with those of a typical metal
Use data from tables or bar charts to describe patterns in the melting and boiling points of the Group 1 elements	Use data from bar charts to identify patterns in the melting and boiling points of the Group 1 elements	**Use data from tables or bar charts to describe patterns in the melting and boiling points of the Group 1 elements**	Use data from tables or bar charts to compare patterns in the melting and boiling points of the Group 1 elements
Use patterns to predict reactions of the Group 1 elements with water	Describe the pattern in reactions of the Group 1 elements with water	**Use patterns to predict reactions of the Group 1 elements with water**	Use the pattern in the reactions of the Group 1 elements with water to predict the reaction of another Group 1 element with water, and justify the answer

Tier 2 vocabulary	Tier 3 vocabulary
reactive	Group 1

Digital resources

Practical: *How do Group 1 elements react?* (Practical sheet, Support sheet, Teacher and technician notes)

See p.99 for the answers to the **Summary questions** for this lesson.

Student Book answers

Think back 1 metals **2** any three from: high melting and boiling points, good conductor of electricity/thermal energy, shiny, high density, malleable, ductile, sonorous **3** reacts with oxygen to make a solid, basic oxide

In-text questions A Any one from: Group 1 elements have low densities, but most other metals have high densities; Group 1 elements have lower melting points than most other metals; Group 1 elements are softer than most other metals. **B** The boiling point decreases from 1330°C (lithium) to 688°C (rubidium). **C** hydrogen

Getting started

Discuss the fact that lithium, a Group 1 element, is found in the batteries of lots of smartphones and tablets, and is incredibly useful to the technology industry. Explain that the vast majority of the world's lithium can currently be found in the salt flats of South America. Ask students to recall where Group 1 is on the Periodic Table, and whether Group 1 elements are metals or non-metals.

Recalling pH values Ask students to recall the pH values for acids, alkalis, and neutral substances

(< 7, > 7, and 7 respectively), and to describe the colours seen when universal indicator is added to each (red, blue, and green respectively).

Group 1 Ask students to recall the properties of typical metals. Discuss how Group 1 metals are similar in their electricity and heat conduction, and are shiny when freshly cut. Using Table 1 in the Student Book, discuss that Group 1 metals are also different from other metals in that they have lower melting points and are softer – they can be cut with a knife!

Main activity

Practical: How do Group 1 elements react?
Discuss the reactivity of Group 1 metals with water, and then demonstrate the reactions of lithium, sodium, and potassium with water. Show the production of the alkaline solution, which gives the group its name of the alkali metals. Students record their observations in their results table. They should discuss and suggest what they would expect to observe from the reactions of rubidium, caesium, and

francium, based on the reactivity trends they have observed already. Students then work through the questions that follow.

If time allows, you may want to show clips of water with rubidium and caesium. Note that the Periodic Table of Videos from the University of Nottingham (available on YouTube) demonstrate genuine chemical reactions, whereas other videos of the same reactions are often inaccurate or staged.

Review and reflect

Students hold up whiteboards with 'True' and 'False' written on them in response to a statement

on the board. Ask students to justify their answers.

Language support

Give students time to define the key word 'reactive' in groups. What does it mean to react? Encourage them to think about the word category it belongs to (adjective). Then invite volunteers to make

suggestions – they might use the words 'respond' or 'interact'. A reactive element easily takes part in chemical reactions, responding to other substances they come into contact with.

Chemistry links

- the varying physical and chemical properties of different elements
- how patterns in reactions can be predicted with reference to the Periodic Table
- the properties of metals and non-metals

Working scientifically links

- make and record observations and measurements using a range of methods for different investigations; and evaluate the reliability of methods and suggest possible improvements
- interpret observations and data, including identifying patterns and using observations, measurements, and data to draw conclusions

Learning objective	Learning outcomes		
	Developing	Secure	Extending
Describe the physical properties of the Group 7 elements	Identify the colours and states at room temperature of the Group 7 elements	**Describe the physical properties of the Group 7 elements**	Compare the physical properties of the Group 7 elements
Use data from tables or bar charts to describe patterns in the melting and boiling points of the Group 7 elements	Use data from bar charts to identify patterns in the melting and boiling points of the Group 7 elements	**Use data from tables or bar charts to describe patterns in the melting and boiling points of the Group 7 elements**	Use data from tables or bar charts to compare patterns in the melting and boiling points of the Group 7 elements
Use patterns to predict reactions of the Group 7 elements with iron	Describe the pattern in reactions of the Group 7 elements with iron	**Use patterns to predict reactions of the Group 7 elements with iron**	Compare the reactions of chlorine and iodine with iron

Tier 2 vocabulary	Tier 3 vocabulary
	Group 7, halogen

Digital resources

Activity: *Exploring Group 7 elements* (Activity sheet, Support sheet, Teacher and technician notes)

Student Book answers

Think back 1 non-metals **2** any two from: low melting and boiling points, poor conductor of electricity/thermal energy, dull in solid state, low density in solid state, brittle, not sonorous **3** fluorine, chlorine, bromine, iodine

In-text questions A Chlorine is pale green, but iodine is grey; chlorine is in the gas state, whereas iodine is a solid. **B** The boiling point increases from fluorine (−188 °C) at the top of the group to iodine (184 °C) at the bottom of the group. **C** iron fluoride

See p.99 for the answers to the **Summary questions** for this lesson.

Getting started

Ask students what causes the classic 'swimming pool smell'. Explain it is the addition of small amounts of chlorine and chlorine-containing compounds to the water, which kills bacteria and can make water clean and safe to swim in.

Introducing Group 7 Ask students to recall the typical properties of non-metals. Discuss where to find Group 7 on the Periodic Table, the elements in Group 7, and that the Group 7 elements are often called the halogens.

If possible, show samples of chlorine, bromine, and iodine in a fume cupboard, or show them on the board. Show how the colours of the Group 7 elements get darker from top to bottom of the group. Ask students to give the states of the three halogens at room temperature.

Main activity

Group 7 elements with iron If there is a fume cupboard available, demonstrate the reaction of iron and chlorine. If not, use videos to compare the reactivity of Group 7 elements (the halogens) down the group. Write the word equation for the reaction of iron and chlorine on the board and ask students to predict the word equation for the reaction of bromine and iodine.

Activity: Exploring Group 7 elements Students use the information on the Activity sheet to complete the table describing the properties of the Group 7 elements, and then use this information to answer the questions that follow. Elicit from students the best ways to extract information from large sections of text and how they might complete the information tables.

Review and reflect

Students complete a plus, minus, interesting (PMI) grid to reflect on their learning in this lesson. To complete a PMI grid, students divide a page into three columns, and add the headings 'plus (+)', 'minus (–)', and 'interesting'. In the plus column, they list positive examples and applications from the lesson; in the minus column, they list any drawbacks or challenges; and in the interesting column, they describe interesting facts. If time, discuss what went well/badly with their method of finding information from the text, and what they might do differently next time.

Language support

Explain to students that the key word 'halogen' means 'salt forming'. Therefore, all of the elements in Group 7 react with metals to form a salt.

Chemistry links

- the varying physical and chemical properties of different elements
- how patterns in reactions can be predicted with reference to the Periodic Table
- the properties of metals and non-metals

Working scientifically links

- present observations and data using appropriate methods, including tables and graphs
- interpret observations and data, including identifying patterns and using observations, measurements, and data to draw conclusions

Learning objective	Learning outcomes		
	Developing	Secure	Extending
Describe the physical properties of the Group 0 elements	Identify the physical properties of the Group 0 elements	**Describe the physical properties of the Group 0 elements**	Compare the physical properties of the Group 0 elements with those of the Group 7 elements
Use data from tables or bar charts to describe patterns in the melting and boiling points of the Group 0 elements	Use data from bar charts to identify patterns in the melting and boiling points of the Group 0 elements	**Use data from tables or bar charts to describe patterns in the melting and boiling points of the Group 0 elements**	Use data from tables or bar charts to compare patterns in the melting and boiling points of the Group 0 elements
Use patterns to predict properties of the Group 0 elements, and their uses	Describe the properties of the Group 0 elements	**Use patterns to predict properties of the Group 0 elements, and their uses**	Evaluate how the properties of Group 0 elements make them suitable for unfamiliar uses

Tier 2 vocabulary	Tier 3 vocabulary
unreactive	Group 0, noble gases

Digital resources

Activity: *Trends in the noble gases* (Activity sheet, Support sheet, Teacher and technician notes)
Video: *The Periodic Table*

Student Book answers

Think back 1 metals **2** He, Ne, Ar, Kr, Xe

In-text questions A The boiling point increases from helium (−269 °C) at the top of the group to xenon (−108 °C) at the bottom of the group. **B** A substance is unreactive if it takes part in very few chemical reactions. **C** Argon is a better thermal insulator than air.

See p.99 for the answers to the **Summary questions** for this lesson.

Getting started

Display the images in Figures 1–3 in the Student Book on the board (double-glazed windows, bar code scanner, balloons) and ask students what these things have in common. They all make use of elements from the same group, Group 0, in the Periodic Table. Ask students what they think makes the Group 0 elements suitable for these uses.

Introducing Group 0 Discuss where to find Group 0 on the Periodic Table and what the elements in Group 0 are called. Introduce the name 'noble gases' and ask students why they think these elements have that name. Reinforce that Group 0 elements are inert and unreactive.

Main activity

Activity: Trends in the noble gases Show students the melting point trends for Group 0 elements, and discuss the trends in physical properties and trends in chemical reactivity.

Then ask them to consider data on the boiling points of the Group 0 elements (see Table 1 in the Student Book) and use this data to plot a bar chart.

Students then answer the questions that follow, describing the trends in melting and boiling points, and matching each element to its common use.

Review and reflect

Ask students to define the key words 'reactive' and 'unreactive' with respect to the Group 1, Group 7, and Group 0 elements, and to recall as many trends in physical and chemical properties as they can from those three groups.

Give an example of a use for one of the Group 0 elements (helium – balloons, argon – in the gap between panes of glass in a double-glazed window, neon – in 'neon' signs) and ask students to justify why that element is suitable for that use.

You can also watch the video on Kerboodle to consolidate students' learning.

Language support

Ask students if they have heard the word 'noble'. They might have come across the adjective when studying history; often kings and queens were said to be noble. In everyday usage, it means when somebody shows fine personal qualities. The noble gases are unreactive – that is, they avoid reacting when provoked – which is considered to be a noble personality trait in humans.

Getting started

Encourage students to review their learning in this chapter. The 'Summary questions' in the Student Book can be used formatively during lessons. For the 'What have I learned?' pages, students can answer the questions one at a time after each topic, or as a single summative activity. This could be done as a whole-class or group activity, or set as an independent task.

Whichever approach is adopted, the questions are designed to give you and students feedback about progress and identify targets for development.

Student reflection

Allow students time to reflect on how confident they feel about each topic. Remind them to use the learning objectives provided in their Student Book for guidance. They should focus on whether there were any questions they found difficult or easy, and on how well they prepared for the summative assessment at the end of the chapter. Listen to and deal with students' reflections sensitively so that they feel comfortable to report areas they are not confident with.

Learning objectives and learning outcomes

Each lesson is guided by the learning *objectives*. The learning objectives are provided at the beginning of each topic in the Student Book. They outline what students are going to learn in each topic.

In contrast, the learning *outcomes* in this Teacher's Guide are statements that describe the knowledge or skills that students should acquire by the end of each topic. They are linked to the learning objectives, but are *not* often seen by students. The learning outcomes are used by teachers to assess and measure if or how each learning objective has been achieved.

Answer key

Chapter 1: The Periodic Table

1 shiny, sonorous, ductile, malleable, good conductor of electricity/thermal energy
2 any 10 correct elements
3 gold
4 A, B

1.1 Three elements

1 copper – shiny, easy to shape into thin sheets, good conductor of thermal energy, good conductor of electricity; sulfur – brittle, does not conduct electricity
2 copper – electric cables because copper is a good conductor of electricity; germanium – fibre optic cables because germanium can change the direction of light
3 Copper and germanium are shiny, but sulfur is not; copper is a good conductor of electricity but germanium and sulfur are not; germanium and sulfur are brittle, but copper is not.

1.2 Physical properties of metals and non-metals

1 properties, without
2 metals – copper, magnesium, zinc; non-metals – chlorine, oxygen, sulfur
3 Metals are good conductors of electricity and thermal energy, but most non-metals are not; metals are shiny but non-metals are not; metals have high densities but non-metals have low densities; metals are malleable and ductile but non-metals are brittle; metals are sonorous but non-metals are not; metals have high melting point but non-metals have low melting points.

1.3 Chemical properties of metals and non-metals

Working scientifically: Element A forms a base oxide, so it is a metal. Element B forms an acidic oxide so it is a non-metal. Element C can be basic or acidic, so it is likely to be a metalloid.

1 non-metal oxides – acidic, gas at 20 °C; metal oxides – basic, solid at 20 °C
2 the chemical properties of a substance describe its chemical reactions
3 The product of the reaction of sodium with oxygen is a basic solid, but the product of the reaction of sulfur and oxygen is an acidic gas.

1.4 Groups and periods

Maths skills: bar chart should have: Group 1 elements on *x*-axis and relative atomic radius on *y*-axis, 0–25 range on *y*-axis, intervals of 1, with bars plotted correctly

1 groups, periods
2 Density increases from top to bottom of the group.
3 In both periods, the melting point increases from left to right for the first four elements, and the melting point of the other elements are low.

1.5 The elements of Group 1

Working scientifically: density of the element increases from top to bottom of Group 1 elements, with exception of sodium and potassium – sodium slightly denser than potassium

1 conduct, low, softer
2 a

b hardness decreases going down the group.
c 0.4; potassium comes between sodium and rubidium in Group 1, so it is likely to be softer than sodium but harder than rubidium
3 hydrogen; all other elements in the group react with water to make hydrogen gas

1.6 The elements of Group 7

Maths skills: bar chart should have: elements on *x*-axis and boiling point on *y*-axis, suggested –40–200 range and intervals of 20, with bars plotted correctly

1 halogens, right, non-metals, chloride, less
2 chlorine – green gas; bromine – orange liquid; iodine – grey solid
3 In Group 7, melting point increases from fluorine (-220 °C) at the top of the group to iodine (114 °C) at the bottom of the group. But in Group 1, melting point decreases from lithium (180 °C) at the top of the group to rubidium (39 °C) at the bottom of the group. Argon's melting point is between −248 °C and −158 °C.

1.7 The elements of Group 0

1 non-metals, colourless, low, gas, unreactive
2 Helium has a lower density than air.
3 Melting point increases from helium (–270 °C) at the top of the group to xenon (–112 °C) at the bottom of the group; –189 °C.

What have I learned about the Periodic Table?

1 a From top to bottom of the group, [1 mark] melting point increases. [1 mark]
  b About 1750 °C [1 mark for a value within the range of 1700–1800 °C]
2 a any one from: low melting point, dull [1 mark]
  b Non-metal [1 mark] since its properties are consistent with those of a typical non-metal. [1 mark]
  c Y. [1 mark]
3 a One of the products of the reaction is formed in the gas state. [1 mark]
  b The solution formed is alkaline. [1 mark]
  c sodium + water → sodium hydroxide + hydrogen [3 marks – 1 for correct reactants, 1 for correct reactants, 1 for arrow drawn correctly]
  d i One of the products is hydrogen. [1 mark]
    ii The reaction of potassium with water is more vigorous. [1 mark]
  e Reactions get more vigorous from top to bottom of the group (from lithium to potassium). [1 mark]
4 From left to right of the period (sodium to chlorine), relative size decreases. [1 mark]
5 a any two from: fluorine, chlorine, bromine, iodine, astatine [1 mark each, maximum 2 marks]
  b do not conduct electricity [1 mark], poor conductors of heat [1 mark]
  c i bromine [1 mark]
    ii increases from top to bottom of the group [1 mark]
    iii any answer between −219 and −8 °C [1 mark]

Introduction to chapter

In this chapter, students will learn about pure substances and mixtures, how to determine if a substance is pure, and the differences between a solute, a solvent, a solution, and solubility. They will compare mixtures and compounds, and learn about different ways of separating the substances in a mixture: filtration, evaporation, distillation, and chromatography. In doing so, they will learn when each separation technique is appropriate. Students will practise representing and analysing data by plotting solubility data, then using their results to describe how solubility changes with temperature.

Core concepts

- Pure substances, mixtures, solutes, solvents, solutions, dissolving, and solubility
- Using a temperature–time graph to determine if a substance is pure
- Differences between mixtures and compounds
- Using the particle model to explain dissolving and evaporation
- Predicting the mass of a solution made from given masses of solute and solvent
- Plotting solubility data from data in a table
- How solubility changes with temperature
- The process of filtration and its uses, and types of mixtures that can be separated by filtration
- How to use distillation to separate a solvent from a solution
- Determining whether to use evaporation or distillation to separate a substance from a solution
- How to use chromatography to separate the substances in a mixture
- How to use evidence from chromatography to identify unknown substances in mixtures

What have students already learned?

- The definitions of an atom, an element, a molecule, and a compound
- The definitions of melting and boiling points
- The three states of matter, and the changing states of matter
- The particle model for the three states of matter

What will students learn next?

- The bonding and structure of compounds and mixtures
- How to determine properties of mixtures
- How to separate substances using filtration, distillation, evaporation, and chromatography

Think back

1 Describe how to separate sand from a mixture of sand and water.

2 Draw a diagram to show some particles in a grain of sugar. Show each particle as a circle.

3 Draw a diagram to show some particles in liquid water. Show each particle as a circle.

4 Describe how particles leave a liquid by evaporation.

Teaching strategy

Modelling To support students in their understanding of what happens when separating different substances, use the particle model. This allows students to visualize an otherwise abstract concept, and makes it easier for students to apply their knowledge and understanding of these processes to new situations. The use of building bricks and/or food stuffs as real-life examples can help students solidify this abstract concept. As with most models, there are limitations, which can be discussed and highlighted.

Substances and mixtures It is important to use the key vocabulary 'substance' and 'mixture' correctly to avoid forming misconceptions. These words are very useful when building knowledge of bonding, structure, and separation techniques. A pure substance has the same chemical make-up throughout, it has fixed proportions, and it cannot be easily separated into the elements that make it up. However, a mixture is made up of more than one substance (elements or compounds) that are not chemically bonded. A mixture can be separated into its component parts and it does not have fixed proportions of its constituent elements, so the proportions of each substance in a mixture can be changed.

Common learning misconceptions

- All particles are the same. (Particles have different numbers of sub-atomic particles.)

- Particles are all perfect squares.

- The particles in a liquid are not touching their nearest neighbours. (Liquids can flow, which means that particles do touch.)

- Boiling and evaporation are the same thing.

- Gases have no mass. (Everything that exists has mass.)

- When particles dissolve, they disappear.

- A pure substance contains more than one type of particle.

- A mixture is just a substance containing more than one element.

- Mixtures are the same as compounds.

- Compounds display the properties of the elements they contain.

- Compounds cannot be broken down into their elements.

Broader context

In lots of industries, such as the petrochemical industry, agricultural industry, and food industry, substances are often produced or used in mixtures. Therefore, it is necessary to learn how to separate the different substances in a mixture to ensure the right substance is made and used. It also prevents waste or harmful substances from continuing down the production line.

2.1 Pure substances

Chemistry links

- the concept of a pure substance
- the identification of pure substances

Working scientifically links

- present observations and data using appropriate methods, including tables and graphs
- interpret observations and data, including identifying patterns and using observations, measurements, and data to draw conclusions

Learning objective	Learning outcomes		
	Developing	Secure	Extending
Define a pure substance in science	Identify the definition of a pure substance in science	**Define a pure substance in science**	Compare the meaning of pure in science and in everyday life
Use a temperature–time graph to determine if a melting substance is pure	Identify the melting point of a substance on a temperature–time graph	**Use a temperature–time graph to determine if a melting substance is pure**	Use temperature–time graphs to compare the purity of two different substances

Tier 2 vocabulary	Tier 3 vocabulary
impure, pure	

Digital resources

Activity: *Temperature–time graphs* (Activity sheet, Support sheet, Teacher and technician notes)

Student Book answers

Think back 1 a material that is not a mixture **2** a group of two or more atoms, strongly joined together **3** thermometer

In-text questions A It has other substances mixed with it. **B** It contains more than one substance.
C The middle section of the line is sloped, showing that the sample does not have a fixed melting point.

See p.116 for the answers to the **Summary questions** for this lesson.

Getting started

Ask students if they have ever tasted tap water in other places and thought it tasted different from the tap water they have at home (if it is safe to drink in your location). Show Figure 1 in the Student Book, which is an image of a man having a vaccine. Discuss that vaccines contain pure water, but that this is not obtained from taps. Tap water is not pure and contains other substances mixed with it. The substances change depending on where in the country the tap water comes from due to water processing methods. This is why tap water from different places tastes different.

Introducing pure substances Show images of a chocolate bar and a gold bar. Discuss the differences between the chocolate and gold bars, and ask which item they think is pure. Explain that the gold bar is pure because it contains only gold atoms, but the chocolate bar is not pure since it contains multiple substances such as fats, glucose, and cocoa. Tell students that scientists say the chocolate is *impure*.

Main activity

Temperature–time graphs Show the temperature–time graphs in Figures 5 and 6 in the Student Book for the pure and impure samples, X and Y, of stearic acid. Explain that they show the temperature of stearic acid taken every minute as it is heated. Discuss the differences between the graphs. Explain that pure stearic acid, sample X, has a fixed melting point, and the temperature stays at 70 °C until all of the solid stearic acid has melted. The impure stearic acid, sample Y, melts between 70 °C and 80 °C. It does not have a fixed melting point.

Similarly, the pure gold has a fixed melting point whereas the impure chocolate does not – it goes gooey.

Activity: Temperature–time graphs Students are provided with data for a sample that had been heated for 5 minutes, and the temperature taken every minute. They plot temperature against time using the provided axes, then answer the questions that follow.

Review and reflect

As a class, use a 'knowledge of' planning grid to plan the answer to the exam question: *Explain how you can use melting point data to identify whether a substance is pure or impure, including giving the meaning of those words.*

Discuss what is expected of them in the task, the strategies they might use, and how they feel they would be able to successfully answer the question. Students should then attempt to answer the question in their books.

Language support

Show students Figure 3 in the Student Book of pure juice. Explain that the key word 'pure' has different meanings in science and in everyday life. Scientists do not describe juice as pure because it contains more than one substance, including water and fructose.

Chemistry link

- mixtures, including dissolving

Working scientifically links

- make and record observations and measurements using a range of methods for different investigations; and evaluate the reliability of methods and suggest possible improvements
- present observations and data using appropriate methods, including tables and graphs

Learning objective	Learning outcomes		
	Developing	Secure	Extending
Define a mixture in science	Identify the definition of a mixture	**Define a mixture in science**	Give examples of mixtures
Compare mixtures and compounds	Identify the definitions of a mixture and a compound	**Compare mixtures and compounds**	Compare unfamiliar mixtures and compounds

Tier 2 vocabulary	Tier 3 vocabulary
mixture	

Digital resources

Activity: *Comparing mixtures and compounds*
(Activity sheet, Teacher and technician notes)
Video: *Mixtures and identifying substances*

Student Book answers

Think back 1 one substance only, with identical particles **2** a substance made up of atoms of two or more elements, with the atoms strongly joined together **3** the characteristics of a substance or material that describe what it looks like, feels like, or how it behaves

In-text questions A contains two or more substances, which may be elements or compounds, that are not joined together **B** For example: a mixture's substances are not joined together, but the atoms of a compound's elements are strongly joined together; the components of a mixture are usually easy to separate, but to separate those of a compound you need to do chemical reactions to separate it into its elements. **C** to help stabilize the DNA in the vaccine

See p.116 for the answers to the **Summary questions** for this lesson.

Getting started

Show students Figure 1 in the Student Book of bath bombs. Ask students if they have ever used a bath bomb. Sometimes they contain glitter, oils, or flower petals. Elicit what bath bombs are made of, or if they have ever made them at home.

Introducing mixtures Introduce a bath bomb as a mixture. Write the definition of a mixture, as something that contains two or more substances, on the board. To make clear the distinction between a mixture and a compound, recall the definition of a compound as a substance made of atoms of two or more elements, with the atoms strongly joined together.

Modelling mixtures Combine dried kidney beans and rice in a large beaker. Vary the amount of beans in the mixture by adding more to the beaker, eliciting that the mixture contains two types of particle that are not joined together. Therefore, these particles can be separated out fairly easily, and the amount of the different particles in the mixture can be easily changed by adding more. Pour the mixture through a colander to separate out the rice and beans.

Main activity

Activity: Comparing mixtures and compounds
Discuss the differences between mixtures and compounds. Fill in the table on the board during the demonstration that compares iron, sulfur, iron sulfide, and a mixture of iron and sulfur through a class discussion. Highlight that the compound iron sulfide does not have the same magnetic property as the element iron, but that the iron in the mixture still retains this magnetic property. Show it is relatively easy to separate the iron from the sulfur in the mixture, but not when it is in the compound.

More mixtures Introduce the idea that there are lots of mixtures that occur in nature, such as rocks, sea water, and air. You can also discuss the use of paint, which is a mixture too. Paint is made up of substances that have different uses in the mixture.

Students should then copy the completed table from the board, then answer the questions that follow.

Review and reflect

Ask students to read the list of mixtures, compounds, and elements on the board, and then copy all of the elements onto a whiteboard. Discuss and check their answers. They should then write all of the mixtures onto their whiteboard, and finally all of the compounds.

You can also watch the video on Kerboodle to consolidate students' learning.

Language support

Recall with students the meaning of the term 'pure substance'. In pairs, encourage them to say out loud a sentence to their partner containing the term. Their partner will then say if it is correct or incorrect.

Review as a class at the end. This will demonstrate students' understanding and identify any ongoing misconceptions.

Chemistry links

- the properties of the different states of matter (solid, liquid, and gas) in terms of the particle model, including gas pressure
- mixtures, including dissolving

Working scientifically links

- make and record observations and measurements using a range of methods for different investigations; and evaluate the reliability of methods and suggest possible improvements
- apply mathematical concepts and calculate results
- interpret observations and data, including identifying patterns and using observations, measurements, and data to draw conclusions

Learning objective	Learning outcomes		
	Developing	Secure	Extending
Define a solution, a solute, a solvent, and what it means to dissolve a substance	Identify the definitions of a solute, a solvent, a solution, and dissolving	**Define a solution, a solute, and a solvent, and describe what it means to dissolve a substance**	Explain the relationship between a solute, a solvent, a solution, and dissolving
Use the particle model to explain dissolving	Describe dissolving	**Use the particle model to explain dissolving**	Use the particle model to explain dissolving in an unfamiliar situation
Predict the mass of a solution from given masses of solute and solvent	Determine the total mass of solvent and solute present	**Predict the mass of a solution from given masses of solute and solvent**	Predict the missing mass of a solute or solvent, given the masses of a solution and either the solute or solvent

Tier 2 vocabulary	Tier 3 vocabulary
dissolve, dissolving, solution	solute, solvent

Digital resources

Activity: *Conservation of mass* (Activity sheet, Support sheet, Teacher and technician notes)

Student Book answers

Think back 1 contains two or more substances, whose particles are not joined together **2** regular pattern **3** randomly from place to place, still touching their neighbours and moving over each other

In-text questions A sugar **B** 90 g + 3 g = 93 g **C** randomly mixed particles, moving around and sliding over each other

See p.117 for the answers to the **Summary questions** for this lesson.

Getting started

Ask students what happens when a teaspoon of sugar is added to a cup of tea. Where does it go? Discuss that a solution is formed: the sugar dissolves in the tea.

Introducing solutions Discuss the meanings of the key words 'solution' (a mixture of a liquid with a solid or gas), 'solute' (the substance that dissolves), 'solvent' (the liquid it dissolves in), and 'dissolving' (the complete mixing of a solute with a solvent). Elicit and write simple definitions on the board, highlighting the differences between them and the spellings.

Show a beaker of water, pour a spatula of sugar into it, and stir. Ask students to identify the solute, solvent, and solution in this example. Discuss that all parts of the solution are the same and the separate substances cannot be seen.

Main activity

Particle model Explain dissolving using the particle model: show Figures 1–3 in the Student Book of particles of sugar in the solid state and water in the liquid state, followed by the image of the sugar water solution. Explain that when sugar dissolves, its particles separate from each other and mix randomly with the water particles. The water particles surround the sugar particles and they all move around, sliding over each other.

Other models Show Figure 4 in the Student Book of the model of a sugar solution using rice and beans. Ask students to identify the solute, solvent, and solution in this model, as well as which substance is represented by the rice, and which by the beans.

Other solvents Ask students if water is the only solvent. Discuss how nail varnish does not come off in the shower as it is not soluble in water. However, it does come off with nail varnish remover, which is made of propanone, another solvent.

Activity: Conservation of mass Demonstrate the conservation of mass by dissolving a known mass of coffee powder in a known mass of water (mass of coffee solution = mass of coffee powder + mass of water). Ask students to identify the solute, solvent, and solution in this example.

Students answer the questions on the Activity sheet, including predicting the mass of a solution made from given masses of solute and solvent.

Review and reflect

Read aloud the definitions of the key words from the lesson: 'solution', 'solute', 'solvent', and 'dissolving'. Students write the correct key word for each definition on their whiteboards. Ask students to give examples of the key words from examples used in the lesson, or in everyday life.

Language support

Students often think that when something *dissolves*, it disappears. To help them understand the meaning of the key word 'dissolve', ask if they have ever tasted seawater. Does it taste the same as bottled or tap water? They should recall that seawater tastes salty. The solute is mixed with the particles of the solvent – in this case, water. If the salt disappeared, you would not be able to taste it.

Chemistry link

- mixtures, including dissolving

Working scientifically links

- make and record observations and measurements using a range of methods for different investigations; and evaluate the reliability of methods and suggest possible improvements
- present observations and data using appropriate methods, including tables and graphs
- interpret observations and data, including identifying patterns and using observations, measurements, and data to draw conclusions

Learning objective	Learning outcomes		
	Developing	Secure	Extending
Define solubility	Describe how to make a saturated solution	**Define solubility**	Use data to compare the solubility of two different substances
Use data from a table to plot a solubility–temperature graph	Describe what a solubility–temperature graph shows	**Use data from a table to plot a solubility–temperature graph**	Use data from a table to plot the solubility–temperature graphs for two different substances and compare them
Describe how solubility changes with temperature for a named substance, given data	From data in a table, identify the temperature at which a solute is most soluble	**Describe how solubility changes with temperature for a named substance, given data**	Use data from a table or line graph to compare how the solubility of two different substances change with temperature

Tier 2 vocabulary	Tier 3 vocabulary
	insoluble, saturated solution, soluble, solubility

Digital resources

Activity: *How does temperature affect solubility?* (Activity sheet, Teacher and technician notes)
Video: *Solutions*

Student Book answers

Think back 1 a mixture of a liquid with a solid or gas, in which all parts of the mixture are the same **2** the substance that dissolves in a solution **3** kg, °C

In-text questions A 36 g/100 g of water **B** most soluble – lithium chloride; least soluble – sodium chloride **C** increases slightly from 36 g/100 g of water at 20 °C to 39 g/100 g of water at 100 °C

See p.117 for the answers to the **Summary questions** for this lesson.

Getting started

Ask: Which dissolves better in water: sugar or salt? Discuss ideas for working out which dissolves better.

What is solubility? Ask students to recall the meanings of the key words 'solution', 'solute', 'solvent', and 'dissolving' or 'dissolve'. Define the key word 'solubility' as the mass of solute that dissolves in 100 g of water to make a saturated solution. Explain that a *saturated* solution contains the maximum mass of a solute that will dissolve. Discuss briefly how to make a saturated solution.

Comparing solubilities Compare the solubilities of four substances at 20 °C – copper chloride, lithium chloride, magnesium chloride, and sodium chloride – using Figure 2 in the Student Book. Encourage students to use the graph to identify which substance is the most soluble.

Insoluble Invite students to suggest the meaning of the key word 'insoluble', and give examples of substances they believe to be insoluble in water. A substance that cannot dissolve in water is insoluble in water (e.g. sand and chalk [calcium carbonate]).

Main activity

Activity: How does temperature affect solubility? Ask students to predict if more sugar will dissolve in hot water or in cold water. Discuss the solubility of sugar at different temperatures using the data in the table.

Compare the solubilities of sugar and salt at 20 °C and 100 °C, and ask which is more soluble at 20 °C. Discuss that different substances have different solubility patterns as temperature increases. The solubility of salt does not increase very much, but the solubility of sugar increases dramatically in comparison.

Students plot a graph of the solubility of sugar with temperature, before answering the questions that follow.

Review and reflect

Call out a substance and ask students to use the graph in Figure 2 in the Student Book to describe the solubility pattern for that substance, using whiteboards.

You can also watch the video on Kerboodle to consolidate students' learning.

Language support

Ensure that students understand the meaning of the key word 'soluble' – it describes a substance that can be dissolved. Encourage them to suggest soluble materials, such as salt, sugar, coffee granules, milkshake powder, etc. Then elicit what the key word 'insoluble' means. The prefix 'in-' means not, therefore, an insoluble material can*not* be dissolved. Build on students' understanding by explaining that the noun 'solubility' describes the level of *ability* that the solute has for dissolving in the solvent.

Chemistry links

- mixtures, including dissolving
- simple techniques for separating mixtures: filtration, evaporation, distillation, and chromatography

Working scientifically links

- interpret observations and data, including identifying patterns and using observations, measurements, and data to draw conclusions
- present reasoned explanations, including explaining data in relation to predictions and hypotheses

Learning objective	Learning outcomes		
	Developing	Secure	Extending
Name the types of mixture that can be separated by filtration	Identify the types of mixture that can be separated by filtration	**Name the types of mixture that can be separated by filtration**	Give some examples of mixtures that can be separated by filtration
Explain how filtration works	Describe how to use filtration to separate a soluble substance from an insoluble one	**Explain how filtration works**	Suggest advantages and disadvantages of filtration as a separation technique
Explain some uses of filtration	Identify some uses of filtration	**Explain some uses of filtration**	Evaluate the use of filtration as a separation technique in given situations

Tier 2 vocabulary	Tier 3 vocabulary
filtering, residue	filtrate, filtration

Digital resources

Practical: *Separating sand and salt* (Practical sheet, Support sheet, Teacher and technician notes)

Student Book answers

Think back 1 for example: paint, vaccines
2 a substance that does not dissolve **3** solid, liquid, gas

In-text questions A any two from: insoluble solid from liquid; small pieces of solid from gases; insoluble solid from a solution **B** filtrate – water; residue – glitter
C for example: face masks, coffee-making, filtering oil, or making water safe to drink

See p.117 for the answers to the **Summary questions** for this lesson.

Getting started

When is filtration used? Explain to students that in laboratories and industry, useful substances usually need to be separated from the substances they are made from or any by-products that are made at the same time. One method of separation used is filtration. Explain that filtration, or filtering, separates several types of mixture: an insoluble solid from a liquid, an insoluble solid from a solution, and small pieces of solid from gases.

How does filtering work? See if students can recall that a mixture in science is something that contains two or more substances that are not joined together. Then introduce them to filtration equipment, also illustrated in Figure 4 in the Student Book. Explain that you have a mixture of dyed water and glitter, which you want to separate. Demonstrate the filtration of the mixture of glitter and dyed water. Ask students to identify each of the pieces of equipment in the filtration experiment as you go, and highlight that the liquid that passes through the filter is called the filtrate and the content left behind is the residue. Ask students to identify the filtrate and residue in this case: the dyed water is the filtrate and the glitter is the residue.

Filtration model Show students a mixture of dried kidney beans and rice, and elicit how they know that this is a mixture. Pour the mixture through a colander to separate the rice and beans. Explain that this is a model for using filter paper: colander = filter paper, kidney beans = residue, and rice = filtrate.

Main activity

Uses of filtration Ask students to recall uses of filtration. Introduce the filter in a car engine, which is made of cotton or wood fibre and traps solid bits of dirt. This allows the liquid oil to pass through, removing the dirt from the oil that would otherwise damage the car engine. You can also discuss the sand filters in water treatment, which trap bits of dirt but allow the water to flow through, removing the bits of dirt and making water safer to drink.

Practical: Separating sand and salt Students separate salt from a mixture of sand and salt by dissolving the salt and then filtering the mixture. They identify the filtrate and residue, before answering the questions that follow about filtration.

Review and reflect

Call out the names of pieces of filtration equipment for students to draw on their whiteboards. Then call out examples of filtration for students to identify the filtrate and the residue in each case.

Language support

Write the key words 'filter', 'to filter', 'filtration', and 'filtrate' on the board. Give students time to think about the meaning of each in pairs or in groups, then go through them one by one as a class. To *filter* (verb) something is to separate mixtures, *filtration* (noun) is the process of filtering, and a *filtrate* (noun) is a substance that has passed through a *filter* (noun).

Chemistry links

- the properties of the different states of matter (solid, liquid, and gas) in terms of the particle model, including gas pressure
- changes of state in terms of the particle model
- simple techniques for separating mixtures: filtration, evaporation, distillation, and chromatography

Working scientifically links

- make and record observations and measurements using a range of methods for different investigations; and evaluate the reliability of methods and suggest possible improvements
- interpret observations and data, including identifying patterns and using observations, measurements, and data to draw conclusions

Learning objective	Learning outcomes		
	Developing	Secure	Extending
Use the particle model to explain evaporation	Describe how to use evaporation to separate the solute from a solution	**Use the particle model to explain evaporation**	Use the particle model to explain evaporation in unfamiliar situations
Explain how to use distillation to separate mixtures	Label the equipment and setup in a distillation experiment	**Explain how to use distillation to separate mixtures**	Use the particle model to explain distillation
Understand when to use evaporation or distillation to separate a named substance from a solution	Describe the uses of evaporation and distillation	**Understand when to use evaporation or distillation to separate a named substance from a solution**	Give reasons for using evaporation or distillation to separate a named unfamiliar substance from a solution

Tier 2 vocabulary	Tier 3 vocabulary
	distillation, evaporation

Digital resources
Practical: *Distillation of inky water* (Practical sheet, Teacher and technician notes)

Student Book answers

Think back 1 a mixture of a liquid with a solid or gas, in which all parts of the mixture are the same **2** liquid, gas **3** condensing

In-text questions A seawater **B** make crystals from solutions, making glue dry, obtaining solid lithium compounds from solution **C** evaporating/boiling, condensing

See p.117 for the answers to the **Summary questions** for this lesson.

Getting started

Ask students where they think salt is obtained from. Most will probably say the sea/seawater. Invite them to suggest methods for obtaining salt from seawater, and why this might be useful.

Evaporation: Show students the setup of equipment used for evaporation. Elicit what this is used for and ask them to identify the solute, solvent, and solution before demonstrating the evaporation of salty water.

Students should be able to see the presence of small salt crystals. Ask them where the water particles have gone and how to get them back. Use the particle model to explain the process of evaporation: on heating, solvent particles evaporate and leave the surface of the solution. The solute particles remain in the container. Encourage students to think about when this evaporation technique might be useful.

Main activity

Practical: Distillation of inky water Demonstrate how pure water is extracted from salty water using distillation. Talk through the main steps in distillation: on heating, water in the salt solution boils, forming steam; salt does not boil because its boiling point is much higher; steam leaves the solution; steam travels through the condenser and cools down, condensing to liquid water; liquid water drips into the flask.

Students add labels to the diagram of the equipment used in distillation, before answering the questions that follow.

Review and reflect

Call out mixtures or solutions and ask students to decide if they would be suitable for separation by evaporation, distillation, or both. Students display their answers on their whiteboards. Encourage them to justify their answers by explaining the distillation and evaporation processes.

Language support

Ask students to draw their own diagram, from memory, of the distillation of salty water activity. They should write the title 'Distillation' above their diagram.

Writing down the name of the process and linking it to a drawing is an effective method of remembering unusual vocabulary.

Chemistry links

- mixtures, including dissolving
- simple techniques for separating mixtures: filtration, evaporation, distillation, and chromatography
- the identification of pure substances

Working scientifically links

- use appropriate techniques, apparatus, and materials during fieldwork and laboratory work, paying attention to health and safety
- make and record observations and measurements using a range of methods for different investigations; and evaluate the reliability of methods and suggest possible improvements
- interpret observations and data, including identifying patterns and using observations, measurements, and data to draw conclusions

Learning objective	Learning outcomes		
	Developing	Secure	Extending
Explain how to use chromatography to separate the substances in a mixture	Label the equipment in a chromatography experiment	**Explain how to use chromatography to separate the substances in a mixture**	Use the particle model to explain how chromatography separates mixtures
Analyse chromatograms to identify substances in mixtures	Use evidence from chromatography to determine how many different substances are in a mixture	**Analyse chromatograms to identify substances in mixtures**	Suggest advantages and disadvantages of using chromatography to identify unknown substances in mixtures

Tier 2 vocabulary	Tier 3 vocabulary
	chromatogram, chromatography

Digital resources

Practical: *Who stole the money?* (Practical sheet, Support sheet, Teacher and technician notes)
Video: *Separating mixtures*

Student Book answers

Think back 1 in a solution, the liquid that a substance dissolves in **2** the complete mixing of a solute with a solvent **3** contains two or more substances, whose particles are not joined together

In-text questions A separates substances in a mixture, if all the substances are soluble in the same solvent **B** two **C** orange

See p.117 for the answers to the **Summary questions** for this lesson.

Getting started

Ask students if they enjoy coloured, sugar-coated chocolates. These sweet coatings on the sweets contain mixtures of dyes. Use this to introduce chromatography as a method of separating mixtures that are soluble in the same solvent.

Colours Discuss with students that some coloured dyes are made of a mixture of other colours. For example, black dyes and inks are often a mixture of blue, yellow, and red dyes or inks.

Colourful sweets Discuss what you intend to show with the demonstration: how we can separate soluble mixtures with just water. Demonstrate chromatography by placing a sugar-coated chocolate in the middle of a piece of filter paper. Place one drop of water on it very slowly using a pipette. Show students how the dyes in the sugar coating separate out, since the shell contains a mixture of colours. Some dissolve in the water more easily than others, and they travel outwards with the water. Discuss what this method of separation can be used for (separating mixtures of soluble substances) and how chromatography can be useful (analysing different samples to find out what they are made from, comparing amounts of vitamins in different foods, and detecting or comparing identical samples).

Main activity

Practical: Who stole the money? Students carry out a chromatography experiment. They investigate a crime scene to identify a thief who used a forged cheque to steal money from a bank. Students prepare a chromatogram of three suspects' inks and compare their chromatograms to decide who the thief is. They then answer the questions that follow.

Review and reflect

Students write a short news article or review of the lesson. They should describe the steps involved in chromatography and explain how chromatography was used to catch the fraudster.

You can also watch the video on Kerboodle to consolidate students' learning.

Language support

Display the key word 'chromatography'. Ask students to break it down into parts. For example, they are likely to find the word 'graph', which refers to writing or recording something. Then explain that 'chroma' means colour in Greek. Link these ideas together by establishing that chromatography is a separation technique that separates a mixture using a solvent. It is often used to separate *coloured* dyes and produces a type of *graph* called a chromatogram.

Getting started

Encourage students to review their learning in this chapter. The 'Summary questions' in the Student Book can be used formatively during lessons. For the 'What have I learned?' pages, students can answer the questions one at a time after each topic, or as a single summative activity. This could be done as a whole-class or group activity, or set as an independent task.

Whichever approach is adopted, the questions are designed to give you and students feedback about progress and identify targets for development.

Student reflection

Allow students time to reflect on how confident they feel about each topic. Remind them to use the learning objectives provided in their Student Book for guidance. They should focus on whether there were any questions they found difficult or easy, and on how well they prepared for the summative assessment at the end of the chapter. Listen to and deal with students' reflections sensitively so that they feel comfortable to report areas they are not confident with.

Learning objectives and learning outcomes

Each lesson is guided by the learning *objectives*. The learning objectives are provided at the beginning of each topic in the Student Book. They outline what students are going to learn in each topic.

In contrast, the learning *outcomes* in this Teacher's Guide are statements that describe the knowledge or skills that students should acquire by the end of each topic. They are linked to the learning objectives, but are *not* often seen by students. The learning outcomes are used by teachers to assess and measure if or how each learning objective has been achieved.

Answer key

Chapter 2: Separation techniques

1 Pour the mixture through filter paper. The sand will remain in the filter paper and the water will pass through.
2 correct diagram of particles in the solid state (i.e. circles in a fixed, regular arrangement)
3 correct diagram of particles in the liquid state (i.e. circles in a random arrangement, touching their neighbours)
4 In a liquid, some particles have more energy than others. The particles with most energy leave the surface of the liquid. Then they move away from the liquid. The particles spread out, forming a gas.

2.1 Pure substances

Working scientifically: Line graphs are used to plot continuous data. Time is the independent variable so plotted on the x-axis; temperature is the dependent variable so plotted on the y-axis.

1 A
2 pure because melting point is fixed
3 in science – one substance only, with identical particles; in everyday life – something that has not been processed (or similar definition)

2.2 Mixtures

1 true – C; corrected version of A – A mixture is made up of different substances that are not joined together; corrected version of B – You can change the amounts of substance in a mixture.
2 For example: mixture – its substances are not joined together, compound – the atoms of its elements are strongly joined together; mixture – usually easy to separate, compound – need to do chemical reactions to separate into its elements.
3 for example: vaccine – preventing disease; paint – make things colourful/protect surfaces

2.3 Solutions

Maths skills: 100 g + 3 g = 103 g
1 solution, solute, solvent, water, salt
2 Sugar particles separate from each other and are surrounded by water particles. The sugar and water particles mix randomly and move around, sliding over each other.
3 75 g – 4 g = 71 g

2.4 Solubility

Maths skills: All of the solutes increase in solubility as the temperature increases, except for cerium (III) sulfate, which decreases in solubility.
1 An insoluble substance does not dissolve. A soluble substance dissolves in a solvent. Solubility increases with temperature, for most solutes. Solubility is the mass of substance that dissolves in 100 g of water.
2 Line graph, with temperature on labelled x-axis and solubility on labelled y-axis. The graph shows that the solubility of zinc bromide increases with temperature.
3 Solubility of lead nitrate increases evenly from about 36 g/100 g of water at 0 °C to about 95 g/100 g of water at 60 °C. The solubility of cerium(III) sulfate decreases with temperature, from about 18 g/100 g of water at 0 °C to about 3 g/100 g of water at 30 °C. The solubility of cerium(III) sulfate does not change between 40 °C and 100 °C.

2.5 Filtration

Working scientifically: most soluble – calcium bromide; least soluble – calcium hydrogencarbonate
1 from top – insoluble residue; liquid filtrate.
2 The material traps solid bits of dirt and liquid oil passes through the gaps between the fibres.
3 Insoluble solid from liquid, for example sand and water; small pieces of solid from gases, for example face masks that separate viruses from air; insoluble solid from a solution, for example coffee solution from ground-up coffee beans.

2.6 Evaporation and distillation

Literacy skills: The liquid is heated and the water rises as steam. It cools as it reaches the curved lid, and condenses. The liquid water flows out, leaving the solid residue at the bottom of the alembic.
1 Heat/warm the solution. Water evaporates, leaving salt behind.
2 When one liquid reaches its boiling point, it evaporates. The gas then rises into the condenser and condenses back into a liquid, which can be collected.
3 (a) – evaporation, because the substance needed (copper chloride crystals) is the solute; distillation, because the substance needed (propanone) is the solvent; distillation, because the substance needed (ethanol) is the solvent

2.7 Chromatography

1
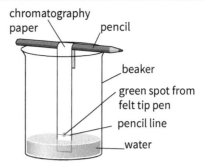

2 Spinach, because the pattern of the spots matches the pattern of spots in Figure 3.
3 Some dyes in the mixture mix with water better than others. All the dyes are attracted to the paper, but some are attracted more strongly than others. In one minute, a dye that is attracted more strongly to the water than to the paper moves further than a dye that is attracted more strongly to the paper.

What have I learned about separation techniques?

1 B, D, F, A, C, E [4 marks for all correct, 3 marks for three correct, 2 marks for two correct, 1 mark for one correct]
2 a mass of salt [1 mark]
   b whether or not the ball floats [1 mark]
   c for example: temperature/mass of golf ball [1 mark]
   d 100 g + 10 g = 110 g [2 marks – 2 for correct answer, 1 if working is correct but answer is incorrect]
   e 20 g [1 mark]
   f 20 g × 2 = 40 g [1 mark]
      mass of water is doubled, so mass of salt must be doubled [1 mark]
3 a
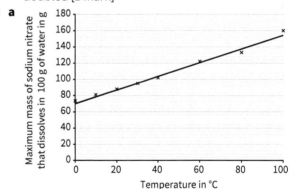

   [1 mark for each correctly labelled axis, 1 mark for each sensibly labelled scale, 1 mark for correctly plotting all the points]
   b [1 mark for correctly drawn line of best fit]
   c As temperature increases, so the mass of sodium nitrate that dissolves also increases. [1 mark]

Chapter 3: Metals and other materials

Introduction to chapter

In this chapter, students will learn about the reactions of metals with acids, with oxygen, and with water, and write word equations for these reactions. They will describe the reactivity series and use this to predict the reactivity of metals with acids, with oxygen, and with water. Displacement reactions are explored, including the displacement reaction of a metal compound with carbon as a method for extracting the metal from its ore. Students will look at the properties and uses of ceramics, some polymers, and some composites.

Core concepts

- Reactions of metals with acids, oxygen, and water

- Comparing the pattern of reactivity of metals with acids, oxygen, and water

- Using the reactivity series to predict reactivity of metals with acids, with oxygen, and with water

- Displacement reactions and when they do/do not occur

- How to extract from their ores, including when carbon can be used; calculating the mass of metal in an ore

- Properties and uses of ceramics, some polymers, and some composites

What have students already learned?

- The position of metals on the Periodic Table

- The definitions of a material, a substance, an atom, an element, a molecule, and a compound; all materials are made of particles

- The difference between a reactant and a product

- Some changes cannot be reversed as new substances are made

What will students learn next?

- How to write chemical formulae

- How to prepare a salt from a metal carbonate or oxide

- How to write ionic equations

- Reactions of acids and reactions of metals

- Redox reactions

- The bonding and structure of compounds and mixtures

- How to determine properties of substances

- Typical properties of transition metals vs Group 1 metals

- Group 7 displacement reactions

Think back

1 Write down a property of brick (a type of building block). Explain how this property makes it useful for building houses.

2 Name the substance made when zinc reacts with oxygen.

3 Write a word equation for the reaction of zinc with hydrochloric acid to make zinc chloride and hydrogen.

4 Suggest how to separate magnetic iron oxide from its mixture with sand.

Teaching strategy

Rusting Clarify to students that rusting only refers to the formation of iron(III) oxide (the 'III' is an oxidation number; at lower secondary, students only need to be familiar with 'iron oxide') and that other metals corrode.

Modelling Using 'general reactions' to model the reactions between substances can help students learn reactions quicker. However, students do need to be confident about the meanings of the key words 'acid', 'metal', and 'salt' for this to be useful.

When explaining displacement reactions, it can be tempting to use analogies about 'fighting' or 'strong' vs 'weak' metals. However, this can introduce misconceptions that atoms fight or have inherent strengths unrelated to the metal's physical properties. It is better to use the reactivity of the metal, linked to the reactivity series, to explain displacement reactions.

Common learning misconceptions

- Mixtures are the same as compounds.
- A substance contains more than one type of material.
- The majority of chemical elements are non-metals.
- Rusting is not a chemical reaction.
- All metals rust.
- Air (oxygen) or water are required for iron to rust. (Iron combines with oxygen in a chemical reaction. The product is iron oxide.)
- Displacement reactions only occur between metals and metal oxides (or between metals and metal salt solutions).
- Salts are all chlorides. (For example, copper sulfate is a salt but not a chloride.)

- The reaction of a metal with acid gives a salt and water.
- Metals 'fight' each other in displacement reactions. (A more reactive metal will displace [push out] a less reactive metal.)
- Aluminium has many outdoor uses, so it must be an unreactive metal.
- Carbon is a metal because it is in the reactivity series.
- Composite materials are compounds, so they have different properties from their component materials.
- All metals react the same.

Broader context

Materials react all the time. Not only do chemists need to make new substances, but industries such as the food sector use chemical reactions every day. Understanding what occurs, why, and when can help students understand these different industries. This chapter also looks at some common materials

and their properties. Understanding how a material behaves or reacts allows us to use it safely and to its full capacity.

3.1 Metals and acids

Chemistry links

- reactions of acids with metals to produce a salt plus hydrogen
- representing chemical reactions using formulae and using equations
- how patterns in reactions can be predicted with reference to the Periodic Table

Working scientifically links

- use appropriate techniques, apparatus, and materials during fieldwork and laboratory work, paying attention to health and safety
- make and record observations and measurements using a range of methods for different investigations; and evaluate the reliability of methods and suggest possible improvements
- present observations and data using appropriate methods, including tables and graphs

Learning objective	Learning outcomes		
	Developing	Secure	Extending
Use a pattern to predict the products of the reaction of a metal with an acid	Identify the pattern in the products of the reaction of a metal with an acid	**Use a pattern to predict the products of the reaction of a metal with an acid**	Predict the products of the reaction of a metal with an acid
Write a word equation for the reaction of a metal with an acid, given the names of the reactants and products	Identify the word equation for the reaction of a metal with an acid, given the names of the reactants and products	**Write a word equation for the reaction of a metal with an acid, given the names of the reactants and products**	Write a word equation for the reaction of a metal with an acid

Tier 2 vocabulary	Tier 3 vocabulary
acid, metal	

Digital resources

Practical: *Reacting metals with acids* (Practical sheet, Support sheet, Teacher and technician notes)

Student Book answers

Think back 1 left of the stepped line **2** For example, any three from: shiny when cut, good conductor of electricity/thermal energy, ductile, malleable, sonorous **3** a compound that forms when an acid reacts with a metal element or metal-containing compound

In-text questions A iron chloride, hydrogen **B** 2 **C** zinc + sulfuric acid → zinc sulfate + hydrogen

See p.136 for the answers to the **Summary questions** for this lesson.

Getting started

Show students the image of the sick hyena in Figure 1 in the Student Book, and explain that the zookeepers did an X-ray and found 20 zinc coins in the hyena's stomach. The zinc coins had reacted with the stomach acid (hydrochloric acid) to produce zinc chloride and hydrogen. Write the word equation for this reaction on the board:

zinc + hydrochloric acid → zinc chloride + hydrogen

Explain that zinc chloride dissolves in water and can travel around in the blood, causing zinc poisoning.

Ask students to recall signs that a chemical reaction is occurring, such as light, sound, smell, heat being given off, or new substances being made.

Main activity

Introducing the reaction of metals with acids Show a strip of magnesium ribbon and a test tube containing dilute hydrochloric acid. Ask students to predict if the two will react. Add the magnesium to the test tube, wait 10 seconds, then place an empty test tube over the mouth of the test tube containing the acid to fill the upturned test tube with hydrogen gas (this may take 1 minute). Ask students to make observations about the reaction. Discuss the observations and whether they think their prediction was correct. Explain that this reaction produces magnesium chloride and hydrogen gas. Show that it is hydrogen gas produced by performing the hydrogen pop test. (With the gas-filled test tube still upside down, move it away from the reaction and – keeping fingers and faces away from the open end – place a lit splint near to its mouth. There should be a squeaky pop as the hydrogen combusts rapidly.)

Write the word equation for the reaction on the board:

magnesium + hydrochloric → magnesium + hydrogen
            acid   chloride

Ask students to determine the products (magnesium chloride + hydrogen) and the reactants (magnesium + hydrochloric acid) in this equation.

What happens with other acids? Introduce the idea that the reactions of metals with an acid produce a salt (e.g. magnesium chloride) and hydrogen. Explain that some metals react more vigorously (strongly) with acids than others, and some do not react at all, such as gold.

Practical: Reacting metals with acids Students carry out four reactions of metals with hydrochloric acid, and practise testing for hydrogen. They note down their observations and answer the questions that follow.

Review and reflect

Give the names of the reactants and products in reactions between metals and acids to form metal salts and hydrogen. Ask students to write word equations for these reactions on their whiteboards.

Give students the names of a metal and an acid from the lesson. Ask them to predict the products of the reaction and write these on their whiteboards.

Language support

Remind or elicit from students that hydrochloric acid makes chloride salts, sulfuric acid makes sulfate salts, and nitric acid makes nitrate salts. Highlight that the spelling of these salts changes from the name of the acid (e.g. sulfuric to sulfate).

Chemistry links

- representing chemical reactions using formulae and using equations
- combustion, thermal decomposition, oxidation, and displacement reactions
- reactions of acids with metals to produce a salt plus hydrogen

Working scientifically links

- interpret observations and data, including identifying patterns and using observations, measurements, and data to draw conclusions
- use appropriate techniques, apparatus, and materials during fieldwork and laboratory work, paying attention to health and safety
- make and record observations and measurements using a range of methods for different investigations; and evaluate the reliability of methods and suggest possible improvements

Learning objective	Learning outcomes		
	Developing	Secure	Extending
Use a pattern to predict the products of the reaction of a metal with oxygen	Identify the pattern in the products of the reaction of a metal with oxygen	**Use a pattern to predict the products of the reaction of a metal with oxygen**	Predict the products of the reaction of a metal with oxygen
Write a word equation for the reaction of a metal with oxygen, given the names of the reactants and products	Identify the word equation for the reaction of a metal with an acid, given the names of the reactants and products	**Write a word equation for the reaction of a metal with oxygen, given the names of the reactants and products**	Write a word equation for the reaction of a metal with oxygen
Compare the patterns in the reactivity of metals with acids and with oxygen	Describe how gold and magnesium react with acids and oxygen	**Compare the patterns in the reactivity of metals with acids and with oxygen**	Predict how a metal will react with oxygen, given information about how it reacts with acids

Tier 2 vocabulary	Tier 3 vocabulary
reactive, unreactive	

Digital resources

Practical: *How do metals react with oxygen?* (Practical sheet, Support sheet, Teacher and technician notes)
Video: *Reactions of acids and reactions of metals*

Student Book answers

Think back 1 properties that describe the chemical reactions of a substance **2** easily take part in chemical reactions **3** magnesium

In-text questions A magnesium oxide
B iron + oxygen → iron oxide **C** reacts vigorously (strongly) with oxygen

See p.136 for the answers to the **Summary questions** for this lesson.

Getting started

Ask students if they have ever seen magnesium burning in oxygen. If yes, what did they observe? Explain that magnesium burns vigorously (strongly) – it reacts with oxygen from the air. The product is magnesium oxide. Show a piece of magnesium ribbon and explain that the duller/grey bits are where the surface atoms of magnesium have reacted with oxygen from the air, forming a thin layer of magnesium oxide.

What is happening to these metals? Show students a shiny new iron nail and a rusty iron nail, and how the shiny iron nail does not instantly become dull. Then cut a piece of lithium on a white tile and show the shiny cut surface rapidly becoming dull. Explain that the iron nail reacts more slowly than the lithium, but both metals have reacted with oxygen to form metal oxides. Clarify that rusting requires moisture and only refers to the formation of iron oxide (specifically iron(III) oxide,

but referred to as 'iron oxide' in lower secondary), while other metals corrode. Explain that most metals react with oxygen (without needing moisture) to form metal oxides, but there are differences. Ask students to predict if gold reacts with oxygen in the same way as lithium. Explain that gold does not react easily with oxygen, which is why it stays shiny.

Writing word equations Recall that air is a mixture of oxygen and other gases, and discuss that burning metals react with the oxygen in the air. Demonstrate the reaction of iron filings burning in oxygen by sprinkling them over a tilted Bunsen flame. Ask students to identify the reactants (iron and oxygen) and product (iron oxide) in this reaction. Write the word equation for this reaction on the board:

$$\text{iron} + \text{oxygen} \rightarrow \text{iron oxide}$$

Main activity

Practical: How do metals react with oxygen?
Demonstrate the reactions of magnesium and calcium burning in oxygen to produce magnesium and calcium oxides respectively. Do not look directly at burning magnesium or burning calcium. Students then carry out the reactions of iron wool and copper with oxygen using a Bunsen flame, and record their observations.

Comparing patterns of reactivity Recall the vigorous reactions of magnesium with a dilute acid

and oxygen. Then remind students that gold is unreactive; it does not react with dilute acids, oxygen, or other substances. Discuss the relative reactivities of some metals with oxygen and dilute acids using the table. Show the relationship between the reactivities: metals that react vigorously with dilute acids also react vigorously with oxygen.

Students then answer the questions that follow on the Practical sheet.

Review and reflect

Give the names of the reactants and products in reactions between metals and oxygen to form metal oxides, and ask students to write word equations for these reactions on their whiteboards.

Give students the name of a metal from the lesson, and ask them to predict the product(s) of the reaction with oxygen and write these on their whiteboards.

Ask students to compare the reactivities of elements with either oxygen or acids.

You can also watch the video on Kerboodle to consolidate students' learning.

Language support

Regularly remind students that an equation is a simple way of showing what happens in a chemical reaction. The reactants are positioned on the left of the arrow,

and the final product(s) on the right of the arrow. The arrow shows the direction of the reaction and means 'react to make'.

Chemistry links

- combustion, thermal decomposition, oxidation, and displacement reactions
- the order of metals and carbon in the reactivity series
- how patterns in reactions can be predicted with reference to the Periodic Table

Working scientifically links

- ask questions and develop a line of enquiry based on observations of the real world, alongside prior knowledge and experience
- make and record observations and measurements using a range of methods for different investigations; and evaluate the reliability of methods and suggest possible improvements
- interpret observations and data, including identifying patterns and using observations, measurements, and data to draw conclusions

Learning objective	Learning outcomes		
	Developing	Secure	Extending
Use a pattern to predict the products of the reaction of a metal with water	Identify the pattern in the products of the reaction of a metal with water	**Use a pattern to predict the products of the reaction of a metal with water**	Predict the products of the reaction of a metal with water
Write a word equation for the reaction of a metal with water, given the names of the reactants and products	Identify the word equation for the reaction of a metal with water, given the names of the reactants and products	**Write a word equation for the reaction of a metal with water, given the names of the reactants and products**	Write the word equation for the reaction of a metal with water
Use the reactivity series to predict how vigorously metals react with acids, oxygen, and water	Describe the reactivity series	**Use the reactivity series to predict how vigorously metals react with acids, oxygen, and water**	Use reactivity data to predict where a metal sits in the reactivity series

Tier 2 vocabulary	Tier 3 vocabulary
	reactivity series

Digital resources

Activity: *Most reactive to least reactive* (Activity sheet, Support sheet, Teacher and technician notes)

Student Book answers

Think back 1 reactive metal – for example: potassium, sodium, lithium, calcium, magnesium; unreactive metal – for example: gold, copper **2** zinc oxide **3** any three from: lithium, sodium, potassium, rubidium, caesium

In-text questions A calcium hydroxide and hydrogen **B** lithium + water → lithium hydroxide + hydrogen **C** calcium

See p.137 for the answers to the **Summary questions** for this lesson.

Getting started

Ask students to look at the metals around them and decide if they react with water. For example, stainless steel taps do not react with water, nor do stainless steel cutlery, gold jewellery, or copper pipes. Then recall the reactions of lithium, sodium, and potassium with water. Discuss that some metals do react with water, and others do not.

How do different metals react with water?
Demonstrate (or show a video of) the (vigorous) reaction of calcium with water and the (too slow to be visible) reaction of magnesium with water. Discuss the differences between the reactions observed. Show

that the reaction of calcium with water produces calcium hydroxide (a white substance) and hydrogen (the bubbles that are formed). Write the word equation for this reaction on the board.

The reactivity series Tell students that the patterns in metal reactions with acids, oxygen, and water are similar. Discuss how the reactivity series lists metals by how vigorously (strongly) they react with other substances. The metals at the top have vigorous reactions, with metals getting less reactive going down the list.

Main activity

Reaction with steam Show students the Royal Society of Chemistry video on YouTube, which demonstrates that the reaction of magnesium with water is slow – no visible reaction occurs. However, when magnesium is reacted with steam, there is a reaction that produces magnesium oxide and hydrogen. Write its word equation on the board:

magnesium + water → magnesium oxide + hydrogen

Discuss that copper is not reactive enough to react with water, even if the water is heated to form steam. Discuss that zinc and iron also react with steam to form hydrogen and a metal oxide.

Activity: Most reactive to least reactive Demonstrate (or show videos of) the reactions of the Group 1 metals

lithium, sodium, and potassium with water. Write word equations for these reactions on the board, showing that the products are a metal hydroxide and hydrogen. Ask students to make observations about the reactivity of the three Group 1 metals. Compare these reactions with those of steam with iron, zinc, and magnesium. Show that magnesium, iron, and zinc are all less reactive than the Group 1 metals as the water must be heated for them to react.

Students then complete the activity, ordering metals by reactivity based on the descriptions given and their observations from the lesson. They use this reactivity series to predict how vigorously metals react with oxygen, dilute acids, and water.

Review and reflect

Give students the name of a metal from the lesson and ask them to predict the products of the reaction with water. They write these on their whiteboards.

Ask students to compare the reactivity of elements with either oxygen, acids, or water, and to explain their answer using the reactivity series.

Language support

Encourage students to create a unique mnemonic, written by them, to help remember the order of metals

in the reactivity series. This is an effective strategy that aids the retention of information.

3.4 Metal displacement reactions

Chemistry links

- the order of metals and carbon in the reactivity series
- how patterns in reactions can be predicted with reference to the Periodic Table
- chemical reactions as the rearrangement of atoms

Working scientifically links

- make predictions using scientific knowledge and understanding
- make and record observations and measurements using a range of methods for different investigations; and evaluate the reliability of methods and suggest possible improvements
- interpret observations and data, including identifying patterns and using observations, measurements, and data to draw conclusions
- present reasoned explanations, including explaining data in relation to predictions and hypotheses

Learning objective	Learning outcomes		
	Developing	Secure	Extending
Describe a displacement reaction	Identify the definition of a displacement reaction	**Describe a displacement reaction**	Give examples of displacement reactions
Identify pairs of substances that do, and do not, react in displacement reactions	Use the reactivity series to identify more and less reactive metals	**Identify pairs of substances that do, and do not, react in displacement reactions**	Explain why a pair of substances can, or cannot, react in a displacement reaction
Predict the products of displacement reactions	Identify the products of a metal displacement reaction	**Predict the products of displacement reactions**	Write a word equation for a displacement reaction

Tier 2 vocabulary	Tier 3 vocabulary
displace, displacement	

Digital resources

Practical: *Will a displacement reaction occur?* (Practical sheet, Support sheet, Teacher and technician notes)

Student Book answers

Think back 1 a list of metals in order of how vigorously (strongly) they react with other substances **2** top **3** react to make

In-text questions A a reaction in which a more reactive metal displaces, or pushes out, a less reactive element from its compound **B** The metal on its own (copper) is less reactive than the metal in the compound (magnesium).

See p.137 for the answers to the **Summary questions** for this lesson.

Getting started

Ask students to recall the definitions of an element, a compound, and a mixture.

Recall where to find copper in the reactivity series. Ask students where we find copper, a very useful metal, in nature, and how we get it ready to use. Discuss that scientists use chemical reactions to remove copper from its compounds. They add sulfuric acid to the rock, which produces copper sulfate solution, and then add some waste iron to the solution. There is a chemical reaction and copper is produced.

Main activity

Introducing displacement reactions Set up a boiling tube containing silver nitrate solution and a coil of copper wire. Ask students to make observations about the colours of the metal and the solution. Put the copper wire into the silver nitrate solution. Ask students to identify the positions of silver and copper in the reactivity series, and to compare their reactivities. Explain that, in a displacement reaction, a more reactive element displaces (pushes out) a less reactive element from its compound. However, if the more reactive metal is already the one in the compound, no reaction takes place. Ask students to predict what they might observe with the more reactive copper as an element, and the less reactive silver as a solution. The more reactive copper will displace the less reactive silver from its compound, silver nitrate. So the copper will go into solution, as copper nitrate, and the silver will come out of solution, as elemental silver. Write the word equation on the board:

copper + silver nitrate → copper nitrate + silver

Highlight to students that the nitrate part stays the same and does not take part in the chemical reaction, but the silver and copper swap. The displacement reaction may not occur quickly – return to it at the end of the lesson.

Products of a displacement reaction Discuss the thermite reaction, which is the displacement reaction between aluminium and iron oxide. Ask students to identify which is the more reactive metal and to predict if a displacement reaction will occur. What will be the products of the reaction? Write the equation on the board and show the metals swapping places. The aluminium (the more reactive metal) displaces iron (the less reactive metal) from the compound:

aluminium + iron oxide → aluminium oxide + iron

Thermite is used in welding for railway repairs (videos can be found online), providing a real-life example of displacement reactions.

Practical: Will a displacement reaction occur?
Students use the reactivity series to predict whether displacement reactions will occur between different combinations of four metals (Mg, Zn, Cu, Fe) and their sulfates. Students then carry out a practical, combining metals with their sulfates on a spotting tile, record their observations, and answer the questions that follow.

Review and reflect

Return to the demonstration of the copper wire in the silver nitrate solution. Ask students to describe what they can now see (they should see silver in the solid state on the coiled wire). Encourage them to explain, in their own words, what has happened to the particles and why. Students should use the reactivity series, the key word 'displacement', and a word equation in their explanation.

Language support

Ask students if they can see a familiar word in the key words 'displace' and 'displacement'. They should suggest 'place', which means a particular position (noun) or to put something in a particular position (verb). Explain that the prefix 'dis-' gives the root word the opposite meaning. Therefore, a displacement reaction refers to a more reactive element pushing out (i.e. removing from its position) a less reactive element from its compound.

Chemistry links

- the order of metals and carbon in the reactivity series
- the use of carbon in obtaining metals from metal oxides

Working scientifically links

- interpret observations and data, including identifying patterns and using observations, measurements, and data to draw conclusions
- present reasoned explanations, including explaining data in relation to predictions and hypotheses
- use and derive simple equations and carry out appropriate calculations

Learning objective	Learning outcomes		
	Developing	Secure	Extending
Describe the two steps needed to extract a metal from its ore	Identify the two steps needed to extract a metal from its ore	**Describe the two steps needed to extract a metal from its ore**	Describe the two steps needed to extract a metal from its ore, and explain why this is necessary
Name metals in the reactivity series that can be extracted by heating their ores with carbon	Identify which metals in the reactivity series can be extracted by heating their ores with carbon	**Name metals in the reactivity series that can be extracted by heating their ores with carbon**	Use the reactivity series to predict and justify whether a given metal can be extracted from its ore by heating with carbon
Calculate the mass of metal in an ore	Identify the mass of metal in an ore	**Calculate the mass of metal in an ore**	Calculate the percentage of metal in an ore

Tier 2 vocabulary	Tier 3 vocabulary
ore	

Digital resources

Activity: *Methods of extracting metals* (Activity sheet, Support sheet, Teacher and technician notes)
Video: *The reactivity series and extracting metals*

Student Book answers

Think back 1 a chemical reaction in which a more reactive element displaces, or pushes out, a less reactive element from its compound **2** zinc **3** any three from: good conductor of electricity, good conductor of thermal energy/electricity, malleable, ductile, sonorous, shiny

In-text questions A 25% × 20 kg = 5 kg **B** step 1
C zinc, iron, lead, copper

See p.137 for the answers to the **Summary questions** for this lesson.

Getting started

Ask students to give any uses of iron they know. An example is that iron is the main part of steel, which is used in making vehicles, as well as other things. Discuss that iron comes from rocks in Earth's crust that contain iron compounds, but that other substances, such as gold, can be found as an element. Metals that are found naturally as compounds need to be extracted before they can be used.

What is an ore? Ask students if it is worth extracting every atom of metal from rocks – is it energy- and cost-efficient? Discuss that some rocks containing metal compounds have very little metal in them and the metal is not worth extracting. Rocks that you can extract metals from, and that contain enough of the metal to make it worth extracting, are called ores.

Introducing metal extraction Show students a reactivity series with carbon placed in between aluminium and zinc. See if they can identify what is wrong with this reactivity series of metals – carbon is not a metal. Justify the presence of carbon in this series by introducing the displacement of metals using carbon.

Which metals can be extracted using carbon? Elicit from students what a displacement reaction is, and discuss that not all metals can be extracted with carbon. As the extraction of a metal with carbon is a displacement reaction, the metal needs to be less reactive than carbon, so carbon can displace (push out) the less reactive metal from its compound. Ask students to predict if aluminium, which is more reactive than carbon, can be extracted from its ore using carbon. Students should decide that it cannot, as aluminium is more reactive than carbon, so will stay in the compound.

Main activity

How much metal is in an ore? Recall that different ores contain different amounts of metal. Companies need to calculate the mass of metal in a sample of an ore to decide if the metal is worth extracting. In order to do this, you need to know the mass of the ore and the percentage of metal in the ore.

$$\text{mass of metal in the ore} = \text{percentage of metal in the ore} \times \text{mass of the ore}$$

Using the example in the Student Book, or another example with a different mass of ore and a different percentage of metal, work through the calculation process with students, calculating the mass of iron in the iron ore.

Activity: Methods of extracting metals Show a demonstration of iron(III) oxide reacting with carbon to produce iron: roll a damp, non-safety match in sodium carbonate, and then iron(III) oxide, and heat it in a blue Bunsen flame. The resulting crushed product can be shown to be magnetic – iron was produced. Discuss the steps involved in separating a metal from its ore.

Students then consider an early method for extracting iron by reading an old 'recipe' and applying their understanding of scientific concepts to answer the questions that follow, explaining the steps in iron extraction and calculating the mass of metal in an ore.

Review and reflect

Students complete a plus, minus, interesting (PMI) grid to reflect on their learning in this lesson. To complete a PMI grid, students divide a page into three columns, and add the headings 'plus (+)', 'minus (–)', and 'interesting'. In the plus column, they list positive examples and applications from the lesson; in the minus column, they list any drawbacks or challenges; and in the interesting column, they describe interesting facts.

You can also watch the video on Kerboodle to consolidate students' learning.

Language support

Display an image or images of ores that clearly show traces of metal. Explain that an ore is a rock that contains a metal or a metal compound. When there is a lot of metal present, it can be extracted (removed) from the rock.

Chemistry link
- properties of ceramics, polymers, and composites (qualitative)

Working scientifically links
- make and record observations and measurements using a range of methods for different investigations; and evaluate the reliability of methods and suggest possible improvements
- interpret observations and data, including identifying patterns and using observations, measurements, and data to draw conclusions
- present reasoned explanations, including explaining data in relation to predictions and hypotheses

Learning objective	Learning outcomes		
	Developing	Secure	Extending
Describe the properties of ceramics	Identify the properties of ceramics	**Describe the properties of ceramics**	Explain the properties of ceramics
Explain how the properties of ceramics make them suitable for their uses	Describe the properties of some ceramics	**Explain how the properties of ceramics make them suitable for their uses**	Evaluate the properties of ceramics for an unfamiliar use

Tier 2 vocabulary	Tier 3 vocabulary
ceramic	

Digital resources

Activity: *Explaining uses of ceramics* (Activity sheet, Support sheet, Teacher and technician notes)

Student Book answers

Think back 1 the different types of stuff that things are made from **2** solid **3** a property that you can observe or measure without changing the material

In-text questions A a hard, brittle material that is made by firing a material, such as clay, at a high temperature **B** physical – any four from: hard, brittle, stiff, solid at room temperature/high melting point, strong when forces press on them, easy to break when pulled, electrical insulator; chemical – do not react with water, acids, or alkalis **C** For example: building – ceramics are strong when forces press on them; jet engine turbine blades – ceramics have high melting points.

See p.137 for the answers to the **Summary questions** for this lesson.

Getting started

Look at Figure 1 in the Student Book. Ask students what wash basins in bathrooms are made from. Wash basins are made of pottery. Discuss what students know about the properties of pottery.

Introducing ceramics Introduce students to ceramics. A ceramic is a hard, brittle material that is made by firing a substance, such as clay, at a high temperature. Discuss that pottery is an example of a ceramic material. Show samples of other ceramic materials: brick, china, and earthenware. Ask students to suggest properties of these materials – they should all be similar.

Properties of ceramics Use one or two of the ceramic samples to discuss that ceramics are hard, brittle, stiff, solid at room temperature (with high melting points), strong, easy to break when pulled, and electrical insulators. Write a list of these properties on the board. Discuss that ceramics also have similar chemical properties to each other, and do not react with water, acids, or alkalis.

Main activity

What gives ceramic materials their properties?
Invite students to suggest explanations for some of the properties (hardness and high melting points) of ceramics. Explain that, in ceramic materials, millions and millions of atoms are joined together in one big structure. There are strong forces between the atoms. A large amount of energy is therefore needed to break the forces between the atoms – this explains the high melting points. The bonds between the atoms are very strong – this explains why ceramic materials are hard.

Activity: Explaining uses of ceramics In groups, students look at and discuss the images of four uses of ceramics. Together they describe the properties of ceramics, identify the uses, and determine which of these properties make them suitable for their uses. Students then individually answer the questions on their Activity sheet.

Review and reflect

Students refer to a list of the properties of ceramics and suggest one use of ceramics that utilizes each property.

Language support

There are a lot of adjectives used to describe the properties of ceramics in this topic, such as 'hard', 'brittle', 'stiff', 'solid', and 'strong'. With the help of the Student Book, draw a mind map on the board with 'ceramics' written in the middle and arrows pointing to its properties. Ensure that students understand the meaning of unfamiliar words like 'brittle' by using realia or familiar examples to demonstrate something that is easy to break.

Chemistry link

• properties of ceramics, polymers, and composites (qualitative)

Working scientifically links

• interpret observations and data, including identifying patterns and using observations, measurements, and data to draw conclusions
• present reasoned explanations, including explaining data in relation to predictions and hypotheses

Learning objective	Learning outcomes		
	Developing	Secure	Extending
Explain how the properties of polymers make them suitable for their uses	Identify the properties of some polymers	**Explain how the properties of polymers make them suitable for their uses**	Compare the uses of two polymers

Tier 2 vocabulary	Tier 3 vocabulary
	natural polymer, polymer, synthetic polymer

Digital resources

Activity: *Choosing suitable polymers* (Activity sheet, Teacher and technician notes)

Student Book answers

Think back 1 a group of two or more atoms, strongly joined together **2** the mass of a substance in a certain volume **3** Different materials have different properties, making them suitable for different uses.

In-text questions A a substance with very long molecules, in which identical groups of atoms are repeated many times **B** flexible, waterproof, durable **C** Its properties make it suitable for this use – it is strong, can have smooth surfaces, and it does not decay in the body.

See p.137 for the answers to the **Summary questions** for this lesson.

Getting started

Ask students what jumpers and tyres have in common. Explain that jumpers and tyres are made from polymers. Discuss that polymers have many uses, and ask students to suggest materials they think might also be polymers.

Modelling polymers Show students an array of polymers, both natural and synthetic (e.g. plastic bottles, carrier bags, wool, nylon, rubber). Describe polymers as long chains, made up of a huge number of repeating groups of atoms. To demonstrate, ask students to link arms in pairs, and then in one long chain. Explain that the properties of polymers can depend on the repeating units, and this makes them extremely useful for many different products.

Main activity

Different polymer properties Discuss some different polymers that are readily available and their uses: natural polymers (wool and rubber) and synthetic polymers (low-density and high-density poly(ethene)). Ask students to deduce and compare differences in common properties (e.g. flexibility, strength, conduction of thermal energy, conduction of electricity, water resistance, and opacity).

Activity: Choosing suitable polymers Students interpret information on different polymers from a table in order to choose suitable polymers for different uses. Students explain their choices and answer the questions that follow.

Review and reflect

Students make a list of polymers they have learned about in the lesson. They categorize these polymers according to whether they are natural or synthetic, then explain the properties they possess that make them suitable for their uses.

Language support

Ask students to break down the key word 'polymer' into two parts: 'poly' and 'mer'. Do they know any other words with the prefix 'poly-'? Encourage them to use a dictionary. Record any words offered in a central place. Can students see any patterns in these words? The prefix 'poly-' means many (e.g. a polygon is a 2D shape with *many* straight sides and angles). Then explain that the suffix '-mer' is often found in scientific contexts and means part. This describes a polymer as a substance with many parts.

Chemistry link

- properties of ceramics, polymers, and composites (qualitative)

Working scientifically links

- interpret observations and data, including identifying patterns and using observations, measurements, and data to draw conclusions
- present reasoned explanations, including explaining data in relation to predictions and hypotheses

Learning objective	Learning outcomes		
	Developing	Secure	Extending
Describe the properties of some composites	Identify the properties of some composites	**Describe the properties of some composites**	Use information given to suggest advantages and disadvantages of the properties of composites
Explain how the properties of composites make them suitable for their uses	Identify the properties of components of composite materials	**Explain how the properties of composites make them suitable for their uses**	Evaluate the properties of composites for an unfamiliar use

Tier 2 vocabulary	Tier 3 vocabulary
	carbon fibre, composite

Digital resources

Activity: *Explaining the properties of some composites* (Activity sheet, Support sheet, Teacher and technician notes)
Video: *Ceramics, polymers, composites*

Student Book answers

Think back 1 what a substance looks like and how it behaves **2** hard, brittle materials that are made by firing materials like clay at high temperatures **3** a substance with very long molecules, in which identical groups of atoms are repeated many times

In-text questions A concrete and steel
B a mixture of materials, each with different properties; has properties that are a combination of the properties of the materials that are in it **C** low density, does not rust, can be formed into any shape

See p.137 for the answers to the **Summary questions** for this lesson.

Getting started

Show the image in Figure 1 in the Student Book of the Burj Khalifa in Dubai, the world's tallest building. Ask students what it is made from. Encourage them to think about why this material is so strong. Inform students that the Burj Khalifa is made from a composite material: reinforced concrete.

Introducing composite materials Discuss composite materials as a mixture of materials. Each material has different properties, and the composite material has properties that are a combination of the properties of the materials that are in it. Explain that composite materials can be incredibly useful, as we can design and tailor their properties to suit our needs.

Mud bricks Show an image of mud bricks and explain that they are a composite material used in the developing world. They consist of mud (strong under compression) mixed with straw or grass (strong under tension), and are allowed to dry. This is a less expensive and more available version of reinforced concrete.

Main activity

Describing the properties of composite materials Introduce reinforced concrete as a composite material, made of steel bars with concrete around them. Ask students to describe the properties of steel (it is strong when stretching forces are applied) and the properties of concrete (it is not damaged by squashing/compression forces). Then invite students to suggest the properties of reinforced concrete (it can withstand, or hold out against, both high squashing forces and high stretching forces).

Introduce carbon fibre-reinforced plastic (CFRP) as a composite material made of carbon fibres and a glue-like polymer. Discuss the properties of the carbon fibres (tubes of carbon that have a low density and do not react with water) and the glue-like polymer (easily formed into different shapes when soft). Invite students to suggest the properties of CFRP (it makes lighter bicycles, does not rust, and can be formed into any shape). CFRP does have some disadvantages though. Elicit what these might be from students (expensive, easy to break if crashed).

Activity: Explaining the properties of some composites Students choose a composite material and write a newspaper article, imagining they were around when the material was invented in order to introduce the material to the world. They should include a description of the composite material, and the materials it is made from. They then give an explanation of the properties of the materials it is made from, and those of the composite material itself, and give a use of the composite, explaining why it is suitable for that use.

Review and reflect

Ask students to describe one of the examples of composites discussed in the lesson, comparing the properties of its starting materials with the properties of the final composite material. They then give a use of the composite material and explain why its properties make it suitable for this use.

You can also watch the video on Kerboodle to consolidate students' learning.

Language support

Elicit from students what a mixture is in science. Ensure that they understand this meaning before introducing the idea of a composite. As the materials are not chemically combined in the mixture, the composite benefits from the properties of each material. Invite students to the board to write down words and phrases for any properties of materials they can remember, encouraging them to explain what the properties mean using their own words and/or actions.

Getting started

Encourage students to review their learning in this chapter. The 'Summary questions' in the Student Book can be used formatively during lessons. For the 'What have I learned?' pages, students can answer the questions one at a time after each topic, or as a single summative activity. This could be done as a whole-class or group activity, or set as an independent task.

Whichever approach is adopted, the questions are designed to give you and students feedback about progress and identify targets for development.

Student reflection

Allow students time to reflect on how confident they feel about each topic. Remind them to use the learning objectives provided in their Student Book for guidance. They should focus on whether there were any questions they found difficult or easy, and on how well they prepared for the summative assessment at the end of the chapter. Listen to and deal with students' reflections sensitively so that they feel comfortable to report areas they are not confident with.

Learning objectives and learning outcomes

Each lesson is guided by the learning *objectives*. The learning objectives are provided at the beginning of each topic in the Student Book. They outline what students are going to learn in each topic.

In contrast, the learning *outcomes* in this Teacher's Guide are statements that describe the knowledge or skills that students should acquire by the end of each topic. They are linked to the learning objectives, but are *not* often seen by students. The learning outcomes are used by teachers to assess and measure if or how each learning objective has been achieved.

Answer key

Chapter 3: Metals and other materials

1 hard/durable/withstands squashing forces; they will last a long time and support the weight of the building
2 zinc oxide
3 zinc + hydrochloric acid → zinc chloride + hydrogen
4 with a magnet

3.1 Metals and acids

Working scientifically: The experiment plan should involve adding the same amount of metal to each acid and comparing observations.
1 a salt, hydrogen, lead, magnesium, gold
2 calcium + hydrochloric acid → calcium chloride + hydrogen
3 products: calcium nitrate and hydrogen
  word equation: calcium + nitric acid → calcium nitrate + hydrogen

3.2 Metals and oxygen

Working scientifically: Jamila holds the metals in tongs and observes how they burn in the flame of the Bunsen burner. The reactions are ordered based on her observations. To improve, the flame should be the same on the Bunsen burner, and the amount and form (shape) of each metal sample should be the same.
1 magnesium, oxides, copper, gold
2 zinc + oxygen → zinc oxide
3 Lithium reacts vigorously with oxygen, producing lithium oxide. Metals react with oxygen with similar vigor to their reactions with acids to form a metal oxide.

3.3 The reactivity series

1 C
2 lithium hydroxide and hydrogen
3 nickel is between iron and lead – nickel reacts with hydrochloric acid, but lead does not; iron reacts with water and air, but nickel does not

3.4 Metal displacement reactions

1 zinc
2 a, c, d
3 a zinc + copper chloride → zinc chloride + copper
  b zinc + lead oxide → zinc oxide + lead
  c magnesium + iron chloride → magnesium chloride + iron

3.5 Extracting metals

Maths skills: (from top to bottom) 50% waste = 500 kg; 84% waste = 840 kg; 30% waste = 300 kg

1 separate the metal compound from the compounds it is mixed with in the rock; use chemical reactions to extract the metal from its compound
2 6% × 400 kg = 24 kg
3 Magnesium is above carbon in the reactivity series. Carbon can only be used to extract metals that are below it in the reactivity series.

3.6 Ceramics

1 hard, brittle, electrical insulator, high melting point
2 B and D, because they have high hardness values, and very high melting points
3 There are very strong forces between the atoms in the structure, and a great amount of energy is needed to break these strong forces.

3.7 Polymers

Maths skills: bar chart should have: polymers on x-axis and density on y-axis, suggested 0.90–1.10 range and intervals of .1, with bars plotted correctly

1 flexible and strong
2 a low density
  b poor conductor of thermal energy
3 PVC is harder than nylon. Nylon is stronger when pulled than PVC.

3.8 Composites

Working scientifically: independent variable: amount of straw in each block; dependent variable: number of masses supported before block breaks; control variables (to ensure fair test): same size blocks, same types of mud and straw in each block; same size masses; same amount of time allocated for each test (e.g. if a block breaks within 1 min)

1 low density, does not rust, can be moulded to any shape
2 concrete withstands pushing forces, steel withstands pulling forces
3 Fibreglass is five times stronger when pulled.

What have I learned about metals and other materials?

1 brittle, [1 mark] electrical insulator, [1 mark] hard, [1 mark] high melting point, [1 mark] stiff [1 mark]
2 a A mixture of materials, each with different properties. [1 mark]
  b Concrete [1 mark] and steel/iron [1 mark]
  c It can withstand high squashing forces and high stretching forces. [1 mark]
3 calcium – bubbles vigorously; copper – no change; potassium – moves on surface of water and purple flame [2 marks for all correct, 1 mark for 1 correct]
4 a any two from: same temperature, same volume of acid, acid of same concentration [1 mark each, maximum 2 marks]
  b wear eye protection [1 mark] because the acid may harm eyes [1 mark]
  c zinc [1 mark] – of the three metals, it is highest in the reactivity series [1 mark]
  d hydrogen [1 mark]
5 a magnesium + oxygen → magnesium **oxide** [1 mark]
  b sodium + water → sodium hydroxide + **hydrogen** [1 mark]
  c zinc + hydrochloric acid → zinc **chloride** + hydrogen [1 mark]
  d iron + **oxygen** → iron oxide [1 mark]
  e potassium + **water** → potassium hydroxide + hydrogen [1 mark]
  f calcium + **hydrochloric** acid → calcium chloride + hydrogen [1 mark]
  g zinc + copper oxide → zinc oxide + **copper** [1 mark]
  h magnesium + iron oxide → magnesium **oxide** + iron [1 mark]
6 a X and Z [1 mark] because in each case, the metal on its own is more reactive/higher in the reactivity series than the metal in the compound. [1 mark]
  b any one from:
    iron + copper oxide → iron oxide + copper
    iron + lead oxide → iron oxide + lead
    [3 marks – 1 for correct reactants, 1 for correct products, 1 for correctly drawn arrow]
7 a i the metal [1 mark]
    ii any two from: volume of acid, concentration of acid, temperature, amount of metal, size of pieces of metal [1 mark each, maximum 2 marks]
    iii so that the investigation is fair [1 mark]
  b Pour the same amount of acid into each test tube [1 mark] and add the same amount of metal to each test tube. [1 mark] The metal that bubbles most vigorously is the most reactive. [1 mark]
  c

metal	observations
iron	
magnesium	
zinc	

[1 mark for correct headings and metal names, 1 mark for correct table layout]

  d to see if the order of reactivity for the three metals is the same for the different acid [1 mark]

Introduction to chapter

In this chapter, students will learn about the composition of Earth and the atmosphere. They are reintroduced to three different types of rock – sedimentary, igneous, and metamorphic rocks – and describe how they are made, their properties and uses, and how their properties make them suitable for their uses. The rock cycle and the carbon cycle are explored, allowing students to consider how materials are recycled naturally. Students will also study the greenhouse effect, global heating, and climate change. They will think about how to look after and protect Earth by preventing climate change and preserving our natural resources through recycling.

Core concepts

- The composition of Earth and its atmosphere
- The processes involved in making sedimentary, igneous, and metamorphic rocks
- The uses and properties of sedimentary, igneous, and metamorphic rocks
- Explaining how these properties make rocks suitable for their uses
- Using the rock cycle to describe how materials in rocks are recycled
- Explaining how uplift provides evidence for the rock cycle
- Describing how carbon moves between carbon stores in the carbon cycle
- Explaining why the concentration of carbon dioxide in the atmosphere did not change for many years
- Describing the greenhouse effect, global heating, and climate change
- Describing impacts of global heating and how to prevent climate change
- Describing how aluminium is recycled
- Describing advantages and disadvantages of recycling

What have students already learned?

- The definitions of a material, a substance, an atom, an element, a molecule, and a compound
- How some changes cannot be reversed as new substances are made
- Materials being made of particles
- The differences between chemical and physical changes
- States of matter and changes of state
- Rocks being made of grains or crystals

What will students learn next?

- Evidence for the composition of Earth's atmosphere
- Evidence, and uncertainties in evidence, for additional anthropogenic causes of climate change
- Common atmospheric pollutants
- Using fuels
- Natural resources and their uses
- The viability of recycling of certain materials
- Assessing environmental impacts associated with all stages of a product's life
- Atom economy and yields

Think back

1 List three properties you can use to sort rocks into groups.

2 Name the states of matter of a substance before and after it melts.

3 Predict which emits (gives out) more radiation per second: the Sun or the surface of Earth.

4 Write two word equations: one for photosynthesis and one for respiration.

Teaching strategy

Students will have seen rocks in nature, but are unlikely to have experienced rock formation in person. We use models to visualize the processes involved in rock formation, allowing students to picture processes that often occur on large scales or over long periods of time. These models, as with most, come with limitations. Although practicals and demonstrations can be exciting and fun, it is also important to highlight the processes and ensure students recall the key words associated with each. Allow students time to reflect on how the models relate to the natural world and the larger-scale processes they are representing.

Common learning misconceptions

- Carbon dioxide is always harmful. (Plants need carbon dioxide to photosynthesize. Photosynthesis is vital to all life on Earth.)
- Rocks with layers are always sedimentary rocks.
- Weathering is the same process as erosion.
- Lava can only flow on land. (Lava flowing under the sea can cause tsunamis. The Mid-Atlantic Ridge under the ocean is made up of a continuous belt of active volcanoes.)
- Rocks always take a long time to form. (Rocks are formed instantly when lava cools.)
- Rocks cannot change their structure.
- Volcanoes are all active.
- Igneous rocks are only found on volcanoes.
- The greenhouse effect just involves the Sun's rays being trapped in the atmosphere.
- The greenhouse effect is always bad. (Without greenhouse gases, the planet would suffer extreme cold temperatures at night as no heat is retained/reflected back to Earth's surface by these gases. This would make Earth uninhabitable.)
- Energy from the Sun is immediately trapped when it enters Earth's atmosphere.
- Climate change means the temperature of the whole surface of Earth increases.
- Rocks cannot move away from where they were formed.
- Recycling is the only way of preserving Earth's resources.
- All types of plastic can be recycled. (Some plastics cannot be recycled because they produce toxic fumes.)

Broader context

It is important for us to be aware of the world we are living in. This chapter helps students understand Earth and its atmosphere, and consider their impact on it. By looking at how rocks form, we can better understand how our Earth developed and how we can look after it. By highlighting the scarcity of some resources, encourage students to reduce, reuse, and recycle.

Climate change and global heating are prominent issues in society. Consequently, they are topics that can feel scary to some students, possibly evoking strong emotions and causing stress. Help students understand the science behind what is happening to alleviate any fears and empower them to take positive actions. The role of governments and big businesses in tackling and preventing climate change should also be highlighted and discussed. This will reassure students that it is not just up to the individual.

Chemistry links

- the composition of Earth
- the structure of Earth
- the composition of the atmosphere

Working scientifically links

- present observations and data using appropriate methods, including tables and graphs
- interpret observations and data, including identifying patterns and using observations, measurements, and data to draw conclusions

Learning objective	Learning outcomes		
	Developing	Secure	Extending
Describe the layers of Earth	Name the layers of Earth	**Describe the layers of Earth**	Compare the physical properties of the layers of Earth
Name the four main gases that make up Earth's atmosphere	Identify some of the main gases that make up Earth's atmosphere	**Name the four main gases that make up Earth's atmosphere**	Compare the quantities of the four main gases in Earth's atmosphere

Tier 2 vocabulary	Tier 3 vocabulary
atmosphere, core, crust, mantle	inner core, outer core, troposphere

Digital resources

Activity: *The structure of Earth* (Activity sheet, Support sheet, Teacher and technician notes)
Video: *Exploring Earth and its atmosphere*

Student Book answers

Think back 1 any two from: cannot be compressed, does not flow, fixed shape unless you apply a force **2** any two from: can be easily compressed, flows, takes the shape of its container **3** a substance made up of one type of atom that cannot be broken down into simpler substances

In-text questions A inner core, outer core, mantle, crust **B** oxygen, silicon, aluminium, iron, calcium, sodium **C** elements: nitrogen, oxygen, argon; compound: carbon dioxide

See p.156 for the answers to the **Summary questions** for this lesson.

Getting started

Ask students about the components of a packet of crisps, and to suggest where we get the components from. Discuss where they come from (potatoes – plants, which use water, carbon dioxide from the air, and nutrients from the soil; salt – from the sea or mines; aluminium [for the bags] – from bauxite rocks; nitrogen [the crisps are packed in nitrogen] – from the air) and highlight that it is necessary to use lots of different parts of Earth, the oceans, and the air in order to make a seemingly 'simple' everyday packet of crisps.

Introducing the composition of Earth Ask students what they think they would find if they dug a very deep hole through to the centre of Earth. Explain that scientists have not dug down to the centre of Earth, but we can still determine the structure of Earth by studying shock waves from earthquakes and examining different rocks. Show an image of the structure of Earth and name each layer, giving a description of that layer.

Main activity

What is in the crust? Ask students which layer of Earth they think we know most about. Discuss the elements that make up some of the compounds found in the crust using the pie chart in Figure 3 in the Student Book.

Earth's atmosphere Describe the atmosphere as an envelope made from a mixture of gases that surrounds Earth. Name the layer of the atmosphere closest to Earth as the troposphere, explaining that it extends to approximately 10 km above the surface of Earth. Ask students to suggest the names of the elements that make up the majority of the troposphere (nitrogen, 78%; oxygen, 21%) and any other substances present.

Show and discuss the pie chart in Figure 4 in the Student Book that illustrates the composition of the atmosphere. Emphasize that this is the composition of dry air, as the amount of water vapour varies significantly, but the composition of other gases is constant.

Activity: The structure of Earth Students label the structure of Earth and describe each layer, including, where possible, the size of the layer, the state of most matter in the layer, and what substances the layer is made up of. They then answer the questions that follow.

Review and reflect

Call out a layer of Earth, including the atmosphere. Students write down as many facts as they can about that layer on their whiteboards. Discuss answers given. Repeat in reverse, calling out facts about a layer, asking students to determine which layer you are describing and to write it on their whiteboards.

You can also watch the video on Kerboodle to consolidate students' learning.

Language support

There are lots of difficult key words for students to learn in this topic, such as 'crust', 'mantle', 'core', 'atmosphere', and 'troposphere'. Drawing labelled diagrams and making models that show the structure of Earth will help them retain new information. Use the words regularly throughout teaching so students become familiar with them, indicating each part as you say each word.

Chemistry link

- the rock cycle and the formation of igneous, sedimentary, and metamorphic rocks

Working scientifically links

- ask questions and develop a line of enquiry based on observations of the real world, alongside prior knowledge and experience
- make and record observations and measurements using a range of methods for different investigations; and evaluate the reliability of methods and suggest possible improvements
- present reasoned explanations, including explaining data in relation to predictions and hypotheses

Learning objective	Learning outcomes		
	Developing	Secure	Extending
Describe the four stages in the formation of sedimentary rock	State the four stages in the formation of sedimentary rock	**Describe the four stages in the formation of sedimentary rock**	Compare the processes of weathering and transport
Describe two properties of sedimentary rocks	Identify two properties of typical sedimentary rocks	**Describe two properties of sedimentary rocks**	Suggest and justify the properties of unfamiliar sedimentary rocks
Explain how the properties of sedimentary rocks make them suitable for their uses	State a use of sedimentary rocks	**Explain how the properties of sedimentary rocks make them suitable for their uses**	Suggest disadvantages of using sedimentary rocks for making statues, and give reasons for your answer

Tier 2 vocabulary	Tier 3 vocabulary
porous, transport	cementation, compaction, deposition, erosion, sediment, sedimentary, weathering

Digital resources

Practical: *Modelling the formation of sedimentary rocks* (Practical sheet, Teacher and technician notes)

Student Book answers

Think back 1 crust **2** inner core **3** scratch it

In-text questions A porous (air or water can get into the gaps between the grains); soft (easy to scratch) **B** weathering, erosion and transport, deposition, compaction or cementation **C** can withstand strong pushing forces; attractive to look at

See p.156 for the answers to the **Summary questions** for this lesson.

Getting started

Show the image in Figure 1 in the Student Book of the sphinx in Egypt and ask students if they know what type of rock it is made from. Explain that it is made from limestone, carved by stonemasons more than 4000 years ago.

Show images of sedimentary rock formations or use realia. Highlight the layers visible in the formations, and explain that limestone, from which the sphinx is made, and the formations being shown, belong to a group of rocks called sedimentary rocks.

What are the properties of sedimentary rocks?
Hand around small samples of sedimentary rocks. You may wish to give out hand lenses and mounted needles for students to make closer visual observations and complete scratch tests. In pairs, ask students to describe the rocks and state any properties. Discuss findings as a class. Explain that sedimentary rocks are porous (there are gaps between the separate grains that allow air or water into them) and soft (the forces between the grains are weak, so they are easy to scratch).

You may wish to extend students by asking them to use a top pan balance and record the mass of their sample of sedimentary rock. After, instruct them to put their sample in water, then remove and re-measure the mass. They should discover that the mass increases as some of the water has been absorbed into the holes or pores in the rock.

How are sedimentary rocks useful? Invite students to suggest uses of sedimentary rocks. Discuss their use as beautiful building materials, and how they can withstand (hold out against) strong pushing forces.

Main activity

Practical: Modelling the formation of sedimentary rocks Students watch a demonstration of the formation of sedimentary rocks using chocolate, completing descriptions of each step of the process: weathering, erosion and transport, deposition, and compaction or cementation. Discuss the origins of the names of the processes to help students differentiate between them. Explain the different types of weathering (freeze–thaw, chemical, and biological), giving examples of each on the board. Students then answer questions on the formation, properties, and uses of sedimentary rocks.

Review and reflect

To check students' knowledge, name a stage in the formation of sedimentary rocks, and ask students to describe it on their whiteboards. Address any misconceptions. Then ask students to write down two properties of sedimentary rocks on their whiteboards, and discuss why these properties mean some limestones are used as building materials.

Language support

There are lots of difficult key words for students to learn in this topic, such as 'sedimentary', 'porous', 'weathering', 'deposition', 'compaction', and 'cementation', and students might confuse their meanings. Drawing labelled diagrams and making models that show the structure of sedimentary rock will help them retain new information. Use the words regularly throughout teaching so students become familiar with them, using gestures and actions to demonstrate the different steps.

Chemistry link

- the rock cycle and the formation of igneous, sedimentary, and metamorphic rocks

Working scientifically links

- make and record observations and measurements using a range of methods for different investigations; and evaluate the reliability of methods and suggest possible improvements
- interpret observations and data, including identifying patterns and using observations, measurements, and data to draw conclusions
- present reasoned explanations, including explaining data in relation to predictions and hypotheses

Learning objective	Learning outcomes		
	Developing	Secure	Extending
Describe how igneous and metamorphic rocks form	Identify how igneous and metamorphic rocks form	**Describe how igneous and metamorphic rocks form**	Compare how igneous and metamorphic rocks form
Describe the properties of igneous and metamorphic rocks	Identify two properties of typical igneous and metamorphic rocks	**Describe the properties of igneous and metamorphic rocks**	Suggest and justify the properties of unfamiliar igneous and metamorphic rocks
Explain how the properties of igneous and metamorphic rocks make them suitable for their uses	State some uses of igneous and metamorphic rocks	**Explain how the properties of igneous and metamorphic rocks make them suitable for their uses**	Compare the advantages and disadvantages of using igneous rocks and metamorphic rocks for roof tiles

Tier 2 vocabulary	Tier 3 vocabulary
durable, lava, magma	igneous, metamorphic

Digital resources

Activity: *What affects crystal size?* (Activity sheet, Support sheet, Teacher and technician notes)

Student Book answers

Think back 1 for example: sandstone, limestone **2** for example: a rock that has gaps that air or water can get into **3** before – liquid; after – solid

In-text questions A not porous, hard, durable **B** High pressure underground squashes the mudstone, which squeezes out water and makes layers of new crystals. **C** not porous, made up of layers that can be split into sheets

See p.157 for the answers to the **Summary questions** for this lesson.

Getting started

Show the image of the Giant's Causeway in Northern Ireland in Figure 1 in the Student Book. Ask students to consider this natural landmark and to suggest what the columns are made from. Discuss that it is made from basalt, formed around 50 million years ago. Encourage students to discuss ideas as to why it forms a very regular crystalline structure, and to suggest properties of the rock.

Observing rocks Provide students with samples of igneous and metamorphic rocks, and hand lenses. Ask them to observe the rocks under the hand lenses. What colours can they see? Can they see the grains and crystals? Are the crystals big or small? Are they hard or soft? Discuss the samples of rock and describe any properties the students have observed.

Igneous and metamorphic rocks Introduce the different types of rock in the samples as igneous and metamorphic, showing examples of each on the board. Discuss how each type is formed and what that means for the properties of each type. Non-porous, hard, and durable igneous rocks are formed when liquid rock cools down. This can happen slowly within Earth's crust, or rapidly outside the crusts (including underwater). Metamorphic rocks are formed when other types of rock are under high pressure and/or temperature but do not melt. They are also non-porous, and are made up of thin sheets.

Main activity

Uses of igneous and metamorphic rocks
Ask students to suggest uses for both igneous and metamorphic rocks, and to discuss why the properties of slate (a metamorphic rock) make it useful for roofing tiles, why the properties of marble (a metamorphic rock) make it useful for worktops, and why the properties of granite (an igneous rock) make it useful for a path.

Activity: What affects crystal size? Provide students with a selection of building bricks each. Give them 15 seconds to connect together as many bricks as

possible into one block. Compare the sizes of each other's blocks, then ask students to break their blocks apart and repeat, but this time only give them 5 seconds. Compare the sizes as a class and ask students why they did not manage to make their brick blocks as big. Explain that this is similar to the formation of crystals in igneous and metamorphic rocks. If they cool quickly, only small crystals can form; if they cool slowly over a longer period of time, much bigger crystals can form. Students then answer the questions that follow.

Review and reflect

Show the image of the Giant's Causeway again. On whiteboards, ask students to give a use for this rock and to explain why the properties make it suitable for this use. Encourage students to think about how they

might approach this question, and what hints they can take from the lesson to help. They should discuss what type of rock it is, how it formed, and the properties of the rock.

Language support

Ask students if they recall the key word 'igneous' from their prior learning. They should understand that this rock forms when liquid rock cools and freezes. Build on this knowledge by explaining the difference between magma and lava – the former is liquid rock under the ground and the latter is liquid rock on the surface of Earth.

Then explain that the key word 'metamorphic' means formed by change. Based on this understanding, see if students can work out what a metamorphic rock might be (any type of rock formed by changing another one). For example, slate starts as a sedimentary rock that is changed naturally.

Chemistry links

- chemical reactions as the rearrangement of atoms
- the rock cycle and the formation of igneous, sedimentary, and metamorphic rocks

Working scientifically links

- make and record observations and measurements using a range of methods for different investigations; and evaluate the reliability of methods and suggest possible improvements
- interpret observations and data, including identifying patterns and using observations, measurements, and data to draw conclusions
- present reasoned explanations, including explaining data in relation to predictions and hypotheses

Learning objective	Learning outcomes		
	Developing	Secure	Extending
Use the rock cycle to explain how the materials in rocks are recycled	Label the types of rock and the processes in the rock cycle	**Use the rock cycle to explain how the materials in rocks are recycled**	Use the rock cycle to explain in detail how the materials in rocks are recycled
Explain how uplift gives evidence for the rock cycle	Describe the process of uplift	**Explain how uplift gives evidence for the rock cycle**	Apply understanding of uplift to explain unfamiliar rock formations

Tier 2 vocabulary	Tier 3 vocabulary
	rock cycle, uplift

Digital resources

Practical: *Modelling the rock cycle* (Practical sheet, Support sheet, Teacher and technician notes)
Video: *Sedimentary, igneous, metamorphic*

Student Book answers

Think back 1 the breaking up of rock of all types into sediments by the action of the weather or environment **2** the settling of sediments in one place **3** rocks formed when thermal energy/heat or high pressure, or both, change existing rock

In-text questions A for example: by weathering, by the action of high pressure, as a result of heating or thermal energy **B** as a result of heating, as a result of the action of high pressure **C** the movement of rock upwards when continents collide

See p.157 for the answers to the **Summary questions** for this lesson.

Getting started

Tell students to imagine they could visit Earth a million years from now. How would the rocks be different? How might the rocks have changed? Encourage them to think about how rocks change nowadays. Have they seen volcanoes? Landslides? Waterfalls or canyons? What are the rocks like at the beach?

Introducing the rock cycle Ask students to describe all they know about the rock cycle. Then display the rock cycle diagram on the board (see Figure 2 in the Student Book) and discuss the key components of the formation of sedimentary, igneous, and metamorphic rocks. Keeping the formations separate, elicit from students some of the processes involved in the rock cycle (weathering, erosion and transport, deposition, compaction or cementation, heating and pressure, melting, cooling and freezing), and highlight the key words they have already met.

Main activity

Rock cycle recycling Discuss the rock cycle, explaining that there are many routes around the cycle. Choose one and discuss the route around it, explaining how the materials in the different types of rock change into other types of rock, and how their materials are recycled over millions of years.

What is uplift? Describe the process of uplift and explain how it has meant we can find fossils from the sea floor at the top of Everest. Discuss how the process of uplift can therefore provide evidence for the rock cycle.

Practical: Modelling the rock cycle Students carry out a short practical where they use wax to model the processes in the formation of sedimentary, metamorphic, and igneous rocks as part of the rock cycle. They then answer the questions that follow. Note that water should NOT be poured onto very hot wax to cool it down – this will start an oil fire that will need to be extinguished using a fire blanket.

Review and reflect

As a class, discuss and name the different processes that students modelled in the practical. Ask students to think about and discuss how their models represented these different processes. Discuss the strengths and limitations of the model.

You can also watch the video on Kerboodle to consolidate students' learning.

Language support

Can students work out what the key word 'uplift' means? It is as simple as it sounds – it means to lift something up. It describes how rocks are forced to the surface of Earth by the movement of the crust.

Chemistry links

- chemical reactions as the rearrangement of atoms
- the composition of the atmosphere
- the production of carbon dioxide by human activity and the impact on climate

Working scientifically links

- interpret observations and data, including identifying patterns and using observations, measurements, and data to draw conclusions
- present reasoned explanations, including explaining data in relation to predictions and hypotheses

Learning objective	Learning outcomes		
	Developing	Secure	Developing
Explain why the concentration of carbon dioxide in Earth's atmosphere did not change for many years	Name two processes that add carbon dioxide to Earth's atmosphere, and two that remove it from the atmosphere	**Explain why the concentration of carbon dioxide in Earth's atmosphere did not change for many years**	Compare two processes causing the relative stability in the concentration of carbon dioxide in Earth's atmosphere for many years
Describe how carbon atoms move from one carbon store to another	Name some carbon stores	**Describe how carbon atoms move from one carbon store to another**	Compare the processes by which carbon atoms move from one carbon store to another

Tier 2 vocabulary	Tier 3 vocabulary
	carbon cycle, carbon store, combustion, dissolving, photosynthesis, respiration

Digital resources

Activity: *Completing the carbon cycle* (Activity sheet, Teacher and technician notes)
Video: *Carbon stores and the carbon cycle*

Student Book answers

Think back 1 the mixture of gases that surrounds Earth **2** 0.04% **3** fuels from under the ground or sea, such as coal and oil; cannot be replaced once they have been used, so will run out

In-text questions A combustion or respiration **B** photosynthesis **C** dissolving

See p.157 for the answers to the **Summary questions** for this lesson.

Getting started

Ask students if they know how much of the atmosphere is made up of carbon dioxide molecules, and whether they think carbon dioxide is a useful gas or a harmful gas. A common misconception is that carbon dioxide is harmful, but most plants and algae need carbon dioxide daily to function, and the greenhouse effect keeps our planet warm enough to sustain life. Therefore, carbon dioxide can be useful.

Carbon and its compounds Invite students to suggest substances that they believe contain the element carbon, and places or objects that they think contain carbon and its compounds. Discuss why carbon is important to all of us, building on earlier discussions about carbon dioxide. Highlight that there are places called carbon stores, where carbon and its compounds may remain for long periods of time.

These can be the atmosphere, the oceans (dissolved carbon dioxide), some sedimentary rocks (e.g. calcium carbonate), fossil fuels (e.g. coal, oil, and natural gas), plants and animals, and the soil.

Carbon dioxide: into and out of the atmosphere
Discuss ways in which carbon dioxide enters and leaves the atmosphere. Respiration and combustion are processes that add carbon dioxide into the atmosphere, and photosynthesis and dissolving are processes that remove carbon dioxide from the atmosphere.

Discuss that the total amount of carbon dioxide in the atmosphere did not change during the 1700s. Encourage students to consider why this was (during this period of time, carbon dioxide was added into and removed from the atmosphere at the same rate).

Main activity

Introducing the carbon cycle Using the image of the carbon cycle in Figure 4 in the Student Book, describe how carbon atoms move between carbon dioxide in the atmosphere and carbon compounds on Earth. Describe how carbon can move rapidly within the carbon cycle, for example, during the combustion of fossil fuels; or extremely slowly, for example, being stored in sedimentary rocks at the bottom of oceans

for long periods of time. Highlight the carbon stores discussed earlier.

Activity: Completing the carbon cycle Students complete a diagram of the carbon cycle, before using this to draw a storyboard/cartoon strip showing a possible journey of one particular carbon atom. Students then answer the questions that follow.

Review and reflect

Using whiteboards, students decide if a process adds carbon dioxide into the atmosphere or removes it from the atmosphere. Then challenge them to sketch the carbon cycle from memory, including labelling as many carbon stores as they can remember and the processes that move carbon and its compounds

between the atmosphere and Earth. Students can check their diagrams against the complete one in the Student Book and add in anything they missed.

You can also watch the video on Kerboodle to consolidate students' learning.

Language support

Ask students to list examples of where they have used the word 'carbon' before. They should already know that carbon is an element and carbon dioxide is a gas that we exhale (breathe out). Using Figure 4 in the Student Book, ask students what they think the carbon

cycle is. Remind them of the definition of a cycle – a series of events that are regularly repeated. Therefore, the carbon cycle is the cycle of carbon as it enters and leaves the atmosphere all the time.

Chemistry links

- the composition of the atmosphere
- the production of carbon dioxide by human activity and the impact on climate

Working scientifically links

- understand that scientific methods and theories developed as earlier explanations are modified to take account of new evidence and ideas, together with the importance of publishing results and peer review
- interpret observations and data, including identifying patterns and using observations, measurements, and data to draw conclusions
- present reasoned explanations, including explaining data in relation to predictions and hypotheses

Learning objective	Learning outcomes		
	Developing	Secure	Extending
Describe the greenhouse effect	Label a diagram to show the greenhouse effect	**Describe the greenhouse effect**	Evaluate the advantages and disadvantages of having carbon dioxide in the atmosphere
Describe global heating	Identify the definition of global heating	**Describe global heating**	Interpret a graph showing how average air temperature has changed over time
Describe how the concentration of carbon dioxide in Earth's atmosphere has changed	Name two greenhouse gases	**Describe how the concentration of carbon dioxide in Earth's atmosphere has changed**	Suggest why the concentration of greenhouse gases in Earth's atmosphere has changed

Tier 2 vocabulary	Tier 3 vocabulary
global warming	global heating, greenhouse effect, greenhouse gas

Digital resources

Activity: *Modelling the greenhouse effect* (Activity sheet, Support sheet, Teacher and technician notes)

Student Book answers

Think back 1 nitrogen and oxygen **2** combustion and respiration **3** any five from: atmosphere, oceans, some sedimentary rocks, fossil fuels, plants and animals, soil

In-text questions A the overall transfer of energy from the Sun to the thermal store of gases in Earth's atmosphere **B** the continuous increase in air temperature at the surface of Earth over time **C** about 416 ppm

See p.157 for the answers to the **Summary questions** for this lesson.

Getting started

Ask students to imagine what would be different if our Earth had no atmosphere. Discuss how, without the atmosphere, the surface of Earth would be much colder, with the average air temperature being around −18 °C. Invite students to suggest what might be affected by this, and highlight that there would be no liquid water, and therefore no life as we know it.

Introducing the greenhouse effect Ask students to discuss what they know about the greenhouse effect, and then share their ideas as a class. Use the opportunity to address any misconceptions, then refer to the diagram in the Student Book to explain it further, emphasizing that the greenhouse effect is

a natural phenomenon. Highlight the misconception that energy from the Sun is trapped immediately in the atmosphere, using Figure 1 in the Student Book to show the transfer of energy from the Sun to Earth, and then from Earth to the gases in the atmosphere or out into space. Explain that the greenhouse effect is the overall transfer of energy from the Sun to the thermal store of gases in Earth's atmosphere. See if students can recall some of the gases in the atmosphere and explain how they all store energy. However, carbon dioxide and methane store much more energy than others. This is why they (along with water vapour) are called greenhouse gases.

Main activity

Global heating Show the graph of the average global air temperatures in Figure 2 in the Student Book. Ask students to describe the trend shown, as well as what the word 'average' means. Explain that the increase in the average global air temperature at the surface of Earth is called global heating, or global warming. Emphasize that it is likely to be human activity that is causing global heating by accelerating the natural greenhouse effect.

What causes global heating? Describe how scientists set up a laboratory on a mountain in Hawaii to measure the concentration of carbon dioxide in the

atmosphere. Using the graph of data collected in Figure 4, ask students to describe the trend shown.

Activity: Modelling the greenhouse effect Students design a model to illustrate the greenhouse effect and global heating, with the aim of using their model to explain these concepts to primary school children. They then complete the table to show how their model represents the greenhouse effect and global heating. (Models could include people wearing coats, a thermos flask, a hot car, a greenhouse, wrapping food in tin foil, putting on a sleeping bag, etc.) Students then answer the questions that follow.

Review and reflect

Using teacher-led questioning, ask students to describe what the greenhouse effect is, how the concentration of carbon dioxide in the atmosphere

has changed, and what is meant by global heating. Address any misconceptions and encourage students to improve on their previous answers.

Language support

Ask students what a greenhouse is, or show an image of a greenhouse. What are they used for? Greenhouses heat up the place where plants are grown using energy from the Sun. Light rays enter the greenhouse and are absorbed by the plants. The plants convert the light into heat (thermal energy), which is then trapped

inside the greenhouse by the glass, keeping it warm. So how can we use this word to describe global heating? Energy from the Sun heats up Earth, and then some of the thermal radiation gets trapped in the atmosphere. We cannot open a window to release it, so planet Earth gets hotter and hotter.

Chemistry links

- the production of carbon dioxide by human activity and the impact on climate
- Earth as a source of limited resources and the efficacy of recycling

Working scientifically links

- understand that scientific methods and theories developed as earlier explanations are modified to take account of new evidence and ideas, together with the importance of publishing results and peer review
- present reasoned explanations, including explaining data in relation to predictions and hypotheses

Learning objective	Learning outcomes		
	Developing	Secure	Extending
Explain why global heating happens	Describe how people add extra carbon dioxide to the atmosphere	**Explain why global heating happens**	Analyse evidence to identify natural sources of greenhouse gases
Describe some impacts of global heating	Identify some impacts of global heating	**Describe some impacts of global heating**	Explain some impacts of global heating
Describe how to prevent climate change	Identify the definition of climate change	**Describe how to prevent climate change**	Suggest how some methods of preventing climate change might work

Tier 2 vocabulary	Tier 3 vocabulary
climate change, deforestation	

Digital resources
Activity: *Preventing climate change* (Activity sheet, Support sheet, Teacher and technician notes)

Student Book answers

Think back 1 the overall transfer of energy to the thermal store of gases in the atmosphere **2** the increase in air temperature at Earth's surface **3** carbon dioxide and methane

In-text questions A for example: breathing, burning fossil fuels for heating or transport, deforestation **B** Laboratory experiments show that carbon dioxide molecules trap thermal energy. **C** long-term changes to weather patterns

See p.157 for the answers to the **Summary questions** for this lesson.

Getting started

Ask students what links Figures 1 and 2 in the Student Book (a forest fire and an aeroplane) and discuss their answers. Elicit that these images depict two human activities (burning forests to make space for crops or cattle, and burning fossil fuels to generate electricity to power aeroplanes) that add extra carbon dioxide into the atmosphere.

What causes global heating? Find out if students know of any other human activities that increase the amount of carbon dioxide in the atmosphere, and discuss them (burning fossil fuels to generate electricity to heat homes and fuel cars/other vehicles, farming animals, etc.). Ask students to recall how the concentration of carbon dioxide in the atmosphere has changed over time, how the average global air temperature has changed over time, and how this, together with other data from experiments in laboratories, shows scientists that the increase in the concentration of greenhouse gases in the atmosphere from human activity definitely causes global heating.

The impacts of global heating Invite students to volunteer any impacts of global warming that they have heard about in the news. Discuss reasons (glaciers and polar ice melting makes sea levels rise, causing flooding on low-lying coasts; local weather patterns change, leading to flooding, or drought and heat waves). Address any misconceptions, such as: it is only the melting of icebergs that is causing sea levels to rise, rather than the combined effect of melting icebergs, ice caps, etc. Describe climate change as long-term changes to weather patterns, which can lead to the extinction of plant and animal species and make it harder to grow sufficient food.

Main activity

How can we stop climate change? Discuss the climate change conference COP26 in November 2021, and describe how world leaders came together to discuss how to prevent climate change. Encourage students to suggest what they might have discussed, and any actions we, as individuals, schools, companies, or countries, can take to stop climate change.

Activity: Preventing climate change Students create a poster explaining why global heating happens, describing some of the damaging impacts of global heating, and giving suggestions as to what countries, governments, and/or individuals can do to stop climate change.

Review and reflect

Show students definitions of global heating and climate change, and ask them to identify which is which. They can then list some impacts of global heating on their whiteboards, before engaging in a whole-class discussion about how to prevent climate change at a local and at a global level.

Language support

Display the key word 'deforestation'. Ask students to work with a partner to try to define the word. To prompt, encourage them to think about what a forest is (a large area of trees). Since the prefix 'de-' means the opposite of something, deforestation refers to the removal and destruction of forests.

Chemistry links

- the composition of Earth
- Earth as a source of limited resources and the efficacy of recycling
- the production of carbon dioxide by human activity and the impact on climate

Working scientifically links

- ask questions and develop a line of enquiry based on observations of the real world, alongside prior knowledge and experience
- make and record observations and measurements using a range of methods for different investigations; and evaluate the reliability of methods and suggest possible improvements
- present reasoned explanations, including explaining data in relation to predictions and hypotheses

Learning objective	Learning outcomes		
	Developing	Secure	Extending
Describe the process of recycling	Identify the definition of recycling	**Describe the process of recycling**	Describe the process of recycling, giving examples
Explain how aluminium is recycled	Identify the stages in recycling aluminium	**Explain how aluminium is recycled**	Use data to compare the process of recycling aluminium with the process of recycling another metal
Describe some advantages and disadvantages of recycling	Identify some advantages and disadvantages of recycling	**Describe some advantages and disadvantages of recycling**	Evaluate the advantages and disadvantages of recycling

Tier 2 vocabulary	Tier 3 vocabulary
recycling	

Digital resources

Activity: *Should we recycle?* (Activity sheet, Support sheet, Teacher and technician notes)
Video: *Climate change and recycling*

Student Book answers

Think back 1 Earth's crust, oceans, and the atmosphere **2** a rock that you can extract a metal from, and that contains enough of the metal to make it worth extracting **3** before – liquid; after – solid

In-text questions A 2035 **B** collecting and processing used objects so that their materials can be used again **C** natural resources will last longer; needs less energy than using new materials; reduces waste and pollution

See p.157 for the answers to the **Summary questions** for this lesson.

Getting started

Ask students to name as many substances as they can that they recycle at home. Add to the list any other substances that can be recycled outside of the home. Reinforce that many types of material, including paper, metals, and plastic, can be recycled.

Where do resources come from? Discuss with students that the materials we use to make everything have to come from somewhere – Earth's crust, atmosphere, or oceans – and that these supplies of new materials will eventually run out. Show Table 1 in the Student Book, which lists some elements and when the ores that we extract the metal from may run out. Highlight that two of these are well within students' lifetimes. Ask them to discuss what we can do about this. Discuss the phrase 'reduce, reuse, recycle', reinforcing that 'reduce' means cutting down on the amount of waste you produce, and 'reuse' means when you or someone else uses an object again, either for its original purpose or for another purpose. Discuss examples of reducing (e.g. putting kitchen waste into a compost bin to use as compost, mending clothes instead of buying new ones) and reusing (e.g. using old milk cartons as bird feeders).

What is recycling? Ask students what recycling means (collecting and processing objects that have been used so that their materials can be used again), and to recall which materials can be recycled. Discuss examples of recycling, such as recycling paper to make new paper, recycling plastic bottles to make clothing and stationery, and recycling aluminium cans to make aluminium sheets to make more cans.

Main activity

Recycling aluminium Using the steps described and Figures 3 and 4 in the Student Book, discuss the process of recycling aluminium: taking the aluminium cans to a factory, breaking up and then melting the cans, cooling and freezing the liquid metal into an ingot, and softening and rolling the ingot into thin sheets to make new cans. Discuss some advantages (e.g. recycling ensures that natural resources can last longer, it uses less energy than it does to extract new materials, it reduces waste and pollution) and disadvantages (e.g. recycling costs a lot of money, it takes a lot of time and effort, some people do not like sorting their waste, recycling lorries use fuel and cause pollution, not everything can be recycled).

Activity: Should we recycle? Students write an informative newspaper article or detailed letter to a friend about recycling. They should explain how aluminium is recycled, and describe some advantages and disadvantages of recycling.

Review and reflect

Students complete a plus, minus, interesting (PMI) grid to reflect on their learning in this lesson. To complete a PMI grid, students divide a page into three columns, and add the headings 'plus (+)', 'minus (–)', and 'interesting'. In the plus column, they list positive examples and applications from the lesson; in the minus column, they list any drawbacks or challenges; and in the interesting column, they describe interesting facts.

You can also watch the video on Kerboodle to consolidate students' learning.

Language support

Students have now learned about the rock and carbon cycles, so see if they can use their knowledge of a cycle to describe the meaning of the key word 'recycle'. You could give them a clue by telling them that the prefix 're-' means to do again. Recycle means to begin the cycle again – that is, to redo or repeat the use of a material or object.

Getting started

Encourage students to review their learning in this chapter. The 'Summary questions' in the Student Book can be used formatively during lessons. For the 'What have I learned?' pages, students can answer the questions one at a time after each topic, or as a single summative activity. This could be done as a whole-class or group activity, or set as an independent task.

Whichever approach is adopted, the questions are designed to give you and students feedback about progress and identify targets for development.

Student reflection

Allow students time to reflect on how confident they feel about each topic. Remind them to use the learning objectives provided in their Student Book for guidance. They should focus on whether there were any questions they found difficult or easy, and on how well they prepared for the summative assessment at the end of the chapter. Listen to and deal with students' reflections sensitively so that they feel comfortable to report areas they are not confident with.

Learning objectives and learning outcomes

Each lesson is guided by the learning *objectives*. The learning objectives are provided at the beginning of each topic in the Student Book. They outline what students are going to learn in each topic.

In contrast, the learning *outcomes* in this Teacher's Guide are statements that describe the knowledge or skills that students should acquire by the end of each topic. They are linked to the learning objectives, but are *not* often seen by students. The learning outcomes are used by teachers to assess and measure if or how each learning objective has been achieved.

Answer key

Chapter 4: Earth

1 for example: size, colour, hardness, density, composition
2 before: solid, after: liquid
3 the Sun
4 photosynthesis: carbon dioxide + water → glucose + oxygen

respiration: glucose + oxygen → carbon dioxide + water (+ energy)

4.1 Earth and its atmosphere

1 crust, mantle, outer core, inner core
2 gas, nitrogen, oxygen, argon, carbon dioxide
3 The crust cannot flow, but the outer core can flow; neither the crust nor the inner core can be compressed.

4.2 Sedimentary rocks

1 porous (air or water can get into the gaps between the grains); soft (easy to scratch); can withstand strong pushing forces
2 Weathering breaks rock into smaller pieces. Erosion breaks rock into smaller pieces and moves them from the original rock. Transport moves sediments far away from the original rock. Deposition is sediments stopping and coming to rest. Compaction involves the weight of sediment on top making sediments below stick together.
3 advantage – strong or can withstand strong pushing forces; disadvantage – easy to scratch or damaged by acidic rain

4.3 Igneous and metamorphic rocks

Maths skills: 1971 – 1740 = 231 years = 12,045 weeks (including leap years) 6,000,000 tonnes/12,045 weeks = 498.13 tonnes each week

1 igneous, igneous, metamorphic, metamorphic, non-porous, hard.
2 They are hard and durable, so are not damaged when people walk on them.
3 Igneous rock – liquid rock freezes to form crystals; metamorphic rock also consists of crystals, but they were formed by the action of pressure on an existing rock, or by the action of heat (without melting) on an existing rock.

4.4 The rock cycle

1 **a** melting **b** cooling/freezing **c** compaction or cementation
2 Fossils in limestone that formed on the seafloor have been found on Mount Everest. This shows that the rock that is now the mountain must have moved upwards
3 metamorphic to sedimentary – metamorphic rock weathered, sediments transported and deposited, action of compaction or cementation forms sedimentary rock; sedimentary to igneous – sedimentary rock is heated and becomes hot enough to melt, liquid rock cools to make igneous rock

4.5 The carbon cycle

1 respiration, combustion, photosynthesis, dissolving, sedimentary, coal
2 For example, from a fossil fuel (store) to the atmosphere (store) by combustion (process). Then from the atmosphere to the ocean (store) by dissolving (process). Then from the ocean to sedimentary rock (store) by deposition (process).
3 Combustion is a chemical reaction, but dissolving is a physical change; combustion adds carbon dioxide to the atmosphere, but dissolving removes carbon dioxide from the atmosphere

4.6 Global heating

Working scientifically: Overall, the concentration of carbon dioxide in the atmosphere has increased between 1969 and 2020. Any data can be taken from the graph as evidence of this.

1 the greenhouse effect, global heating
2 makes Earth warm enough for life, allows water to be in the liquid state
3 For example: Between 1900 and 1925, the global average air temperature was between 13.5 °C and 14.0 °C. The global average temperature has increased since the 1950s, when it was between 13.75 and 14.0 to 2000, when it was about 14.3 °C.

4.7 Climate change

1 fossil fuels, global heating, climate change
2 for example: melting ice caps/glaciers cause flooding; climate change results in extinctions and makes it harder to grow food
3 For example: make walking/cycling safer or improve public transport so that people travel by car less – this works because travel by most cars results in the emission of carbon dioxide; insulate houses – this works because less fuel is needed for heating; grow more food locally – this works because fewer lorries are needed to transport food, so lorries use less fuel.

4.8 Recycling

Maths skills: number of people in your school × 25

1 A, C
2 Aluminium objects are collected, shredded and melted; the liquid is poured into an ingot and cooled until it freezes; the ingot is warmed and rolled into thin sheets, the sheets are made into new aluminium objects.
3 advantages – natural resources will last longer, needs less energy than using new materials, reduces waste and pollution; disadvantages – some people do not like sorting their rubbish, collecting lorries use fuel and make pollution; a statement giving an overall judgement

What have I learned about Earth?

1 igneous, [1 mark] metamorphic, [1 mark] sedimentary [1 mark]
2 from left: oxygen, [1 mark] nitrogen [1 mark]
3 **a** from top: crust, [1 mark] mantle, [1 mark] outer core, [1 mark] inner core [1 mark]
  b from top: solid, [1 mark] solid, [1 mark] solid, [1 mark] liquid [1 mark]
4 **a** hand lens [1 mark]
  b A [1 mark]
  c no [1 mark]
  d B or C [1 mark]
  e A [1 mark]
  f A [1 mark]
  g B or C [1 mark]
5 **a** C [1 mark]
  b A [1 mark]
  c Liquid rock/magma/lava cooled [1 mark] and froze/solidified. [1 mark]
  d Surrounding rocks have eroded, [1 mark] but the granite has not. [1 mark]
  e It was heated by the magma that formed the granite [1] and of the three sedimentary rocks, rock B is the only limestone. [1 mark]

Physics

Introduction to unit

In this unit, students are introduced to the abstract idea of electricity, and gain an understanding of how objects can be charged. They will meet the (fundamental) concept of a 'field' as a region where objects experience forces. They will build circuits and take measurements when learning about current, potential difference, and resistance. They will investigate the shape of the magnetic field around a bar magnet, and explore how electricity and magnetism are linked.

Students are then introduced to the difficult concept of energy. They will compare energy values in foods and fuels, and will look at different energy resources. They will learn about different energy stores and how energy is transferred between stores. They will use their knowledge of energy and power equations to calculate the cost of using domestic appliances.

Students will learn to calculate the speed of an object and look at how distance–time graphs can be used to describe motion. They will extend their Year 7 knowledge of forces with the concept of pressure, applying it to situations where a force can produce a turning effect.

Working scientifically

Each lesson lists the relevant Working scientifically links at the top of the spread.

Physics links

- Energy
- Motion and forces
- Electricity and magnetism

Learning journey

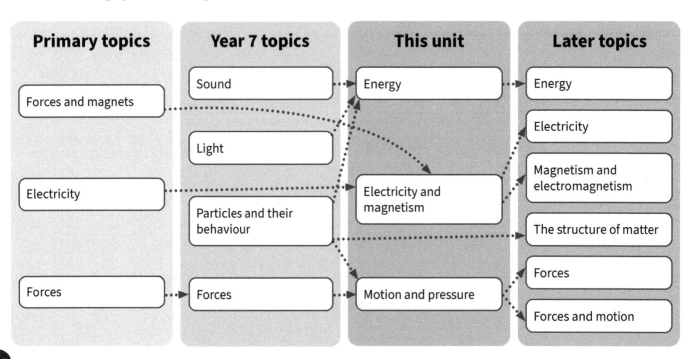

Primary topics	Year 7 topics	This unit	Later topics
Forces and magnets	Sound	Energy	Energy
	Light		Electricity
Electricity	Particles and their behaviour	Electricity and magnetism	Magnetism and electromagnetism
			The structure of matter
Forces	Forces	Motion and pressure	Forces
			Forces and motion

Physics and you

A knowledge of physics helps explain observations that students make of the world around them. Physics also enables students to understand key ideas such as forces, pressure, energy, electricity, and magnetism. Every day, students experience and interact with physics either personally or through the use of machines.

Explain that there are many careers in which physics plays a key role – even if the application of 'school' physics is not obvious. Here are three examples:

- Opticians need to understand how lenses work, how light travels, and how white light can be split into different colours.

- Architects need to understand forces so that buildings are safe in varying conditions, such as weather extremes.

- Airline pilots must understand how the forces acting on an aircraft can affect its behaviour. They need to understand weight distribution, wind speed, and varying atmospheric pressure.

Physics and the world

From cars to computers, physics affects our everyday lives. A life without electricity would be very different. However, we have to reverse those activities that are warming the planet and producing toxic waste. This provides exciting challenges for physicists, other scientists, and engineers. How do we ensure that our electricity generation is not harming the planet, or that our energy transfers are efficient? How do we make the necessary changes while retaining convenience and luxury? The future of our planet depends on this work.

Big questions

How will we keep the lights on?

There are limited supplies of fossil fuels on Earth and their use has adverse impacts on the environment. Scientists and engineers are working hard to find alternative, sustainable forms of power generation. Nuclear power was considered to be a solution, but concerns over safety and managing nuclear waste mean that this is falling out of favour. The use of renewable resources is a more attractive way of generating electricity, and physicists play a key role in developing these methods.

What can we do to reduce climate change?

Replacing fossil fuels with renewable resources will reduce the emission of harmful greenhouse gases. However, using renewables to meet our demand for electricity is a challenge, so we need to reduce our use of fossil fuels quickly. Another challenge is to make our energy use more efficient. This includes insulating homes and businesses; and developing effective, convenient forms of transport. These – and other areas of development – require an understanding of energy transfers, electricity, and many other basic ideas covered in school physics.

Why is electromagnetism so important?

A current flowing through a wire in a magnetic field makes an electric motor work. Many houses have at least 50 electric motors in them and, as technology develops, this number will increase. It is essential to understand electromagnetism to ensure that motors are energy-efficient, and that we can use common household appliances such as electric toothbrushes or vacuum cleaners. In the future, motorized transport will rely on powerful, reliable, and efficient electric motors.

Introduction to chapter

In this chapter, students are introduced to electric fields, current, and magnetism. They will build simple circuits and take measurements of current and potential difference. They will then study electromagnets and plan how to investigate the shape of magnetic fields. Students will also practise changing the subject of an equation.

Core concepts

- Static electricity

- Building circuits and taking measurements

- Effects of magnetic fields and uses of electromagnets

What have students already learned?

- How some forces need contact between two objects, but magnetic forces can act at a distance

- How magnets attract or repel each other, and attract some materials and not others; how to compare and group together everyday materials based on whether they are attracted to a magnet, identifying some magnetic materials

- How to construct a simple series electrical circuit, identifying main components

- Whether or not a lamp will light in a simple series circuit, based on whether or not it is part of a complete loop with a battery; the function of a switch to open and close a circuit

- Some common conductors and insulators, identifying metals as good conductors

- How to compare and give reasons for variations in how components function, including the brightness of bulbs, the loudness of buzzers, and the on/off position of switches

- The use of symbols to represent a simple circuit in a diagram

What will students learn next?

- How to measure resistance using p.d. and current values

- Current, resistance, and voltage relationships for different circuit elements, including their graphical representations

- Quantity of charge flowing as the product of current and time

- How to draw circuit diagrams; equivalent resistance for resistors in series

- The domestic a.c. supply; live, neutral, and earth mains wires; safety measures

- How power transfer is related to p.d. and current, or current and resistance

- The magnetic fields of permanent and induced magnets, and Earth's magnetic field, using a compass to explore them

- The magnetic effects of currents; how solenoids enhance the effect

- How transformers are used and the reasons for their use

Think back

1 Draw a diagram showing two magnets that are repelling. Label the poles.

2 Make a list of three materials or objects that conduct electricity and three that do not.

3 Draw a circuit diagram showing a cell, a lamp, and a switch. Explain why the bulb is not lit when the switch is open (up).

Teaching strategy

Substituting values Students should apply their Year 7 knowledge of equations to help calculate the resistance of a component. Remind them of the best way to set out questions involving equations – that is, write the equation out in full, substitute the values in, then calculate the final answer.

Using ammeters and voltmeters Students are likely to be using ammeters and voltmeters for the first time. Demonstrate how to use the meters and revisit the idea of zero error.

Common learning misconceptions

- All metals are attracted to a magnet. (Only cobalt, nickel, iron, and anything made from iron, such as steel, are magnetic metals.)

- Larger magnets are always stronger than smaller magnets.

- Magnetic poles are always at the end of the magnet.

- Only metals conduct electricity. (Many materials are good conductors of electricity, including you.)

- Objects become positively charged because they have gained protons/electrons have been destroyed.

- All the electrons in an electrical circuit are initially contained in the battery/other source of electricity.

- Potential difference is the same as current.

- Potential difference flows through components.

- A larger battery will always make a motor run faster or a bulb glow brighter.

- Current flows from a battery to a light bulb, but not from the light bulb to the battery.

- A battery gives out a certain current, but if the circuit has lots of resistance, the current will get smaller.

- Electrons that are lost by an object disappear.

- Current flows out of both terminals of a battery or power-pack (the 'clashing' current model).

- Current is used up in a circuit.

- The magnetic pole of Earth in the northern hemisphere is a north pole, and the pole in the southern hemisphere is a south pole. (The magnetic pole near the Earth's north is the magnetic south pole. The north end of the magnet is attracted to the opposite pole.)

- Magnetic poles are charged.

- Voltmeters are connected in series.

Broader context

Electricity is essential to the life that we know. Imagine life without electricity. What would we miss the most? It is very important that students understand how electricity works because it is dangerous when it is not used safely. Salt water is a very good conductor of electricity and we are made up of a large percentage of salt. Consequently, we are very good conductors of electricity. Electric shocks are harmful and could lead to electrocution, which is fatal.

Physics links

- separation of positive or negative charges when objects are rubbed together: transfer of electrons, forces between charged objects
- the idea of electric field, forces acting across the space between objects not in contact

Working scientifically link

- ask questions and develop a line of enquiry based on observations of the real world, alongside prior knowledge and experience

Learning objective	Learning outcomes		
	Developing	Secure	Extending
Describe how charged objects interact	Describe how charged particles interact	**Describe how charged objects interact**	Explain how charged objects can be useful
Describe how objects can become charged	Identify positive and negative charges	**Describe how objects can become charged**	Explain how objects can become charged in unfamiliar scenarios
Define an electric field	Identify objects that have been and are affected by an electric field	**Define an electric field**	Compare and contrast electrostatic and gravitational fields

Tier 2 vocabulary	Tier 3 vocabulary
attract, electric charge, negative charge, neutral, positive charge, repel	atom, electric field, electron, neutron, proton

Digital resources

Activity: *Electrostatics* (Activity sheet, Support sheet, Teacher and technician notes)
Video: *Electrostatics*

Student Book answers

Think back 1 a force that can act when objects are not touching **2** when the poles facing each other are different **3** when the poles facing each other are the same

In-text questions A There are equal numbers of protons and electrons. **B** They will repel/move away.

See p.180 for the answers to the **Summary questions** for this lesson.

Getting started

Types of charge and electric fields Ask students to *think pair share* examples of static electricity. Explain that there are two types of charge: positive and negative. Show students an image of an unlabelled atom, including the subatomic particles. Ask: *What are the particles called? What charge do the particles have?* Label the image as a class, and use it to state the charge of each particle.

Explain that an electric field exists around a charged particle or object. Use the images in Figure 2 in the Student Book to show that charged particles in an electric field experience a repulsive or attractive force.

Discuss any misconceptions, such as: there is nothing smaller than an atom; static electricity and electric fields only occur around metal objects.

Main activity

Charging an object Demonstrate how to charge a polythene rod by rubbing it with a cloth.

Ask: *What happens to the charges when the polythene is rubbed with the cloth? What charge does the polythene rod gain? What charge does the cloth gain?*

Elicit that electrons can be transferred from the cloth to the polythene rod, as they are on the outside of the atoms. This produces a negative charge on the rod, and a positive charge on the cloth.

Students often think an object becomes positively charged because it gains protons – make sure they understand that *only the negative charges can move.* Then balance two rods on an upside-down watch glass

to demonstrate that two charged rods of the same type will repel and two oppositely charged rods will attract.

Show students an image of an electrostatic paint sprayer, and how this is used to evenly coat a metal surface with paint. The paint has a positive charge and the surface to be painted has a negative charge. These charges attract the paint to the metal surface like a magnet. Use this example to discuss how charging objects can be useful.

Activity: Electrostatics Students complete the activity and answer the questions that follow. They can then mark their own or peer mark their answers. Encourage them to use different coloured pens to suggest improvements.

Review and reflect

Hold up a plastic ruler and a cloth. Encourage students to think back to the demonstration with the polythene rod. Display the following statements and ask them to decide which are correct.

When you rub the ruler with the cloth, ...

a) ... some electrons are transferred from the cloth to the ruler.
b) ... some protons are transferred from the cloth to the ruler.

Students should identify statement **a** as being correct.

The ruler is now ...

a) ... positively charged. It has a net or total positive charge.
b) ... negatively charged. It has a net or total negative charge.

Students should identify statement **b** as being correct.

The cloth is now ...

a) ... positively charged. It has a net or total positive charge.
b) ... negatively charged. It has a net or total negative charge.

Students should identify statement **a** as being correct.

Remind students to give reasons for their answers, applying what they have learned about the transfer of particles.

You can also watch the video on Kerboodle to consolidate students' learning.

Language support

Encourage students to copy out the structure of an atom in Figure 3 in the Student Book and add the correct labels. This will act as a useful visual to remind

them of the key vocabulary, and the type of charge of each particle.

163

Physics link

- electric current, measured in amperes, in circuits; and current as flow of charge

Working scientifically links

- evaluate risks
- use appropriate techniques and apparatus during laboratory work, paying attention to health and safety

Learning objective	Learning outcomes		
	Developing	Secure	Extending
Define a current	Identify the unit of current	**Define a current**	Give examples of electric currents in everyday life
Describe how to measure current in a simple circuit	Name the component used to measure current	**Describe how to measure current in a simple circuit**	Describe how to measure current in an unfamiliar circuit
Draw circuit diagrams	Identify a range of circuit symbols	**Draw circuit diagrams**	Identify errors in unfamiliar circuits

Tier 2 vocabulary	Tier 3 vocabulary
battery, current, lightning, motor, switch	ammeter, amp (A), cell, circuit symbol, electron

Digital resources

Practical: *Investigating current* (Practical sheet, Support sheet, Teacher and technician notes)

Student Book answers

Think back 1 electron **2** a region where a charged particle experiences a force **3** cell/battery, lamp, switch

In-text questions A The charges are in an electric field. **B** There is far more charge flowing per second in lightning than in a bulb. **C** The torch would not work.

See p.180 for the answers to the **Summary questions** for this lesson.

Getting started

Explain to students that an electric current can be dangerous and/or useful. Ask: *Can you think of examples where electricity is dangerous or useful?* Share some responses.

Current Set up a simple circuit with a cell, switch, and lamp. Ask students to *think pair share*: *Why does the lamp light up when the switch is closed, but not when the switch is open?* Share ideas until somebody mentions 'current'.

Show the images of free electrons and metal atoms inside the wire in Figures 1 and 2 in the Student Book. Ask: *What is different inside the wire when it is connected to the battery?* Explain that the battery 'pushes' the electrons around the circuit. Discuss any misconceptions, such as: current flows from a battery to a light bulb, but not from the light bulb to the battery; the battery produces the electrons in the wire.

Circuit symbols Working in pairs, ask students to draw the symbols for a cell, lamp, buzzer, switch, and connecting wire. Ask them to draw a circuit diagram containing each of these components. Students can comment on each other's circuits and help correct errors. Invite a volunteer to draw the correct circuit diagram on the board.

Main activity

Using an ammeter Draw a circuit diagram including an ammeter on the board. Elicit from students what the circuit symbol represents, and support them to understand the function of an ammeter (it measures the current through a component in amps). Ask for two volunteers to each set up the circuit. Encourage other students to compare the similarities and differences between the two circuits and suggest changes. Discuss risks and safety measures, such as: turn off the circuit when changing components, keep the circuit away from water, or that wires may become hot.

Practical: Investigating current Students carry out the practical and answer the questions that follow. It is important to check the circuits and correct any errors during the lesson. Students can then mark their own or peer mark their answers.

Review and reflect

The rope model helps us visualize what happens in an electric circuit. Ask for volunteers to stand in a circle holding a rope. One student passes the loop around the circle; the other student(s) allow it to pass lightly over their fingers.

Use the model to address any misconceptions, such as: the student does not 'produce' the rope (cells/batteries do not produce electrons); all of the rope moves at the same time (as do electrons); the rope does not get 'used up' as it moves (neither do electrons).

Language support

The key words 'current' and 'cell' can be confused with other meanings in English, such as a type of dried fruit or a cell in biology. Remind students that a current in physics is the flow of electrical charge around a complete circuit per second. A cell is part of a battery – it is a chemical store of energy that provides the push that moves electrical charge around a circuit.

Physics link

- potential difference, measured in volts; battery and bulb ratings

Working scientifically links

- evaluate risks
- use appropriate techniques and apparatus during laboratory work, paying attention to health and safety
- make predictions using scientific knowledge and understanding

Learning objective	Learning outcomes		
	Developing	Secure	Extending
Define potential difference	Identify the unit of potential difference	**Define potential difference**	Describe examples of potential difference in unfamiliar scenarios
Describe how to measure potential difference in a simple circuit	Name the component used to measure potential difference	**Describe how to measure potential difference in a simple circuit**	Explain why a voltmeter is placed in parallel to a component
State the meaning of the rating of a battery or bulb	Identify components with different ratings	**State the meaning of the rating of a battery or bulb**	Select appropriate components based on their ratings

Tier 2 vocabulary	Tier 3 vocabulary
rating	potential difference, terminal, volt (V), voltage, voltmeter

Digital resources

Practical: *Investigating potential difference* (Practical sheet, Support sheet, Teacher and technician notes)

Student Book answers

Think back 1 cell or battery **2** ammeter **3** The bulb gets brighter.

In-text questions A An ammeter is connected in series in a circuit, but a voltmeter is connected either side of a component/across a component. **B** The higher the rating of a battery, the more energy is transferred to charges.

See p.180 for the answers to the **Summary questions** for this lesson.

Getting started

Show students the defibrillator in Figure 2 in the Student Book. Ask them to *think pair share: What is this piece of equipment? What is it used for? How does it work?*

Share some responses. Explain what defibrillators do – try to use the term 'potential difference' (p.d.) and not 'voltage' from now on to avoid confusion. Defibrillators produce a large potential difference (p.d.) that can be used to restart a person's heart. If it is used on a healthy heart, it can cause a heart attack.

Potential difference (p.d.) Show students images of the following: a phone charger, a laptop, a torch, a television, a washing machine, batteries, a lemon, and a potato. Ask: *What are the similarities and differences between these objects?*

Elicit or explain that the electrical appliances all need electricity, or a potential difference, to work. However, p.d.s vary in size – a phone is charged using a p.d. of about 5 V and televisions use a p.d. of about 230 V. Some of these appliances are mains operated, while others are battery operated. Conversely, batteries, lemons, and potatoes *produce* a p.d. (Both lemons and potatoes contain acids, which allow these materials to behave like a battery.)

Discuss any misconceptions, such as: the bigger the battery, the larger the p.d.; all the electrons in an electrical circuit are initially contained in the battery or other source of electricity.

Explain that chemical reactions take place in a cell to produce a p.d. between the positive and negative terminals.

Main activity

Using a voltmeter Set up a simple circuit with a cell, switch, and lamp. Discuss where the ammeter should be positioned in order to measure the current through the lamp. Show students a voltmeter and explain that it measures p.d. across a component. Ask them to suggest how to connect the voltmeter in the circuit to measure the p.d. across the lamp. Note: you could introduce the key words 'series' and 'parallel' at this stage (the ammeter is in series with the lamp, but the voltmeter is in parallel). Invite a volunteer to draw the correct circuit diagram on the board.

Practical: Investigating potential difference
Students carry out the practical and answer the questions that follow. It is important to check the circuits and correct any errors during the lesson. Students can then mark their own or peer mark their answers.

Review and reflect

Use the rope model to discuss how a battery with a larger p.d. would be represented using the model. Ask: *Why would it be difficult to represent a voltmeter?*

Language support

Ask students to write down the following key words: 'voltage', 'volt', and 'voltmeter'. Discuss the meaning of each word as a class, making links between them to enhance understanding. The voltage is the push of the electrical current around a circuit, a volt is the unit of measurement for voltage, and a voltmeter is the equipment used to measure voltage (in volts). Ensure students understand that potential difference is the same as voltage, and scientists prefer to use this term.

Physics links

- resistance, measured in ohms, as the ratio of potential difference (p.d.) to current
- differences in resistance between conducting and insulating components (quantitative)

Working scientifically links

- pay attention to concern for precision and repeatability
- make predictions using scientific knowledge and understanding
- plan the most appropriate types of scientific enquiry to test predictions, including identifying independent, dependent, and control variables

Learning objective	Learning outcomes		
	Developing	Secure	Extending
Define resistance	Identify the unit of resistance	**Define resistance**	Use a model to explain why a wire gets hotter when there is a current flowing through it
Calculate the resistance of a component	Give the equation for resistance	**Calculate the resistance of a component**	Change the subject of the resistance equation to calculate potential difference or current
Describe the difference between conductors and insulators in terms of resistance	Identify the definitions of a conductor and an insulator	**Describe the difference between conductors and insulators in terms of resistance**	Explain why conductors and insulators have different values of resistance

Tier 2 vocabulary	Tier 3 vocabulary
resistance	conductor, insulator, ohm (Ω)

Digital resources

Activity: *Investigating the resistance of a wire* (Activity sheet, Support sheet, Teacher and technician notes)

Student Book answers

Think back 1 ampere/amp (A) **2** volt (V) **3** graphite

In-text questions A television (the current in the wires is smaller) **B** the lamp **C** more posts, posts closer together, bigger posts

See p.181 for the answers to the **Summary questions** for this lesson.

Getting started

Show students images of a television and a microwave oven. Ask them to *think pair share* similarities and differences between the appliances. Share some responses before explaining that all appliances have a current passing through them, but the size of the current differs due to resistance. Discuss any misconceptions, such as: all appliances have the same current as the current comes from the same socket/power station.

What is resistance? Discuss what resistance means in everyday life, and what 'electrical resistance' means.

Set up a circuit with a cell, an ammeter, and a lamp. Then leave a gap. Ask students to use the key word 'resistance' to explain why the lamp lights up if a conductor is connected in the gap, but not when an insulator is connected.

Calculating resistance Ask students to suggest which two things in the circuit affect the size of the current. Explain that the current depends on the resistance of the circuit and the potential difference provided by the cell.

Resistance, current, and p.d. are related by the equation:

$$\text{resistance } (\Omega) = \frac{\text{potential difference (V)}}{\text{current (A)}}$$

Work through the example in the Maths skills box in the Student Book to practise using this equation.

Main activity

Activity: Investigating the resistance of a wire
Show students the circuit used to investigate the resistance of different lengths of wire. Ask them to identify what each of the variables are in this experiment. Discuss how many lengths of wire should be tested and how many repeat measurements taken. Ask students to suggest the column headings for the results table and the axis labels on the graph. Demonstrate how to take measurements. A complete set of example measurements is on the Activity sheet.

Students then answer the questions that follow. Note that the wire can get hot, so make sure that the potential difference used is not high.

Review and reflect

Students complete a plus, minus, interesting (PMI) grid to reflect on their learning in this lesson. To complete a PMI grid, students divide a page into three columns, and add the headings 'plus (+)', 'minus (−)', and 'interesting'. In the plus column, they list positive examples and applications from the lesson; in the minus column, they list any drawbacks or challenges; and in the interesting column, they describe interesting facts.

Language support

Ask students what it means to resist something. Encourage a discussion around resistance. Explain or elicit that it means to oppose (go against) or withstand an action or effect – for example, a rebellious student might *resist* a teacher's instruction and not do as they are told. In a circuit, all components oppose the current, even the wire to some extent. They reduce the flow of charge. This is called resistance in a circuit.

1.5 Changing the subject

Physics link
- potential difference, current, and resistance

Working scientifically link
- apply mathematical concepts and calculate results

Learning objective	Learning outcomes		
	Developing	Secure	Extending
Change the subject of an equation	Substitute values into a given equation	**Change the subject of an equation**	Change the subject of an unfamiliar equation
Change the subject of the resistance equation to calculate values for current and potential difference	Substitute values into equations for current and potential difference	**Change the subject of the resistance equation to calculate values for current and potential difference**	Use the resistance equation to explain the effect of changing one variable on another

Tier 2 vocabulary	Tier 3 vocabulary
relationship	Hooke's Law

Digital resources

Activity: *Gallery walk* (Activity sheet, Support sheet, Teacher and technician notes)

Student Book answers

Think back 1 resistance $(\Omega) = \dfrac{\text{potential difference (V)}}{\text{current (A)}}$

2 weight (N) = mass (kg) × gravitational field strength (N/kg) **3** The extension of a spring is proportional to the force up to the elastic limit.

In-text questions A The chair is the thing that I am sitting on. Sitting is what I am doing on the chair.

B $I = \dfrac{V}{R}$ **C** $0.1 = \dfrac{2}{20}, 20 = \dfrac{2}{0.1}$

See p.181 for the answers to the **Summary questions** for this lesson.

Getting started

Show students the image of the cat in Figure 2 in the Student Book. Ask students to *think pair share: Make up a sentence about the image where the **cat** is the subject. Now change the sentence so the **mat** is the subject.*

Now show students the image of the rope model in Figure 1. Ask: *What is the relationship between the three values?*

Discuss that the relationship can be illustrated by the resistance equation that students learned last lesson. If the p.d. and resistance are known, the current can be calculated, but the equation has to be rearranged.

Changing the subject Demonstrate how the equation can be rearranged to make p.d. the subject.

Then ask students to work in pairs to make current the subject, showing all the stages of their workings. Discuss some answers so that students can comment on their peers' work.

Work through another example, such as rearranging force = mass × acceleration to make mass, and then acceleration, the subject.

Ask students to make notes. Show them the method in the Student Book under the heading 'How can I check that I have done it correctly?', as some students may find it easier to substitute the values into the equation before changing the subject.

Main activity

Activity: Gallery walk Ask students to work through the 'gallery walk' questions set out around the room. At the front of the room, have 'hints' and a mark scheme available for each question: students can use these if they are struggling, and when they have finished each question and need to mark their work. Encourage them to use a different coloured pen to make any improvements to their method of changing the subject.

Review and reflect

Show examples of incorrectly rearranged equations. Ask students to identify the mistake and write the correct answer on their whiteboards.

Language support

Explain to students that the word 'rearrange' is often used in science when talking about rearranging an equation, whereas 'change the subject' of the equation is more commonly used in maths. However, both refer to the same transferable skill and can be used interchangeably.

Elicit from students the meanings of resistance, current, and potential difference before practising changing the subject of equations. Testing students' knowledge of these scientific concepts regularly in class will improve their ability to retain the information.

Physics link

- electric current in series and parallel circuits, currents add where branches meet

Working scientifically link

- interpret observations and data, including identifying patterns and using observations, measurements, and data to draw conclusions

Learning objective	Learning outcomes		
	Developing	Secure	Extending
Describe the difference between series and parallel circuits	Identify series and parallel circuits	**Describe the difference between series and parallel circuits**	Evaluate why some circuits are better suited to be parallel or series
Describe how current changes in series and parallel circuits	Identify where to place ammeters in a series circuit	**Describe how current changes in series and parallel circuits**	Calculate current values in unfamiliar circuits
Describe how potential difference changes in series and parallel circuits	Identify where to place voltmeters in a series circuit	**Describe how potential difference changes in series and parallel circuits**	Calculate potential difference values in unfamiliar circuits

Tier 2 vocabulary	Tier 3 vocabulary
parallel, series	

Digital resources

Practical: *Observing series and parallel circuits* (Practical sheet, Support sheet, Teacher and technician notes)
Video: *Understanding circuits*

Student Book answers

Think back 1 the charge flowing per second

2 resistance $(\Omega) = \dfrac{\text{potential difference (V)}}{\text{current (A)}}$

3 the p.d./battery

In-text questions A Any two from: in a parallel circuit, if one bulb breaks the others stay on; components can be turned on and off independently; parallel circuits have more than one loop or branch. **B** 4 **A C** The rope goes at the same speed everywhere.

See p.181 for the answers to the **Summary questions** for this lesson.

Getting started

Series and parallel circuits Divide students into groups of five. Give each group a large sheet of paper with two circuit diagrams (one series and one parallel) and a marker pen. You may use the ones in Figures 3 and 4 in the Student Book with the ammeter symbols removed.

Ask students to write facts about each circuit next to the diagrams. Discuss ideas and describe the difference between series and parallel circuits. For example, a series circuit only has one loop but a parallel circuit has more than one loop.

Measuring current and p.d. in a circuit Ask: *Can you remember where an ammeter and a voltmeter need to be placed in a circuit to measure current and p.d.?* Invite a volunteer to draw an ammeter in the series circuit so it measures the current through both lamps. Discuss whether the position chosen is correct. Invite another volunteer to draw the positions of three voltmeters, to measure the p.d. across the cell and each lamp. Ask other students to comment on these positions or suggest improvements. Discuss any misconceptions, such as: the current is bigger nearer the cell.

Main activity

Practical: Observing series and parallel circuits Students investigate circuit rules for series and parallel circuits by carrying out mini-experiments set out around the room. They visit each circuit and write down their measurements and observations.

Review and reflect

Discuss students' results and use large diagrams of the four mini-experiments to write the readings of each meter. Ask students to suggest patterns in what happens to the current and p.d. in each type of circuit.

You can also watch the video on Kerboodle to consolidate students' learning.

Language support

Show students a running track. Can they think of another name to describe it? It could also be called a circuit – a series circuit. You could ask students to stand in a circle holding hands, or linking arms, to demonstrate this. All of the students are in series, that is, they are positioned one after the other. Now take a couple of students out of the circuit to form a new circuit. Two students should each still hold onto one hand in the original circuit. Explain that this now represents a parallel circuit.

Physics links

- non-contact forces: forces between magnets
- magnetic poles, attraction and repulsion
- magnetic fields by plotting with compass, representation by field lines
- Earth's magnetism, compass and navigation

Working scientifically link

- make and record observations and measurements using a range of methods for different investigations; and suggest possible improvements

Learning objective	Learning outcomes		
	Developing	Secure	Extending
Define a magnetic field	Identify a region where a magnetic field is present	**Define a magnetic field**	Compare and contrast electric, magnetic, and gravitational fields
Describe how to investigate and represent the shape of a magnetic field	Give one way to observe magnetic fields	**Describe how to investigate and represent the shape of a magnetic field**	Plan an investigation to observe how magnetic fields interact
Describe Earth's magnetic field	Identify the north and south poles of Earth	**Describe Earth's magnetic field**	Explain how a compass works

Tier 2 vocabulary	Tier 3 vocabulary
magnet, magnetic material, north pole, south pole	magnetic field, magnetic field line

Digital resources

Practical: *Drawing magnetic fields* (Practical sheet, Support sheet, Teacher and technician notes)

Student Book answers

Think back 1 north and south **2** iron **3** a region where a mass experiences a force

In-text questions A A magnetic material will be attracted to a magnet, but cannot repel it. **B** In a magnetic field, there is a force on a *magnetic material*; in a gravitational field, there is a force on a *mass* (all things that have mass). **C** Aluminium is not a magnetic material/the filings would not align with the field.

See p.181 for the answers to the **Summary questions** for this lesson.

Getting started

Use a 'hot potato' activity to assess prior knowledge.

Show students the image of ferrofluid (magnetic liquid) and the 'levitating paperclip' set-up in Figures 1 and 3 in the Student Book to prompt their thinking about magnetism.

Ask students to work in pair as part of a larger group of 8–10. Give each pair a piece of paper with a heading related to magnetism (e.g. 'levitating paperclip', 'magnetic materials', or 'magnetic poles'). Give students 30 seconds to write down key ideas related to their heading before passing the paper to the next pair of students. Students read the key ideas and add their own. Once each piece of paper has been passed around the group, discuss ideas as a whole class. Discuss any misconceptions, such as: all metals are magnetic.

Main activity

Demonstrating magnetic fields Demonstrate the magnetic field around a bar magnet using iron filings. Ask students to predict what will happen to the iron filings when they are sprinkled around the bar magnet. Ask: *What do the iron filings show? Why do they show this pattern? Would the same happen if you sprinkled sugar around the magnet?*

Discuss the similarities and differences between magnetic fields, electric fields, and gravitational fields.

Practical: Drawing magnetic fields Although iron filings show the pattern of the magnetic field, they do not show it very clearly and do not show the direction of the magnetic field lines. Show students how to use a compass to begin plotting the magnetic field lines around the bar magnet, explaining that the compass points in the direction of the field lines around the magnet.

Ask students to complete the Practical sheet, where they follow a method to practise this technique of drawing magnetic fields. They then answer the questions that follow.

Students can peer mark each other's diagrams. They should include one thing that was done well and one improvement that could be made.

Review and reflect

Hang a bar magnet by a fine thread so that it is not moving (see Figure 7 in the Student Book).

Ask students to predict what will happen if you push or turn the magnet, and to explain their answer.

Language support

Students might already be familiar with the word 'field' in an everyday context. A field is an area of land in the countryside where farmers grow crops. However, in science, a field refers to a special area, or region, in which something experiences a force.

Find out if students can think of examples of fields in science (electric, gravitational, and magnetic). Reinforce that a magnetic field is a region where there is a force on a magnet or a magnetic material.

Physics link
- the magnetic effect of a current, electromagnets

Working scientifically links
- make predictions using scientific knowledge and understanding
- make and record observations and measurements

Learning objective	Learning outcomes		
	Developing	Secure	Extending
Describe the magnetic field around a current-carrying wire	Identify the magnetic field around a wire	**Describe the magnetic field around a current-carrying wire**	Compare the magnetic fields of a current-carrying wire and a permanent bar magnet
Describe how to make an electromagnet	List the equipment needed to make an electromagnet	**Describe how to make an electromagnet**	Explain how to test the strength of an electromagnet
Describe how to change the strength of an electromagnet	Identify factors that affect the strength of an electromagnet	**Describe how to change the strength of an electromagnet**	Use diagrams to explain why different electromagnets have different field strengths

Tier 2 vocabulary	Tier 3 vocabulary
core	electromagnet, magnetize

Digital resources

Practical: *Changing the strength of electromagnets* (Practical sheet, Support sheet, Teacher and technician notes)

Student Book answers

Think back 1 a region where a magnetic material experiences a force **2** using iron filings or a plotting compass **3** The field lines are close together.

In-text questions A The field lines get further apart. **B** You could not turn it off because it would still be magnetic.

See p.181 for the answers to the **Summary questions** for this lesson.

Getting started

Show students images of a bar magnet, an electromagnet used in a bell, and an electromagnet used in a scrap yard. Ask students to *think pair share*: *What are the similarities between these images? What are the differences?* Discuss any misconceptions, such as: all silver-coloured items are attracted to a magnet; larger magnets are always stronger than smaller magnets.

Demonstrating the magnetic field around a wire and a coil of wire Ask students to predict what will happen to a compass when it is placed near a current-carrying wire. Use a compass to plot some field lines.

This should show that there is a magnetic field around the wire, and the magnetic field lines are circular. Show Figure 4 in the Student Book. Say: *The magnetic field lines are circular and become further apart as the distance from the wire increases. What does this tell us about the magnetic field?*

Explain to students that the magnetic field around just one wire is not very strong, so an electromagnet is made from lots of loops (circles of wire). Show students the magnetic field pattern around a coil of wire (a solenoid) and compare it with the field of a bar magnet.

Main activity

Practical: Changing the strength of electromagnets In pairs, students carry out three mini-experiments where they observe how the strength of an electromagnet changes as the current increases, how its strength changes as the number of loops in the coil of wire increases, and how the core material affects its strength. Students make a prediction about each variable before recording their results and drawing conclusions.

Review and reflect

Use the 'snowballing' technique for students to share their observations and draw conclusions. Each pair joins with another pair, and then the group of four joins with another group of four. At each stage, students discuss their results and how each variable affected the strength of the electromagnet. Students can also discuss any difficulties they encountered when carrying out the experiments. A spokesperson from each group of eight can then share their findings with the rest of the class.

Language support

Write the key word 'electromagnet' on the board. Give students time to discuss between themselves what this might be. The part 'electro' sounds like it is linked to electricity. An electromagnet is a temporary magnet produced using an electric current.

Physics link

- the magnetic effect of a current, electromagnets, DC motors (principles only)

Working scientifically link

- ask questions based on observations of the real world, alongside prior knowledge and experience

Learning objective	Learning outcomes		
	Developing	Secure	Extending
Describe some uses of electromagnets	Give some uses of electromagnets	**Describe some uses of electromagnets**	Explain why the properties of electromagnets make them suitable for different uses
Compare permanent magnets and electromagnets	Identify examples of permanent magnets and electromagnets	**Compare permanent magnets and electromagnets**	Evaluate the use of permanent magnets and electromagnets for different purposes
Describe how a simple motor works	Identify simple motors in everyday life	**Describe how a simple motor works**	Explain how different factors can affect the speed of a motor

Tier 2 vocabulary	Tier 3 vocabulary
motor	relay

Digital resources

Activity: *Researching the uses of electromagnets* (Activity sheet, Support sheet, Information sheet, Teacher and technician notes)
Video: *Magnetic fields and electromagnets*

Student Book answers

Think back 1 wire, battery, nail/piece of iron **2** Any two from: add more loops in the coil of wire, use a bigger current, use a magnetic core. **3** iron/steel, nickel, cobalt

In-text questions A north and south **B** Neither is a magnetic material. **C** Permanent magnets would not be strong enough.

See p.181 for the answers to the **Summary questions** for this lesson.

Getting started

Permanent magnets and electromagnets
Ask: *Can you think of some uses of permanent magnets in your homes? Why are electromagnets not used in these examples?*

Demonstrate making a homopolar motor and/or show students a fully constructed Westminster motor. Describe how a motor needs both an electromagnet and a permanent magnet to be able to spin (turn).

Ask students to suggest some examples of where motors are used and how the motor can be made to spin faster. If there is time (or another lesson), students could construct their own homopolar motor and investigate which variables affect how fast it spins.

Main activity

Activity: Researching the uses of electromagnets
In groups of four, students research uses of

electromagnets and create a poster or information leaflet.

Review and reflect

Ask students to present their research to the rest of their group. Ask one member of each group to describe a use that they did not research to the rest of the class. Give students the opportunity to ask questions about any of the uses.

You can also watch the video on Kerboodle to consolidate students' learning.

Language support

Ask students if they have ever taken part in a relay race. Encourage them to describe how this works – in a team, runners take turns running different sections of a running track or circuit. In physics, a relay is an

electrical device. It uses current flowing through one circuit to switch on and off a current in a second circuit.

Getting started

Encourage students to review their learning in this chapter. The 'Summary questions' in the Student Book can be used formatively during lessons. For the 'What have I learned?' pages, students can answer the questions one at a time after each topic, or as a single summative activity. This could be done as a whole-class or group activity, or set as an independent task.

Whichever approach is adopted, the questions are designed to give you and students feedback about progress and identify targets for development.

Student reflection

Allow students time to reflect on how confident they feel about each topic. Remind them to use the learning objectives provided in their Student Book for guidance. They should focus on whether there were any questions they found difficult or easy, and on how well they prepared for the summative assessment at the end of the chapter. Listen to and deal with students' reflections sensitively so that they feel comfortable to report areas they are not confident with.

Learning objectives and learning outcomes

Each lesson is guided by the learning *objectives*. The learning objectives are provided at the beginning of each topic in the Student Book. They outline what students are going to learn in each topic.

In contrast, the learning *outcomes* in this Teacher's Guide are statements that describe the knowledge or skills that students should acquire by the end of each topic. They are linked to the learning objectives, but are *not* often seen by students. The learning outcomes are used by teachers to assess and measure if or how each learning objective has been achieved.

Answer key

Chapter 1: Electricity and magnetism

1 a correctly labelled diagram of a bar magnet with two north poles facing or two south poles facing
2 conduct – for example: metals (allow three listed metals), graphite, seawater; do not conduct – for example: wood, plastic, rubber, glass, concrete, ceramics, air
3 a correctly drawn simple circuit diagram with the circuit symbols for a cell, a lamp, and a switch
   When the switch is open, the circuit is not complete, so charge/current cannot flow to light up the bulb.

1.1 Charging up

1 charge, negative, electrons, attract, field
2 Electrons are transferred from the sweater to the balloon. The negatively charged electrons are attracted to the positively charged protons on the wall, so the balloon sticks to the wall.
3 Gravitational and electric fields both produce forces. You cannot see or feel a gravitational or electric field. They both produce non-contact forces. Gravitational fields are produced by masses. Electric fields are produced by charges. Gravitational fields produce forces that only attract. Electric fields produce forces that attract and repel.

1.2 Circuits and current

1 charge, second, electrons, ammeter, amps, A
2 a series circuit with battery of cells, motor, and switch (with annotations explaining how it can be switched on/off to control the circuit)
   b The electrons move/a current flows.
3 a Have two people pulling the rope. One pulls one way, and the other pulls in the opposite direction. The rope does not move, so no current flows/the lamp goes out.
   b Have a third person who grabs the rope and stops it when you open the switch; the current does not flow.

1.3 Potential difference

Working scientifically: Observe how long batteries of different sizes last in a series circuit with several bulbs, recording the time when the bulbs stop working. The age and type of batteries, component types, number of components, and circuit set-up must be controlled.

1 force, energy, a voltmeter, rating, rating on
2 The buzzer would sound louder because the three cells transfer more energy than the two.
3 **a** The current is like the amount of rope passing a point per second (do not allow current is the rope); the battery is like the person pulling the rope.
   b You can add a person watching how much rope goes past per second, but you cannot measure the pull or the energy transferred.

1.4 Resistance

Maths skills: 12 V/0.6 A = 20 Ω

1 difficult, p.d., current, electrons, energy, conductors, insulators
2 motor: resistance = p.d./current = 12 V/0.1 A = 120 Ω
   lamp: resistance = p.d./current = 12 V/0.4 A = 30 Ω
3 **a** There are no charges free to move.
   b The charges are now free to move.

1.5 Changing the subject

1 relationship, subject, dividing
2 **a** W = mg; dividing both sides by g: m = W/g
   b W = mg; dividing both sides by m: g = W/m
3 The extension depends on the force and spring constant. A bigger force means bigger extension, and a bigger spring constant means a smaller, extension. So x = F/K.

1.6 Series and parallel

Maths skills: 0.1 A because if you add components to a series circuit, the current decreases, so it is half of the original current 0.2 A.

1 one, more than one, parallel, series
2 resistance = p.d./current; as more bulbs are added, the current decreases; if the current is smaller, the resistance will be greater.
3 **a** current = p.d./resistance = 6 V/10 Ω = 0.6 A
   b 6 V
   c The ammeter reading would decrease to 0.3 A. The voltmeter reading would decrease to 3 V.

1.7 Magnets and magnetic fields

Working scientifically: The table would have the different types of magnet listed, with columns for the number of paperclips picked up by each magnet. To collect reliable results, readings should be repeated three times with a mean result calculated.

1 north, south, repel, attract, force, filings
2 A compass needle always points in a north–south direction. The compass needle lines up in Earth's magnetic field (which does not change).
3 **a** There is a force on the steel ball because it is a magnetic material in a magnetic field. The force due to each magnet is equal in size but opposite in direction, so they cancel out and the ball does not move.
   b The force due to the magnet on the left would be bigger, so the ball would move towards the magnet on the right.

1.8 Electromagnets

1 current, a magnetic field, more, stronger, magnetic field

2 Wind a wire around the nail. Attach the ends of the wires to the battery using the leads and crocodile clips.
3 There is a magnetic field around a wire carrying a current. The field is stronger if there are more loops of wire because the fields add together. The magnetic material inside the coil becomes magnetized when you put it in a magnetic field. This increases the strength of the electromagnet.

1.9 Using electromagnets

1 lift, relay, turns, cannot
2 **a** coil of wire, two permanent magnets
   b A current flows in the coil of wire. The coil becomes an electromagnet. The forces between the coil and the permanent magnets make it spin.
3 An electromagnet is on the wall. A magnetic material is on the door. The magnetic material on the door is attracted to the electromagnet, so the doors stay open while a current flows. When the fire alarm button is pressed, the current to the electromagnet is cut, so the magnetic material on the doors is no longer attracted to it. The doors close.

What have I learned about electricity and magnetism?

1 **a** electrons [1 mark] **b** attract [1 mark] **c** charges [1 mark]
2 **a** S on the left, N on the right [1 mark]
   b A – attract [1 mark], B – repel [1 mark]
   c You can turn it on and off/you can make it much stronger. [1 mark]
3 **a** wire, [1 mark] a nail/metal rod, [1 mark] battery [1 mark]
   b increase, [1 mark] decrease, [1 mark] decrease [1 mark]
4 **a** suitable parallel circuits with two cells, a bulb, and a switch on one branch [1 mark], and another bulb and switch on another branch around the first bulb and switch [1 mark]
   b parallel [1 mark]
   c Y, [1 mark] X, [1 mark], X and Y [1 mark]
   d Attach an ammeter [1 mark] between each bulb and switch. [1 mark]
5 **a** correctly drawn circuit diagram, as described [1 mark for four correct circuit symbols, 1 mark for correct position of voltmeter across bulb]
   b the push of the battery/energy transferred in a component [1 mark]
   c resistance = p.d./current = 6 V/0.4 A = 15 Ω [2 marks]
   d the potential difference that the lamp is designed to work at [1 mark]
   e current = p.d./resistance = 6 V/10 Ω = 0.6 A [2 marks]
6 The best answers will explain in detail how the bar becomes charged and is able to attract the small pieces of paper. [6 marks maximum] Examples of correct scientific points:
   Both the bar and cloth contain atoms.
   Atoms contain electrons, protons, and neutrons.
   Electrons are negatively charged.
   Protons are positively charged.
   When you rub the bar, electrons move from the cloth to the bar (or vice versa).
   The bar becomes negatively charged/cloth becomes positively charged (or vice versa, as above).
   The bar repels the electrons on the top of the pieces of paper.
   The top of the pieces of paper become positively charged.
   The paper is attracted to the bar.

Introduction to chapter

In this chapter, students are introduced to energy resources, stores, and transfers. They will look at how electricity is generated by renewable and non-renewable energy resources. They will learn about stores of energy and methods of transfer between stores, in particular, by particles, radiation, and forces. Students will also study the links between energy, work done, and power; and will have the opportunity to apply their maths skills to real-life scenarios when calculating work done, power, and the cost of using household appliances and devices.

Core concepts

- Energy resources
- Energy stores and transfers
- Work done, energy, and power

What have students already learned?

- How some materials change state when they are heated or cooled, and the temperature at which this happens can be researched and measured in degrees Celsius (°C)

What will students learn next?

- Energy changes in a system involving heating, doing work using forces, or doing work using an electric current; how to calculate the stored energies and energy changes involved

- How to calculate work done

- Power as the rate of transfer of energy

- Conservation of energy; in a closed system; dissipation

- How to calculate energy efficiency for any energy transfers

- Renewable and non-renewable energy sources used on Earth, including changes in how these are used

Think back

1 Draw particle diagrams for ice (water in the solid state), liquid water, and steam (water in the gas state). Describe the motion (movement) of the particles in each state.

2 Name the unit of temperature we use in science, and the instrument we use to measure temperature.

3 Calculate the weight of a person with a mass of 50 kg on Earth, where g = 10 N/kg.

Teaching strategy

Scientific vocabulary This chapter has many key words that students may have encountered in everyday life, but have specific meanings in science (e.g. 'work done' and 'power'). Energy is a difficult concept to teach because it is an abstract idea that is difficult to define. Energy and transfers of energy are taught in terms of stores instead of types or forms. We cannot observe energy or measure amounts of energy directly, but we can look at how objects have gained or lost energy.

Using simple gears and levers Students will use simple gears and levers to investigate how forces transfer energy between stores. Talk about the different skills they will practise, such as evaluating risks, making predictions using scientific knowledge and understanding, recording measurements in a table, and identifying trends and patterns in their results.

Common learning misconceptions

- Energy is something that is tangible.

- Energy transfers are always 100% efficient.

- Heat is a substance that can flow from place to place.

- An object at rest has no energy. (All objects have potential energy.)

- Energy and force are interchangeable terms. (Energy is the ability to do work. A force acts on an object.)

- Energy, in food or fuel, gets used up.

- Energy is fuel.

- Energy is confined to its origin (e.g. in food, the electric company).

- Thermal conductors and insulators are opposites, not part of a continuum.

- Hot objects can cool down without something else around them getting hot. (Energy can only be transferred, not created or destroyed.)

- Energy is only transferred upwards by heating.

- Cold can be transferred.

- When you heat a substance, particles get hotter.

- Work is synonymous with labour or a job, and not to do with forces.

- Power and energy are the same thing.

- Heat and temperature are the same thing.

Broader context

Energy is essential to all life on Earth. Energy can be in many different forms, including chemical energy that we use when we eat and electrical energy generated in power plants. Scientists are working hard to ensure that we all have enough food to provide the energy that we need to stay healthy. They are also assessing the different methods of generating electricity. Historically, electricity has been generated through combustion reactions in power plants. This has contributed to climate change and global warming. Scientists are working with technologists to develop new methods that are better for the climate.

Physics link

- comparing energy values of different foods (from labels) (kJ)

Working scientifically link

- present reasoned explanations, including explaining data in relation to predictions and hypotheses

Learning objective	Learning outcomes		
	Developing	Secure	Extending
Compare the energy values of foods and fuels	Identify foods with high and low energy values	**Compare the energy values of foods and fuels**	Predict energy values based on different proportions of food groups
Compare the energy needed for different activities	Identify different situations or activities that need greater intakes of energy	**Compare the energy needed for different activities**	Explain the diets of different groups of people, relating this to their energy needs

Tier 2 vocabulary	Tier 3 vocabulary
energy, fuel	joule (J), kilojoule (kJ)

Digital resources

Activity: *Energy in foods and fuels, and for activities* (Activity sheet, Support sheet, Teacher and technician notes)

Student Book answers

Think back 1 for example: coal, wood, gas **2** petrol/diesel **3** walking

In-text questions A 200 000 J **B** 400 kJ **C** 60 kJ

See p.200 for the answers to the **Summary questions** for this lesson.

Getting started

Ask students: *What did you have for breakfast? Why is it important to eat breakfast?* Show the class pictures of an apple and a plate of chips. Ask: *What are the differences between these foods?* Guide discussion towards 'energy' being mentioned. You could demonstrate setting sugar alight to show that it is a store of energy.

Energy values of food and fuels Show students Figure 2 in the Student Book. Ask what the images have in common. Show the image of a food label in Figure 1. Ask students: *Can you think of any other quantities that can be measured in two or more different units? Why do foods have this information on the labels? Why is the amount of energy stated per 100g?*

Discuss any misconceptions, such as: energy is only found in living things; fruit and vegetables do not contain energy; energy is a fuel.

Energy for different activities Ask students to *think pair share*: *How much energy from food should a person have on average per day?* Discuss students' suggestions until you agree that it depends on many factors such as gender, age, job, and activities carried out. Refer to examples of people with different energy requirements in Figure 3 in the Student Book.

Main activity

Activity: Energy in foods and fuels, and for activities Give students a list of foods and fuels such as soups, crisps, ready meals, coal, oil, and so on. In pairs, they predict the order of the foods and fuels in increasing energy per 100g. Then put the labels of these foods and fuels around the room. Students record the energy per 100g of each food and fuel and put them in order of increasing energy.

After the first task, students compare the energy requirements of different activities by putting them in order. They can also convert the energy values from joules into kilojoules in order to have a better understanding of which foods would provide the required energy for these activities.

Review and reflect

Ask students to form small groups and compare the order they put the foods and fuels in. They discuss if they were surprised by any of the energy values. Each group can then share their ideas with the rest of the class.

Language support

The kilojoule is the scientific unit used to measure energy that is contained in food. Kilojoules and calories are both used to measure this, which leads to confusion. It could be compared to measuring distance in miles, although the standard scientific unit of measurement is the kilometre.

2.2 Energy resources

Physics link

- fuels and energy resources

Working scientifically link

- ask questions based on observations of the real world, alongside prior knowledge and experience

Learning objective	Learning outcomes		
	Developing	Secure	Extending
Describe how fossil fuels are formed	Name three fossil fuels	**Describe how fossil fuels are formed**	Compare the differences between fossil fuels
Describe the difference between a renewable and a non-renewable energy resource	Identify renewable and non-renewable energy resources	**Describe the difference between a renewable and a non-renewable energy resource**	Compare the long-term use of renewable and non-renewable energy resources
Describe how electricity is generated by renewable and non-renewable resources	Label the parts of a power station	**Describe how electricity is generated by renewable and non-renewable resources**	Evaluate the suitability of different energy resources for different locations

Tier 2 vocabulary	Tier 3 vocabulary
energy resource, fossil fuel, non-renewable, renewable	nuclear power station, thermal power station, uranium

Digital resources

Activity: *Renewable or non-renewable?* (Activity sheet, Support sheet, Information sheet, Teacher and technician notes)

Student Book answers

Think back 1 joule (J) **2** 2 kJ **3** any two from: coal, oil, gas, wood

In-text questions A Coal is formed from trees; oil is formed from sea creatures; both take millions of years to form. **B** You need water for cooling and to make steam in a power station. **C** Both use a generator; wind turbines turn a generator directly, but biomass is burned to heat water and produce steam to turn a turbine and generator.

See p.200 for the answers to the **Summary questions** for this lesson.

Getting started

Ask students to write down a known fact about an energy resource on a sticky note and to stick it onto the board. Discuss some of these facts but do not say if they are correct. Explain that they will be learning more about these resources, so you will return to the sticky note facts at the end of the lesson.

Renewable and non-renewable energy resources

Show students samples of different resources, such as wood, oil, coal, a solar cell, and the images in Figure 3 in the Student Book. Encourage them to suggest two groups that the samples and images could be divided into. Discuss the groups suggested.

Fossil fuels and power stations Ask students to *think pair share*: *What are fossil fuels and how are they formed?* Share students' ideas.

Use Figure 2 to discuss how fossil fuels are used to produce electricity, including the advantages and disadvantages of using fossil fuels. Ask: *How is this different from how a wind turbine generates electricity?*

Discuss any misconceptions, such as: fossil fuels must be renewable because they are formed from the remains of dead plants and animals; fossil fuels will last forever as they are still being formed.

Main activity

Activity: Renewable or non-renewable? Working in pairs and as part of a larger group, students research and write an extended response about an energy resource.

Ask them to spend a few minutes in their pairs planning what they will need to include in their

answer. Then give each pair of students one energy resource to focus their answer on. Students use the resources around the room to research their energy resource, plan their response by writing down relevant notes, and then write an extended response to the question.

Review and reflect

Students join together in their groups so that each energy resource has been covered in that group. Students read out their answers and other group members give positive feedback and suggestions for improvements. If time, students could peer review each other's answers based on success criteria.

Revisit some of the sticky notes from the start of the lesson and ask students if they agree or disagree with the statements.

Language support

Ask students what uranium is. They might remember it from the Periodic Table – uranium is an element. A nuclear power station generates electricity by splitting (breaking up) uranium atoms. This process releases

energy. There are arguments in favour of and against nuclear energy, which is non-renewable. However, it is more sustainable and does not release greenhouse gases into the atmosphere.

Physics links

- other processes that involve energy transfer: changing motion, dropping an object, completing an electrical circuit, stretching a spring, metabolism of food, burning fuels
- energy as a quantity that can be quantified and calculated; the total energy has the same value before and after a change
- comparing the starting with the final conditions of a system; and describing increases and decreases in the amounts of energy associated with movements, temperatures, changes in positions in a field, in elastic distortions, and in chemical compositions
- using physical processes and mechanisms, rather than energy, to explain the intermediate steps that bring about such changes

Working scientifically link

- make and record observations

Learning objective	Learning outcomes		
	Developing	Secure	Extending
Describe the energy stores in everyday transfers	Name a range of everyday energy stores	**Describe the energy stores in everyday transfers**	Describe the energy stores in unfamiliar energy transfers
Describe how energy changes and is transferred between stores	Give ways in which energy can change and be transferred between stores	**Describe how energy changes and is transferred between stores**	Describe how energy changes and is transferred in unfamiliar scenarios
Use the law of conservation of energy	Describe ways energy can be dissipated	**Use the law of conservation of energy**	Apply the law of conservation of energy to an unfamiliar scenario

Tier 2 vocabulary	Tier 3 vocabulary
elastic, nuclear, thermal	chemical store, dissipated, electromagnetic, energy store, gravitational potential, kinetic, law of conservation of energy

Digital resources

Practical: *Observing energy transfers* (Practical sheet, Support sheet, Teacher and technician notes)
Video: *Energy resources*

Student Book answers

Think back 1 any two from: coal, oil, gas **2** millions of years **3** Fossil fuels are reliable – they do not rely on factors like wind and amount of sunlight.

In-text questions A Money can be transferred, and there is always the same total amount of money at the end as there is at the beginning. **B** any situation where an electrical appliance is used **C** when energy is transferred to the thermal store of the surroundings, not to the water

See p.200 for the answers to the **Summary questions** for this lesson.

Getting started

Ask: *If you brought money to school, how much would you have left if you did not spend any?*

Explain that today's lesson is about energy and, like money, energy cannot just disappear and you cannot end up with more than you had at the start. This is the law of conservation of energy.

Show students an image of Angel Falls. Explain that the temperature of the water at the bottom of the waterfall is higher than at the top. Ask: *Why?* Discuss responses but do not confirm the answer.

Energy is a difficult concept. Ask: *What does the word 'energy' mean to you? How could you use the word 'energy' in a sentence?* Discuss answers.

Energy stores Discuss the list of energy stores in Table 1 in the Student Book. Discuss any misconceptions, such as: light, sound, and electricity are stores of energy; an object at rest has no energy; energy is a fuel.

Energy transfers Explain that energy can be transferred between stores. Demonstrate this using glass beakers to represent energy stores and a coloured liquid to represent energy. Ask students to *think pair share: How can this model be used to represent the transfer of energy between stores and the law of conservation of energy?* Guide discussion to the idea that the liquid (energy) starts in one beaker (store) and can be transferred to other beakers (stores), but the total amount of liquid (energy) is conserved.

Describe some ways that energy can be transferred. For example, burning gas to heat a pan of water transfers energy from the chemical store of the gas to the thermal store of the water; turning on a hand fan transfers energy from the chemical store of the battery to the kinetic store of the fan blades. If there is time, you could use a model steam engine connected to a dynamo and bulb and describe the energy stores and transfers.

Main activity

Practical: Observing energy transfers Students identify energy stores before and after an energy transfer by carrying out a series of mini-experiments and observing what happens.

Review and reflect

Ask students to peer mark each other's answers. Discuss any common mistakes that students made.

Refer back to the Angel Falls image and question. Can students now explain why the temperature of the water is higher at the bottom of the waterfall? (The gravitational potential energy is converted first to kinetic energy of the falling water, and finally to heat energy as it comes to rest at the bottom of the waterfall.)

You can also watch the video on Kerboodle to consolidate students' learning.

Language support

Display the word 'gravitational'. Do students recognize the whole word or any parts of it? They will probably be reminded of the word 'gravity' from prior learning. Gravity is a non-contact force that acts between two masses. Therefore, 'gravitational' is an adjective that relates to movement towards a centre of gravity. Gravitational potential (stored) energy is the energy of an object as a result of its position in a gravitational field.

2.4 Energy and temperature

Physics links

- the total energy has the same value before and after a change
- comparing the starting with the final conditions of a system; and describing increases and decreases in the amounts of energy associated with movements, temperatures, changes in positions in a field, in elastic distortions, and in chemical compositions
- using physical processes and mechanisms, rather than energy, to explain the intermediate steps that bring about such changes

Working scientifically links

- make and record observations
- make predictions using scientific knowledge and understanding

Learning objective	Learning outcomes		
	Developing	Secure	Extending
Describe the difference between energy and temperature	Give the units of energy and temperature	**Describe the difference between energy and temperature**	Explain why heating a material can cause the temperature to increase in terms of particle motion
Describe the factors that affect the change in temperature of a substance	Give some factors that can affect the temperature increase of a substance	**Describe the factors that affect the change in temperature of a substance**	Calculate the energy required to increase the temperature of different substances
Describe equilibrium	Identify scenarios in which equilibrium has been reached	**Describe equilibrium**	Predict the effect of different factors on the position of equilibrium

Tier 2 vocabulary	Tier 3 vocabulary
temperature, thermometer	equilibrium

Digital resources

Activity: *Thermal energy transfers* (Activity sheet, Support sheet, Teacher and technician notes)

Student Book answers

Think back 1 joule (J) **2** degree Celsius (°C) **3** a way in which energy can be calculated

In-text questions A If you had put your hand in hot water, and then put it in the warm water, it would feel cold. **B** There are a lot more particles in the bath, even if they are not moving as fast. **C** The average speed of the particles decreases.

See p.201 for the answers to the **Summary questions** for this lesson.

Getting started

Show the image of the volcano in Figure 1 in the Student Book. Ask: *Why do rocks melt?* Students should suggest that the rocks get very hot. Explain that a lot of energy is needed to heat the rock up to a high enough temperature (about 1200 °C).

The words 'energy' and 'temperature' are often mixed up. This lesson will help students learn why and how they are different.

Activity: Thermal energy transfers Students work together to complete the ranking activity outlined in Question 2 on the Activity sheet. They place labelled cards in order of increasing energy stored in the thermal store, from least to most energy: glass of water at 20 °C, large swimming pool at 15 °C, bath at 38 °C. Invite volunteers to stick their cards on the board in the order they have chosen. Discuss why they have chosen this order. Return to their answers at the end of the lesson.

Hot sparks Show students an image of a sparkler and ask them to *think pair share*: *Why don't the sparks from a sparkler burn you?* Encourage students to think about the difference between energy and temperature.

Support students to understand this difference – energy in a thermal store is a measure of the motion of *all* the particles; temperature is a measure of the *average speed* of motion of the particles. Temperature does not depend on how many particles there are. Compare the units of energy and temperature.

Main activity

Thermal equilibrium Place a test tube of hot water into an insulated beaker of cold water. Measure the temperature of both. Ask students to predict the temperature of the water in the test tube and in the beaker after 15 minutes. Write some suggestions on the board.

While waiting for the 15 minutes to elapse, ask students to think about what happens to the objects in terms of thermal energy transfer.

After 15 minutes, compare the demonstration results with students' predictions. Discuss their ideas about energy transfer, including any misconceptions, such as: the cold from an object travels to the hotter object.

What affects temperature rise? Heat up beakers of water and oil behind a safety screen to compare how much the temperature increases if different heating methods or amounts of each liquid are used. Ask: *Which beaker will have the biggest increase in temperature? Why? What factors affect the increase in temperature of a substance?* Share students' ideas and then compare with the actual results.

Activity: Thermal energy transfers Students answer questions on what they have learned this lesson.

Review and reflect

Return to students' rankings completed at the beginning of the lesson. Allow students time to discuss in pairs or in a group if they are still in agreement with their answers, and to give reasons for this. Go through the correct answers as a class, addressing any misconceptions as you go.

Language support

Can students define the word 'equal' in their own words? They are likely to suggest 'the same'. Then display the key word 'equilibrium'. It is a complicated-looking word but it has a simple meaning. Equilibrium describes a state when opposing forces are balanced, or the same.

2.5 Energy transfer: particles

Physics link

- the total energy has the same value before and after a change

Working scientifically links

- make and record observations
- interpret observations and data, including identifying patterns and using observations, measurements, and data to draw conclusions

Learning objective	Learning outcomes		
	Developing	Secure	Extending
Describe how energy is transferred by particles in conduction	Identify scenarios in which conduction occurs	**Describe how energy is transferred by particles in conduction**	Use the particle model to explain why conduction occurs at different rates in different substances
Describe how energy is transferred by particles in convection	Identify scenarios in which convection occurs	**Describe how energy is transferred by particles in convection**	Explain how convection occurs in unfamiliar scenarios
Explain how an insulator can reduce energy transfer	Give some everyday examples of conductors and insulators	**Explain how an insulator can reduce energy transfer**	Use the particle model to compare conductors and insulators

Tier 2 vocabulary	Tier 3 vocabulary
	conduction, conductor, convection, convection current, insulator, radiation

Digital resources

Practical: *Investigating conduction* (Practical sheet, Support sheet, Teacher and technician notes)

Student Book answers

Think back 1 faster **2** a material that does not allow a current to pass through easily **3** graphite (or seawater)

In-text questions A aluminium **B** good **C** at the bottom

See p.201 for the answers to the **Summary questions** for this lesson.

Getting started

Hold a burning splint. Ask: *The burning end of the splint is at about 1000 °C, so how is it possible to hold the other end?*

Then heat the water at the top of a test tube that has ice at the bottom (fix the ice with gauze). Ask: *How is it possible to heat the water in the test tube so that the ice does not melt but the water at the top of the tube boils?*

Ask students to *think pair share* their ideas about both questions. Discuss students' ideas and write some on the board, but do not say if they are correct at this stage.

Main activity

Conduction Explain that one method of transferring energy between stores by particles is conduction. Focus on thermal energy at this stage. Show an image of a saucepan, or a real one. Ask: *Why is the saucepan made of metal but the handle is made of plastic?* Guide discussion towards the key words 'conductor' and 'insulator'.

Invite volunteers to act as particles to model how thermal energy is transferred through the non-metal and the metal by the particles. Emphasize that it is the collisions between free electrons and atoms (not atoms with other atoms) that cause rapid energy transfer. The model can also be used to show that liquids and gases are poor conductors because the particles are far apart. Ask students to draw labelled diagrams to describe conduction in a non-metal and in a metal, using the Student Book to help. Discuss any misconceptions, such as: the particles themselves get hotter.

Practical: Investigating conduction In pairs, students use different equipment to measure energy transfers and compare how well materials act as thermal conductors in this experiment. They then answer the questions that follow.

Demonstrating convection Demonstrate convection taking place by, for example, heating the circular bits of paper from a hole punch in water, heating potassium permanganate crystals in water, or the coal mine shaft demonstration. Encourage students to describe what they can see and explain why convection takes place using Figure 4 in the Student Book. Discuss other situations in everyday life where something is heated by convection. Discuss any misconceptions, such as: the particles themselves become less dense or lighter.

Review and reflect

Students work in groups of four to discuss their observations from the main activity. Ask each group to suggest common features of conductors and common features of insulators.

Revisit the two questions from the beginning of the lesson and ask students to reflect on their earlier ideas, suggesting improvements.

Language support

Students should recall that a current is a flow. This does not just apply to electricity. A convection current is the flow, or movement, of heat (thermal energy) caused by hotter particles rising and then falling as they cool.

Physics links

- the total energy has the same value before and after a change
- other processes that involve energy transfer: burning fuels
- temperature difference between two objects leading to energy transfer from the hotter to the cooler one, through radiation

Working scientifically links

- make and record observations
- interpret observations and data, including identifying patterns and using observations, measurements, and data to draw conclusions
- identify independent, dependent, and control variables

Learning objective	Learning outcomes		
	Developing	Secure	Extending
Define radiation	Identify the difference between temperature and radiation	**Define radiation**	Explain the difference between temperature and radiation
Name the waves of the electromagnetic spectrum	Identify waves that are part of the electromagnetic spectrum	**Name the waves of the electromagnetic spectrum**	Explain how the properties of different waves relate to their uses
Compare energy transfer by conduction, convection, and radiation	Identify everyday examples of conduction, convection, and radiation	**Compare energy transfer by conduction, convection, and radiation**	Give reasons for energy transfer in unfamiliar scenarios

Tier 2 vocabulary	Tier 3 vocabulary
	electromagnetic spectrum, infrared radiation, radiation, thermal imaging camera

Digital resources

Practical: *Which colour objects are the best emitters?* (Practical sheet, Support sheet, Teacher and technician notes)
Video: *Energy transfers*

Student Book answers

Think back 1 light **2** reflects **3** gases and liquids

In-text questions A the Sun, a light bulb **B** a cup of hot tea **C** dark colours

See p.201 for the answers to the **Summary questions** for this lesson.

Getting started

Show students Figure 1 in the Student Book. Ask them to *think pair share*: *What can you see in the image? Why can't you usually see the footprints you leave behind?* Discuss students' ideas.

Radiation Show students the image of the fire in Figure 2. Ask: *Which types of radiation does the fire give out?* Discuss how visible light, infrared, and ultraviolet are part of a family of waves known as the electromagnetic spectrum. Discuss how waves of different frequency have different uses. Show images of a microwave, a radio, an X-ray, nuclear waste,

a remote control, a torch, and a blacklight. Ask students to match the names of the waves to the images. Discuss the fact that, in general, the higher-frequency waves are more dangerous.

Absorbing and reflecting infrared radiation
Show students a thermal image of a house and ask: *How is this image useful to people?* (e.g. finding out where the house is well or poorly insulated, or where there is damage) You could give students pieces of heat-sensitive paper to investigate this further.

Main activity

Falling corks Demonstrate how different colours absorb different amounts of infrared radiation using two squares of aluminium – one shiny, the other painted dull black – heated at equal distances from a flame. Then stick a cork to the back of each square with petroleum jelly. Ask students to predict which cork will fall off first.

Discuss where students have noticed that dark colours absorb more radiation; or where white, shiny surfaces are used to reflect radiation.

Emitting infrared radiation Explain that thermal energy cannot be transferred through space by conduction and convection because space is a vacuum (where there are no particles). Energy can be

transferred through space by radiation as particles are not needed, but the type and amount of radiation emitted by an object can vary.

Practical: Which colour objects are the best emitters? Discuss what factors might affect how much radiation is emitted. Students measure the fall in water temperature in different coloured cans (black and silver) to determine which colour is the best emitter of radiation. They record their results at regular intervals, identify the variables in the experiment, and draw a conclusion. They then answer questions comparing conduction, convection, and radiation. Discuss that the lids are used in this practical not only for safety, but also to stop radiation from escaping.

Review and reflect

Show students key words and phrases from the chapter so far and ask them to write a question on their whiteboard using one of the key words or phrases is the answer. Students can then ask each other their questions.

You can also watch the video on Kerboodle to consolidate students' learning.

Language support

Review the meanings of the key words 'conduction', 'convection', and 'radiation', ensuring that students clearly understand the difference between these methods of energy transfer. Conduction refers to the transfer of energy through solids (in most cases),

convection refers to the transfer of energy through liquids and gases, and radiation is the transfer of energy as a wave (in contrast to particles). Remind students that liquids and gases do not conduct energy well.

Physics links

- the total energy has the same value before and after a change
- simple machines give bigger force but at the expense of smaller movement (and vice versa): product of force and displacement unchanged
- work done

Working scientifically links

- make and record observations
- interpret observations and data, including identifying patterns and using observations, measurements, and data to draw conclusions

Learning objective	Learning outcomes		
	Developing	Secure	Extending
Define work in physics	Identify the definition of work in physics	**Define work in physics**	Explain why no work is done when an object moves in a circle
Calculate work done	Give the factors that will affect work done	**Calculate work done**	Change the subject of the work done equation to calculate force or distance
Apply the law of conservation of energy to simple machines	Describe a simple machine	**Apply the law of conservation of energy to simple machines**	Explain how a force multiplier works

Tier 2 vocabulary	Tier 3 vocabulary
lever, ramp, simple machine, work	joule (J), newton-metre (Nm)

Digital resources

Practical: *Gears and levers* (Practical sheet, Support sheet, Teacher and technician notes)

Student Book answers

Think back 1 newton **2** force of Earth on an object **3** Energy cannot be created or destroyed, only transferred between stores.

In-text questions A You are not exerting a force over a distance. **B** When you apply a force with your hand, you get a bigger force acting on the lid.
C work done (J) = force (N) × distance (m) = 80 N × 1 m = 80 J

See p.201 for the answers to the **Summary questions** for this lesson.

Getting started

Show students the image of the winding road in Figure 1 in the Student Book. Ask: *Why do roads in the mountains wind backwards and forwards, and not go straight up the mountain?* Discuss students' ideas.

What is work? Show students images of a person lifting a weight, a person holding something heavy, a person pushing a trolley, and a person working at a desk. Ask students to *think pair share*: *In which images are people doing work?* Students will probably have different ideas about what work means. Explain what 'work' means in science (transferring energy by using a force).

Calculating work done Introduce the equation to calculate work done and go through a few practice examples using the Student Book as a support.

For example:

Calculate the work done when you slide a book a distance of 20 cm across a table with a force of 6 N.

Ask students to use their whiteboards to show their workings. This will help you identify any misunderstandings or common errors.

Example answer:

work done = ?
force = 6 N
distance = 20 cm = 0.2 m
work done (J) = force (N) × distance (m)
= 6 × 0.2
= 1.2 J

Main activity

Using simple machines Set up a pulley and gears system. Ask students to *think pair share*: *What does this simple machine do? What is it used for?* (e.g. in elevators, window blinds, theatre curtains, flagpoles, and construction equipment) Guide discussion to the idea that it is a simple machine that makes a job easier to do.

Practical: Gears and levers Students carry out two short practical activities using gears and levers.

After completing the practicals, ask students to share what they have learned about using simple machines. Students should be aware that a simple machine reduces the force that is needed to do a job. Remind students of the law of conservation of energy – you cannot create energy, so the amount of energy transferred when using a simple machine is the same as without the machine. This means that if the force is smaller, the distance moved in the direction of the force must be bigger.

Review and reflect

Revisit the question from the beginning of the lesson. Ask students if they can improve their answer using ideas about work and forces.

Show students Figure 5 in the Student Book and see if they can use the idea of the ramp as a simple machine to explain why the mountain roads are winding.

Language support

Encourage students to list all of the machines they can think of. What do they have in common? What do they do for us? A simple machine is something that makes our lives easier, such as inclined planes (ramps), screws, levers, pulleys and gears, and wheels and axles. It reduces the force you need to do a job.

Physics links

- comparing power ratings of appliances in watts (W, kW)
- domestic fuel bills, fuel use, and costs

Working scientifically links

- make and record observations
- interpret observations and data, including identifying patterns
- make predictions using scientific knowledge and understanding

Learning objective	Learning outcomes		
	Developing	Secure	Extending
Describe the difference between energy and power	Identify the definition of power	**Describe the difference between energy and power**	Explain how power can vary in unfamiliar situations
Calculate energy and power	Identify the units of work done, energy transferred, and power	**Calculate energy and power**	Change the subject of the power equation to calculate time
Calculate the cost of using appliances at home	Give the link between kilowatts and kilowatt hours	**Calculate the cost of using appliances at home**	Change the subject of the kilowatt hour equation to calculate time, power, or cost

Tier 2 vocabulary	Tier 3 vocabulary
mains electricity	kilowatt (kW), kilowatt hour (kWh), power rating, watt (W)

Digital resources

Activity: *Power ratings* (Activity sheet, Support sheet, Teacher and technician notes)
Video: *Energy, forces, and power*

Student Book answers

Think back 1 work done (J) = force (N) × distance (m) **2** joule **3** 1000

In-text questions A energy transferred (J) = power (W) × time (s) = 800 W × 10 s = 8000 J **B** In science, energy is measured in joules (J); on an electricity bill, it is measured in kilowatt hours (kWh).

See p.201 for the answers to the **Summary questions** for this lesson.

Getting started

Ask students to *think pair share*: *Why do some microwave ovens cook popcorn faster than others? Why do some electric heaters warm up a room faster than others?* Share students' ideas and agree that different appliances have different power ratings, measured in watts (W) or kilowatts (kW).

Power ratings Ask students: *What is the difference between energy and power? How are they linked?* Discuss misconceptions, such as: power and force are the same thing.

Calculating energy, work, and power Introduce equations that can be used to calculate energy, work, and power. Go through a couple of examples as a class for practice. Start by building on the example from *2.7 Energy transfer: forces* (see page 197 in this Teacher's Guide):

If it takes 0.4 s to slide the book across the table, calculate the power.

Example answer:

work done = 1.2 J (see page 197)
time = 0.4 s
power = ?
$$power\ (W) = \frac{work\ done\ (J)}{time\ (s)}$$
$$= \frac{1.2}{0.4}$$
= 3 W

Remind students that this is how they should set out their answers when doing similar calculations.

The cost of energy Explain that electricity companies use the unit of kilowatt hours (kWh) instead of joules (J) to calculate your bill. Work through an example calculation, showing how power is measured in kW and time is measured in hours.

For example:

An oven has a power rating of 2000 W.

a) How much energy is transferred in 5 hours?

b) The cost of each kWh is about 17p. How much will it cost to run the oven for 5 hours?

Example answer:

a) energy transferred = ?
   power = 2000 W = 2 kW
   time = 5 hours
   energy transferred (kWh) = power (kW) × time (h)
   = 2 × 5
   = 10 kWh

b) 10 × 17p = 170 p to run for 5 hours

Main activity

Activity: Power ratings Students predict the order of the power ratings of different appliances. Give students the power rating of a washing machine (e.g. 1700 W) so that they have something to compare the appliances with. Explain that power can also be measured in kilowatts and show students how to convert kW into W. Students examine each appliance to find out its power rating and record it with the correct unit in a table. They then compare their observations with their prediction and discuss any unexpected results.

You can also watch the video on Kerboodle to consolidate students' learning.

Review and reflect

Ask students to peer mark their partner's answers. Encourage them to use different coloured pens to make changes or improvements. Volunteers can work through some of the answers on the board, with other students giving feedback at each stage.

Language support

Display the key word 'watt'. Have students seen this word before? Explain that a watt is the unit of power. A power rating in watts (on devices and household appliances) shows us how much energy is transferred per second. It is the equivalent of one joule of energy used each second. Now challenge students to describe a kilowatt and a kilowatt hour.

Getting started

Encourage students to review their learning in this chapter. The 'Summary questions' in the Student Book can be used formatively during lessons. For the 'What have I learned?' pages, students can answer the questions one at a time after each topic, or as a single summative activity. This could be done as a whole-class or group activity, or set as an independent task.

Whichever approach is adopted, the questions are designed to give you and students feedback about progress and identify targets for development.

Student reflection

Allow students time to reflect on how confident they feel about each topic. Remind them to use the learning objectives provided in their Student Book for guidance. They should focus on whether there were any questions they found difficult or easy, and on how well they prepared for the summative assessment at the end of the chapter. Listen to and deal with students' reflections sensitively so that they feel comfortable to report areas they are not confident with.

Learning objectives and learning outcomes

Each lesson is guided by the learning *objectives*. The learning objectives are provided at the beginning of each topic in the Student Book. They outline what students are going to learn in each topic.

In contrast, the learning *outcomes* in this Teacher's Guide are statements that describe the knowledge or skills that students should acquire by the end of each topic. They are linked to the learning objectives, but are *not* often seen by students. The learning outcomes are used by teachers to assess and measure if or how each learning objective has been achieved.

Answer key

Chapter 2: Energy

1 In ice, the particles are in a fixed, regular arrangement. They are vibrating on the spot. In liquid water, the particles are in a random arrangement but still touching their neighbours. They are free to move, and move faster than in the solid state. In steam, the particles move faster still, and are far apart in a random arrangement.
2 °C; thermometer
3 weight = mass × g = 50 × 10 = 500 N

2.1 Food and fuels

Maths skills: 50g of chocolate has 750 kJ energy stored (see Table 1). Running uses 60 kJ per min (see Table 2). 750 kJ/60 kJ = 12.5 minutes of running; 150 m travelled per min = 12.5 x 150 = 1875 m distance ran
1 food, fuels, joules, breathing, growing
2 There are 1000 kJ in 100 g of chips, so there are 2000 kJ in 200 g of chips.
Cycling uses 26 kJ per minute so you need to cycle for 2000 kJ/26 kJ/minute = 77 minutes.

3 a The student identifies the time they spend doing activities, then calculates the energy for each activity by multiplying the time by the energy per minute.
  b The student works out the amount of apples and the amount of chips needed for their daily activities, then comments on the contrast in amounts.

2.2 Energy resources

1 non-renewable, fossil fuel, renewable
2 Burning gas heats water to produce steam. Steam drives a turbine. The turbine drives a generator. The generator generates electricity.
3 In thermal power stations, water is converted to steam. Steam drives turbines, which drive generators. Water is used in hydroelectric, wave, and tidal energy resources, where it directly drives a turbine, which drives a generator.

2.3 Energy adds up

1 created, destroyed, chemical, thermal, can
2 a The battery has chemical energy.
  b Chemical energy is transferred to thermal energy and light.

3 **What we have:** *Before:* unburnt wood, oxygen, cold/raw food. *After:* less wood, ash, oxygen, cooked food
Thinking about energy: *Before:* There is more energy in the chemical store associated with the wood (and oxygen). *After:* There is more energy in the thermal store associated with the food. There is less energy in the chemical store associated with the wood and oxygen. There is more energy in the thermal store associated with the air.

2.4 Energy and temperature

Literacy skills: "Shut the door, you'll let the heat out!" Thermal energy moves from high to low temperatures.
1 temperature, a thermometer, temperature, energy, more, equilibrium
2 a cup of water at 30 °C, a saucepan of water at 30 °C, a saucepan of water at 50 °C
3 The hotter the tray, the more its particles vibrate. When you take the tray out of the oven, energy moves from the thermal store of the tray to the thermal store of the air. The air heats up/particles move faster. The tray reaches the same temperature as the air (equilibrium) and the particles in the tray vibrate less.

2.5 Energy transfer: particles

Working scientifically: Use different temperatures of water. Time how long it takes each [beaker/boiling tube] of water to cool to a certain temperature. Use beakers of the same size and same type of thermometer. *Risk:* be careful when handling boiling or very hot water to avoid spillage. Use tongs and safety glasses.
1 conduction, convection, can move, slowly
2 **a** Particles in a solid are close together, so pass on the vibration; the particles in a gas/liquid are too far apart.
b The particles in a gas or in a liquid can move; the particles in a solid cannot. Convection involves the movement of particles to transfer energy.
3 The metal element heats the water near it, and the hot water becomes less dense. Hot water floats up. Cooler (denser) water sinks to replace it. A convection current forms, and the water circulates until all the water is hot.

2.6 Energy transfer: radiation

1 radiation, emit, temperature, microwaves, visible, X-rays, particles, a gas
2 **a** White surfaces reflect infrared radiation so the houses will absorb less and stay cooler.
b to reflect infrared back into the flask
3 conduction/convection overlap – both need particles
convection/radiation overlap – happen in liquids/gases
conduction/radiation overlap – happens in some solids
all three overlap – types of energy transfer

2.7 Energy transfer: forces

1 force, distance, machine, lever, force, ramp, conservation, energy
2 **a** lever
b work done = force × distance = 200 N × 0.25 m = 50 J
3 climbing Mount Everest: work done = force × distance = 600 N × 10 000 m = 6 000 000 J

climbing upstairs to bed: work done = force × distance = 600 N × 2.5 m = 1500 J
comparing the two: 6 000 000 J ÷ 1500 J = 4000
so climbing Mount Everest requires 4000 times the work

2.8 Energy and power

Maths skills: A 7500 W   **B** 0.1 Kw   **C** energy = power × time; power = energy/time
1 joules, watts, second, kilowatt hours, lower, less
2 **a** energy = power × time = 10 kW × 1.5 hours = 15 kWh
b cost = 15 kWh × 15 p/kWh = 225 p, or £2.25
3 The energy that you pay for in kWh depends on the power and the time that you use it for. If the power is greater, the time will be shorter, so the number of kWh would be the same. The cost per kWh is the same, so it costs the same.

What have I learned about energy?

1 wind, solar, geothermal [1 mark]
2 **a** C [1 mark]   **b** kW, watts, kilowatts, W [1 mark]
3 **a** The purple solid dissolves. The purple water moves up, across the top of the water, and then down. [1 mark] The Bunsen burner heats the water around the solid, [1 mark] and the purple colour diffuses throughout the water in a convection current. [1 mark]
b Water is heated, so the water molecules move faster. [1 mark] The water expands/becomes less dense. [1 mark] Hot water rises, and is replaced by cold water. [1 mark] Energy from burning gas is transferred to water, which moves around the beaker. [1 mark]
c infrared [1 mark]
4 **a** 100 mins [1 mark]
b smaller [1 mark] as you would use more energy when walking quickly, so would take less time [1 mark]
5 **a** gravitational potential [1 mark]
b **i** Energy is conserved/cannot be lost. [1 mark]
ii Some energy is transferred/dissipated to the thermal store as the ball falls through the air. [1 mark]
c There is a force (of gravity) acting on the ball. [2 marks]
6 **a** gravity [1 mark]
b 300 N × 1 m = 300 J [3 marks: 2 for calculation, 1 for unit]
c the time it took to lift [1 mark]
d power = energy/time, so divide answer to part (b) by the time it took in seconds [1 mark]
7 energy = 8000 kJ = 8 000 000 J [1 mark]
time = 1 day = 24 × 60 × 60 s = 86 400 s [1 mark]
power = energy/time = 8 000 000 J/86 400 s [1 mark]
= 93 W (= 92.59) [1 mark]
Yes, it would be even brighter than 60 W. [1 mark]
8 The best answers will explain in detail how insulation reduces energy bills. [6 marks maximum] Examples of correct scientific points:
Energy is transferred from a warm house to the cold air outside. Energy is transferred by conduction, convection, and radiation. To keep a house at the same temperature, it needs to be heated. A lot of insulators trap air. Air is a poor conductor. Insulators reduce the rate of transfer of energy to the surroundings. The rate at which you need to heat the house to maintain the temperature decreases. A lower-power heater is needed/ heating is required for less time. This reduces the number of kWh of energy used. This will cost less money.

Introduction to chapter

In this chapter, students are introduced to speed, pressure, and turning forces. They will look at how motion can be described using distance–time graphs, and will be introduced to pressure in gases, in liquids, and on solids. Students will also study situations where a force has a turning effect. Throughout the chapter, they will have the opportunity to develop their maths skills by using equations to calculate speed and pressure.

Core concepts

- Speed and distance–time graphs
- Pressure
- Turning forces

What have students already learned?

- How simple machines, including levers, pulleys, and gears, allow a smaller force to have a greater effect

What will students learn next?

- How to interpret graphs of distance, time, and speed
- How pressure in fluids acts in all directions; variation in Earth's atmosphere with height, with depth for liquids, upthrust force
- Links between pressure and temperature of a gas at constant volume, related to the motion of its particles

Think back

1 Describe a situation where the forces on a moving object are balanced, and another where they are unbalanced.

2 Compare the way in which particles are arranged and move in the liquid state and the gas state.

3 Calculate the area of a square with a side of 10 cm, and the area of a rectangle of sides 10 cm and 20 cm.

Teaching strategy

Drawing and interpreting data graphically Remind or elicit from students the maths skills they will need to draw and interpret distance–time graphs:

- drawing and labelling a pair of coordinate axes
- plotting points and joining them accurately with straight lines
- reading the scales on the axes.

Students will determine average speed by finding the change in distance over a period of time and carrying out a suitable division. They should be able to label and describe an object's motion using a distance–time graph.

Volume and temperature Students will watch demonstrations to see how volume and temperature affect gas pressure, and how depth affects liquid pressure. They will also investigate why some objects float and some objects sink. Talk about the different skills they will practise, such as presenting observations and data (including graphs); paying attention to objectivity and concern for accuracy, precision, repeatability, and reproducibility; making predictions using scientific knowledge, and understanding and planning the most appropriate type of scientific enquiries to test predictions.

Common learning misconceptions

- Pressure and force are the same thing. (A force is a push or a pull that can change the speed, shape, or direction of an object. Pressure is the measure of how much force is acting on a given area.)
- Pressure arises from moving liquids or gases.
- Moving fluids cause higher pressures.
- Pressure in liquids and gases can be stronger in one direction than another.
- Objects float in water because they are light and sink because they are heavy. (Floating or sinking is

dependent on the area of the object in contact with the water and the amount of upthrust produced.)

- Gas pressure is caused by collisions between gas particles.
- Air does not exert a force because it is too light. (Air has mass so it exerts a force.)
- Pressure only acts downwards. (Pressure acts in all directions.)

Broader context

Forces are all around us and they impact us in some way every second of our lives. Every time we move, we are surrounded by particles bumping into us and causing friction. This friction opposes our motion.

We also use forces to speed up or slow down. It is important to measure motion accurately to calculate how much fuel a rocket needs to reach space and come back safely, or even to get to class on time.

Physics links

- speed and the quantitative relationship between average speed, distance, and time (speed = distance ÷ time)
- relative motion: trains and cars passing one another

Working scientifically links

- apply mathematical concepts and calculate results
- present observations and data using appropriate methods, including tables and graphs
- pay attention to objectivity and concern for accuracy and precision

Learning objective	Learning outcomes		
	Developing	Secure	Extending
Calculate average speed	Identify the correct units for speed, distance, and time	**Calculate average speed**	Change the subject of the speed equation to calculate distance and time
Describe the difference between average and instantaneous speed	Identify examples of average and instantaneous speed	**Describe the difference between average and instantaneous speed**	Compare the average and instantaneous speeds on different sections of the same journey
Describe examples of relative motion	Identify situations in which relative motion is seen	**Describe examples of relative motion**	Compare relative motion of objects in an unfamiliar situation

Tier 2 vocabulary	Tier 3 vocabulary
average speed, speed	instantaneous speed, metres per second (m/s), relative motion

Digital resources

Activity: *Calculating speed* (Activity sheet, Support sheet, Teacher and technician notes)

Student Book answers

Think back 1 metre (m) **2** second (s) **3** Write out the equation, including any units; put/substitute the values (numbers) into the equation; calculate the answer; write the unit.

In-text questions A m/s **B** Just before it hits the ground **C** 80 km/h

See p.216 for the answers to the **Summary questions** for this lesson.

Getting started

Show students images of a car, a cheetah, and a person going downhill on a bike. Ask students to *think pair share*: *Which object has the fastest speed? What does speed mean? Why is it important that we can work out the speed of an object?* Discuss students' answers and explain that speed is a measure of how far something can travel in a particular time, and can be measured in different units.

Instantaneous and average speed Discuss the ideas of instantaneous speed and average speed. Show students the equations for speed and average speed, and work through the example of calculating speed in the Maths skills box.

Relative motion Ask: *Have you ever been travelling in a car on the motorway when a motorbike overtakes you? If the motorbike overtaking you is travelling at 113 km/h (70mph) and you are travelling at 105 km/h (65 mph), why does it seem like the motorbike is travelling much slower than 113 km/h?* Explain that relative motion means how fast one object is travelling compared with another.

Main activity

Activity: Calculating speed Students work in pairs to time each other moving a set distance in different ways, calculate their average speeds, and then answer the questions that follow.

Review and reflect

Ask students to peer mark their questions and use different coloured pens to make comments and improvements.

Language support

Write the term 'relative motion' on the board and look at the two words separately. Ask students who their relatives are. These are family members, so 'relative' implies a connection or dependency. Then elicit from students the meaning of motion. They should remember that it means movement. Therefore, relative motion is a measurement of an object's motion compared with that of another object (either stationary or moving).

Physics link

- the representation of a journey on a distance–time graph

Working scientifically links

- apply mathematical concepts and calculate results
- present observations and data using appropriate methods, including graphs

Learning objective	Learning outcomes		
	Developing	Secure	Extending
Interpret a distance–time graph	Label a distance–time graph with descriptions of an object's motion	**Interpret a distance–time graph**	Explain why a distance–time graph matches a specific journey
Use data from a distance–time graph to calculate average speed	Identify areas of different speeds on a distance–time graph	**Use data from a distance–time graph to calculate average speed**	Calculate instantaneous speed on a distance–time graph

Tier 2 vocabulary	Tier 3 vocabulary
acceleration	distance–time graph

Digital resources

Activity: *Plotting motion graphs* (Activity sheet, Support sheet, Teacher and technician notes)
Video: *Motion*

Student Book answers

Think back 1 speed (m/s) = distance travelled (m) ÷ time taken (s) **2** instantaneous speed = speed at a certain time; average speed = total distance ÷ total time **3** 1–2 m/s

In-text questions A The slopes do not change.
B a straight line that is shallower than the line for the car
C instantaneous

See p.216 for the answers to the **Summary questions** for this lesson.

Getting started

Ask students: *Describe your journey to school. What was your average speed?* Explain that you can tell the story of a journey and work out your speed using a distance–time graph.

Distance–time graphs: walking Show students the simple distance–time graph in Figure 1 in the Student Book of a girl walking to school. Ask them to work in pairs to describe the journey, using whiteboards.

Share answers, then ask: *What would the graph look like if Lucy accelerated (walked faster)?*

Distance–time graphs: accelerating Show students the graph showing acceleration in Figure 7. The slope changes gradually, not suddenly. Instantaneous speed at a certain time can be worked out by drawing a tangent to the curve at that time and calculating the gradient of the tangent.

Main activity

Activity: Plotting motion graphs Students plot a graph of a bus journey to school and answer questions to describe the journey.

Review and reflect

Watch the video on Kerboodle to consolidate students' learning.

Language support

A formula triangle can help students remember how to calculate speed. Encourage them to make their own to help them understand and visualize the relationship between speed, distance, and time.

3.3 Pressure in gases

Physics link

- atmospheric pressure decreases with increase of height, as weight of air above decreases with height

Working scientifically link

- interpret observations and data, including identifying patterns and using observations, measurements, and data to draw conclusions

Learning objective	Learning outcomes		
	Developing	Secure	Extending
Describe how volume and temperature affect gas pressure	Identify factors that affect gas pressure	**Describe how volume and temperature affect gas pressure**	Explain how changing particular factors affects gas pressure
Describe atmospheric pressure	Give the cause of atmospheric pressure	**Describe atmospheric pressure**	Compare the atmospheric pressure of different planets
Describe how atmospheric pressure changes with height	Identify altitudes and different locations at which atmospheric pressure will be higher or lower	**Describe how atmospheric pressure changes with height**	Use the particle model to explain why changing altitude affects atmospheric pressure

Tier 2 vocabulary	Tier 3 vocabulary
compressed, density	atmospheric pressure, gas pressure

Digital resources

Activity: *Observing pressure in gases* (Activity sheet, Support sheet, Teacher and technician notes)

Student Book answers

Think back 1 air resistance/drag **2** where opposing forces do not cancel out **3** They speed up.

In-text questions A It expands/gets bigger. **B** It increases. **C** The mass is bigger at the bottom of the mountain than it is at the top.

See p.216 for the answers to the **Summary questions** for this lesson.

Getting started

Blowing up a balloon Start to blow up a balloon and ask: *What will happen if I blow into it too much? Why do you think this will happen?* Encourage students to use ideas about particles. Write ideas on the board but do not say if they are correct at this stage as you will return to it later.

Collapsing bottle Demonstrate the 'collapsing bottle' or 'collapsing can' experiment. Discuss what happens to the water in the bottle or can when it is heated. Ask: *Why does the bottle/can collapse?* Write ideas on the board for discussion.

Pressure in gases Indicating to the balloon and the bottle (or can), ask: *What causes gas pressure?* Discuss students' ideas before providing an explanation. Discuss any misconceptions, such as: gas pressure is caused by collisions between gas particles.

Main activity

Activity: Observing pressure in gases
Invite volunteers to help with the air pressure demonstrations outlined in the Teacher and technician notes. For each demonstration, ask: *Can you describe what is happening?* Explain that air pressure is important as it explains, for example, weather patterns and how aeroplanes can fly. Ask: *What causes air pressure? Why don't we feel the air pushing on us? Is atmospheric pressure the same everywhere?* Discuss any misconceptions, such as: air does not exert a force because it is too light; pressure only acts downwards.

For the 'two balloons' experiment outlined in the Teacher and technician notes, ask students to *think pair share*: *Why is the balloon from the freezer smaller than the balloon at room temperature?* Then show a video of a balloon being put into liquid nitrogen and ask the same question. Write ideas on the board. Encourage students to comment on and add to the ideas.

Use Figure 2 in the Student Book to explain how pressure and temperature are linked.

For the final experiment, when you are demonstrating the effect of increasing the pressure on the volume of a small balloon in a sealed syringe, ask: *Why does the balloon get smaller?* Use Figure 3 in the Student Book to explain how pressure and volume are linked.

Review and reflect

Revisit the questions from the beginning of the lesson. Ask students to improve their answers. Then show the 'magic egg' demonstration. Ask students to write a simple explanation individually, then in pairs, and then in groups of four, before creating one final explanation and sharing it with the class.

Language support

See if students can recall the word 'atmosphere'. This is a mixture of gases that surround Earth. Using this knowledge, what do they think atmospheric pressure is? This is the force of the air above the surface of Earth as gravity pulls the air particles towards Earth.

Physics link

- pressure in liquids increasing with depth; upthrust effects, floating and sinking

Working scientifically links

- ask questions and develop a line of enquiry based on observations of the real world, alongside prior knowledge and experience
- make predictions using scientific knowledge and understanding

Learning objective	Learning outcomes		
	Developing	Secure	Extending
Describe how liquids exert a pressure in all directions	Describe how particles cause pressure	**Describe how liquids exert a pressure in all directions**	Apply knowledge of liquid pressure to unfamiliar situations
Describe how liquid pressure changes with depth	Identify areas in which liquid pressure is greater	**Describe how liquid pressure changes with depth**	Use the particle model to explain why liquid pressure changes with depth
Explain why some everyday objects float and some sink	Identify objects that will float or sink	**Explain why some everyday objects float and some sink**	Compare floating and sinking in unfamiliar liquids

Tier 2 vocabulary	Tier 3 vocabulary
	incompressible, liquid pressure, upthrust

Digital resources

Activity: *Floating and sinking* (Activity sheet, Support sheet, Teacher and technician notes)
Video: *Pressure in gases and liquids*

Student Book answers

Think back 1 collisions between gas particles and a surface **2** It increases/gets bigger. **3** the upwards force of water or air on an object

In-text questions A 90° **B** There is little space between the particles in a liquid, so it cannot be compressed. There is a lot of space between particles in a gas, so it can be compressed. **C** The ship has a large area in contact with the water.

See p.217 for the answers to the **Summary questions** for this lesson.

Getting started

Show students a polystyrene cup and ask: *How can you use water to squash the cup without touching it?* Share some students' answers and discuss why water exerts a pressure and why a submarine is not squashed at the bottom of the sea.

Pressure in liquids Ask: *What happens when you try to compress a sealed syringe with air inside, or one with water inside?* Invite a volunteer to try. Ask students to *think pair share*: *Why can you compress a gas but not a liquid?* Encourage students to use ideas about particles in their answers.

Floating and sinking Show students a selection of different objects, such as a stone, a rubber bung, a leaf, a table tennis ball, a cork, a coin, an eraser, and a plastic bottle. Ask: *Can you explain which of these objects will float in water and which will sink?* Students are likely to explain floating in terms of density. Discuss any misconceptions, such as: heavy things sink and light things float.

Show students a simple image of a boat on water, with force arrows labelled with upthrust and weight, to explain upthrust. Alternatively, you can use Figure 5 in the Student Book.

Main activity

Show students two same-sized plastic bottles: one with a number of holes at the same depth, the other with three holes vertically down one side. Block the holes and fill the bottles with water. Ask students to predict what will happen when the holes are unblocked.

Ask: *What does this tell you about pressure in liquids?* Sketch simple diagrams of the two bottles on the board, showing how the water comes out of the holes

at 90° and then falls due to the force of gravity. The flows of water from the holes lower down in the bottle come out with greater force and travel further than the ones higher up. Explain that this shows that the deeper you go, the greater the liquid pressure. This is because the weight of the liquid above is greater.

Activity: Floating and sinking Working in pairs, students investigate how to make a lump of modelling clay float, then explain their observations.

Review and reflect

Discuss students' observations from the activity to check their understanding of why objects float and sink. Ask: *How is it possible for a very heavy oil tanker to float?*

You can also watch the video on Kerboodle to consolidate students' learning.

Language support

Ask students to press their hand on their desk. Can they change the shape of the desk or squash it? (No.) Explain that the desk must be incompressible. Write the word on the board and say it together a few times. Elicit or explain

that the verb 'compress' means to press or squash into a smaller shape, and the prefix 'in-' means not (see also the example 'insoluble'), so the key word 'incompressible' means that it cannot be compressed or squashed.

Physics link

- pressure measured by ratio of force over area – acting normal to any surface

Working scientifically links

- ask questions and develop a line of enquiry based on observations of the real world, alongside prior knowledge and experience
- make predictions using scientific knowledge and understanding
- plan the most appropriate types of scientific enquiry to test predictions

Learning objective	Learning outcomes		
	Developing	Secure	Extending
Describe pressure on a solid, and give the direction that it acts in	Identify situations in which pressure is acting on a solid	**Describe pressure on a solid, and give the direction that it acts in**	Describe the relationship between pressure and force, and between pressure and area
Calculate pressure	Identify the units of pressure, force, and area	**Calculate pressure**	Change the subject of the pressure equation to calculate force or area
Describe situations where high or low pressures are useful	Identify situations in which pressure is higher or lower	**Describe situations where high or low pressures are useful**	Explain the effect of changing area or force on pressure

Tier 2 vocabulary	Tier 3 vocabulary
pressure	newtons per metre squared (N/m²), pascal (Pa)

Digital resources

Activity: *Investigating pressure on solids* (Activity sheet, Support sheet, Teacher and technician notes)
Video: *Pressure on solids*

Student Book answers

Think back 1 at right angles, 90° to the surface **2** newton (N) **3** centimetre squared (cm²); metre squared (m²)

In-text questions A It is the same; they are all at right angles/90°. **B** N/m², N/cm², pascal (Pa) **C** Wide straps have a big area, so the weight is spread over a larger area, making a smaller pressure.

See p.217 for the answers to the **Summary questions** for this lesson.

Getting started

Show students the image of a footprint in Figure 1 in the Student Book and ask: *What causes these footprints to be made?* Discuss students' ideas and explain that a person has exerted pressure on the surface. Then demonstrate a balloon popping when pressed against one drawing pin, but show that it does not pop when pressed against several pins at the same time. Ask students to *think pair share* why the balloon does not pop, but do not tell them the correct answer at this stage. Discuss any misconceptions, such as: pressure only acts downwards.

Calculating pressure Ask students to *think pair share*: *Suggest how more/less pressure can be exerted so that the footprints are deeper/shallower. The legs on a table make dents in the carpet. What can you do to stop this happening?*

Guide discussion towards the equation to calculate pressure. Work through the example of a box with a weight of 35.2 N placed on the floor. The area of the box in contact with the floor is 2.2 m². Calculate the pressure exerted by the box on the floor.

High and low pressure Show students images of a polar bear on ice, a camel in the desert, a knife, and a drawing pin. Ask: *Why do some of the objects have a large area in contact with the surface and some have a small area?* Encourage students to use ideas about force/weight and pressure in their answers.

Main activity

Activity: Investigating pressure on solids In pairs, students predict if the pressure they exert on the ground is greater when they stand on one foot or on both feet. Students plan the method for their investigation (and, if time, carry it out), before answering the questions that follow. Be aware that students may be uncomfortable weighing themselves in front of others.

Review and reflect

Discuss students' observations from the activity to check their understanding. Students peer review their investigation plan. Then return to the questions at the beginning of the lesson to see if students want to change, or can develop, their answers explaining different scenarios involving pressure on a solid.

You can also watch the video on Kerboodle to consolidate students' learning.

Language support

Remind students that we measure force in newtons. It is named after the scientist Sir Isaac Newton. When it is written out in full, it has a lower-case 'n' (e.g. one newton). However, the symbol has an upper-case 'N' (e.g. 1 N).

Physics link
- moment as the turning effect of a force

Working scientifically links
- interpret observations and data, including identifying patterns and using observations, measurements, and data to draw conclusions
- pay attention to objectivity and concern for repeatability and reproducibility

Learning objective	Learning outcomes		
	Developing	Secure	Extending
Define the moment of a force	Identify scenarios in which there will be the turning effect of a force	**Define the moment of a force**	Explain turning effects of forces in unfamiliar situations
Calculate the moment of a force	Give the units of moment, distance from a pivot, and force	**Calculate the moment of a force**	Change the subject of the moment equation to calculate a force or the distance from a pivot
Apply the law of moments	Identify situations in which moments are balanced or unbalanced	**Apply the law of moments**	Apply the law of moments to unfamiliar situations

Tier 2 vocabulary	Tier 3 vocabulary
pivot	centre of gravity, centre of mass, law of moments, moment, newton-metre (Nm)

Digital resources

Practical: *Measuring moments* (Practical sheet, Support sheet, Teacher and technician notes)
Video: *Moments*

Student Book answers

Think back 1 work done (J) = force (N) × distance in the direction of the force (m) **2** far apart **3** balanced = no net force; unbalanced = net force

In-text questions A Work is force × distance moved in the direction of the force; a moment is force × distance moved perpendicular to the force. **B** The large apple exerts a bigger force, so has to be placed at a smaller distance from the pivot to balance a smaller force at a larger distance. **C** The point of the pencil, which acts as the pivot, is very narrow. It is difficult to position the pencil's centre of gravity, halfway up the pencil shaft, above the pivot. Usually, the centre of gravity is left or right of the pivot, so the pencil falls.

See p.217 for the answers to the **Summary questions** for this lesson.

Getting started

Show the image of the tightrope walker in Figure 1, and the image of a paint tin being opened with a screwdriver in Figure 3 in *2.7 Energy transfer: forces*, in the Student Book. Ask students to *think pair share*: *Why does the tightrope walker use a long pole? Why is a screwdriver being used to open the tin lid?*

Challenge a volunteer to push the classroom door shut using one finger close to the hinges, and then to compare it with pushing the door shut using one finger near the handle. Discuss the student's observations and introduce the idea of a pivot and a moment (the turning effect of a force).

Main activity

Calculating moments Show students examples of levers, such as using a screwdriver to lift the lid of a paint tin. Explain that they are 'force multipliers' – a larger force acts than is supplied. Ask students to suggest two ways in which the force on the paint tin lid can be increased. Guide discussion to the conclusion that the longer the lever, and the further the effort force acts from the pivot, the greater the force on the paint tin lid. This can be demonstrated using, for example, screwdrivers of different lengths to lift the paint tin lid. Discuss any misconceptions, such as: a bigger turning effect occurs when the force is near to the pivot. Introduce the equation for the moment of a force and work through the example in Figure 4 in the Student Book.

Unstable objects Challenge volunteers to stand up straight next to a wall, with their heels, back, and head against the wall. They must then bend forward to touch their toes, but while keeping their heels and bottom against the wall. Ask: *Can you do this*

without falling over? Why? Write some ideas on the board without saying if they are correct at this stage. Encourage students to comment on each other's ideas.

Challenge another volunteer to decide if it is easier to topple a marker pen stood on its end, or a Bunsen burner stood upright. Ask students if they can explain why.

Centre of gravity Use students' ideas to introduce the term 'centre of gravity' (mass) and its position with respect to the pivot for a stable and an unstable object.

Practical: Measuring moments Introduce the terms 'clockwise moments' and 'anticlockwise moments'. Demonstrate how to set up the equipment for the practical. Students work in pairs to investigate the law of moments, before answering the questions that follow.

Review and reflect

Ask pairs of students to discuss their observations about the law of moments. Then ask them to join with another pair, and then with another four students to draw a final conclusion. Share conclusions with

the class. Ask students to identify if their results are reproducible and explain why.

You can also watch the video on Kerboodle to consolidate students' learning.

Language support

To introduce students to the new vocabulary, you could show them how to make a see-saw using a ruler and another object to balance it on, such as a pencil or an eraser. Explain that this is called the pivot in science.

Using this demonstration and the ones suggested above, help them understand that a moment is a measure of the turning effect of a force. Model using the key words regularly throughout these demonstrations.

Getting started

Encourage students to review their learning in this chapter. The 'Summary questions' in the Student Book can be used formatively during lessons. For the 'What have I learned?' pages, students can answer the questions one at a time after each topic, or as a single summative activity. This could be done as a whole-class or group activity, or set as an independent task.

Whichever approach is adopted, the questions are designed to give you and students feedback about progress and identify targets for development.

Student reflection

Allow students time to reflect on how confident they feel about each topic. Remind them to use the learning objectives provided in their Student Book for guidance. They should focus on whether there were any questions they found difficult or easy, and on how well they prepared for the summative assessment at the end of the chapter. Listen to and deal with students' reflections sensitively so that they feel comfortable to report areas they are not confident with.

Learning objectives and learning outcomes

Each lesson is guided by the learning *objectives*. The learning objectives are provided at the beginning of each topic in the Student Book. They outline what students are going to learn in each topic.

In contrast, the learning *outcomes* in this Teacher's Guide are statements that describe the knowledge or skills that students should acquire by the end of each topic. They are linked to the learning objectives, but are *not* often seen by students. The learning outcomes are used by teachers to assess and measure if or how each learning objective has been achieved.

Answer key

Chapter 3: Motion and pressure

1 for example: balanced – a car travelling at constant speed; unbalanced – a car accelerating or decelerating
2 liquid – particles are in a random arrangement, moving freely but still touching their neighbours; gas – particles are in a random arrangement, far apart, and moving quickly
3 $10 \times 10 = 100 \text{ cm}^2$; $10 \times 20 = 200 \text{ cm}^2$

3.1 Speed

Maths skills: $42/2.5 = 16.8 \text{ km/h}$
1 distance travelled, time taken, total distance, total time, instantaneous, relative
2 average speed = total distance ÷ total time
$= 100 \text{ m} \div 12.5 \text{ s} = 8 \text{ m/s}$
3 Their relative motion is 70 km/h away from each other.
4 a speed = distance/time
speed × time = distance × time/time
speed × time/speed = distance/speed
time = distance/speed

b distance = 6 km, = 6000 m
sound: time = 6000 m/330 m/s = 18 seconds
light: time = 5000 m/300 000 000 m/s = 0.000 02 s

3.2 Motion graphs

1 distance, time, gradient, stationary, increasing
2 a distance = 4000 m – 2400 m = 1600 m
time = 45 min – 35 min = 10 min = 10 × 60 = 600 s
speed = distance ÷ time = 1600 m ÷ 600 s = 2.67 m/s
b 0 m/s
3 a Both graphs start at a distance of zero and finish at a distance of 3 km, because the students travel the same total distance
b The slope of the graph for the car is steeper than that for the person walking because the car travels faster than the person.

3.3 Pressure in gases

1 collide with, bigger, smaller, smaller, fewer
2 a There is less oxygen as you go up a mountain because gas pressure is reduced. The density of oxygen is low.

b It would take up too much space if it were not compressed. The oxygen pressure will be very high if the gas is compressed.

3 a The pressure decreases. The particles are not colliding with the sides of the can so much because the steam has condensed to water.

b The atmospheric (water) pressure outside the can is higher than the pressure inside. The atmospheric pressure from the outside exerts a force on all sides of the can and it collapses.

3.4 Pressure in liquids

Literacy skills: Objects, like a passenger boat, float when the upthrust force balances the weight of the object. The area of the boat in contact with the water is big enough to produce enough upthrust.

1 all, increases, weight, bigger, upthrust

2 a Water pressure from the bottom creates the force upthrust. The clay boat floats because the upthrust balances out the weight of the boat.

b The area of the ball in contact with the water is too small, so there is not enough upthrust to make it float. The force pushing down is greater than the force of upthrust pushing up.

3 a It increases.

b The difference in pressure between the top and the bottom of the ball produces a (upthrust) force that depends on the area of the ball in contact with the water. When you let the ball go the upthrust is bigger than its weight so the ball moves up.

3.5 Pressure on solids

Maths skills: B force = pressure x area

1 force, area, big, small, N/m^2

2 area of two hands = $150\ cm^2 \times 2 = 300\ cm^2$
pressure = force ÷ area = $600\ N \div 300\ cm^2 = 2\ N/cm^2$

3 a force = pressure × area
= $101\ 000\ N/m^2 \times 1.5\ m^2$
= $151\ 500\ N$

b $151\ 500\ N/1000\ N$ per panda = 151 pandas

c The air is exerting a force in all directions, not just downwards, so the air inside the car exerts a force upwards to balance the downwards force.

3.6 Turning forces

Maths skills: Mother's weight is 4x greater than child's, so mother could sit at 0.5 m and child at 2 m (0.5 × 4 = 2).
mother = 600 × 0.5 = 300 Nm; child = 150 × 2 = 300 Nm

1 turning, force, distance, equilibrium, law, weight, gravity

2 moment = force × distance
= $5\ N \times 0.75\ m$
= 3.75 Nm

a The girl would have to move closer to the pivot. The boy's moment has been reduced because the distance to the pivot is smaller, so she would need to reduce her moment to maintain equilibrium.

b There are now two clockwise moments on the see-saw. The girl would need to move further from the pivot so that there is a bigger anticlockwise moment to balance it.

What have I learned about motion and pressure?

1 m/s, [1 mark] mph, [1 mark] km/s [1 mark]

2 B [1 mark]

3 a i B [1 mark]
ii D [1 mark]

b Speed = distance/time [1 mark]
= 200 m/40 s [1 mark]
= 5 m/s [1 mark]

c At B, the cyclist is stationary. [1 mark] At C, the cyclist is moving at constant speed. [1 mark] At D, the cyclist is moving at a faster speed. [1 mark]

4 a 90° [1 mark]

b There is a difference in pressure between the top and bottom of the balloon [1 mark] and force = pressure × area, so there is a buoyancy force/upthrust on the balloon. [1 mark]

c If the balloon were smaller, the difference in pressure and the area would be smaller, [1 mark] so the force would be smaller. [1 mark]

5 a P = F/A [1 mark]
= $700\ N/200\ cm^3$ [1 mark]
= 3.5 [1 mark] N/cm^3 [1 mark]

b It will halve [1 mark], since the area is double, so the pressure is half. [1 mark]

c The area of their feet is smaller. [1 mark]

6 a clockwise moment = force × distance = 1.5 N × 0.3 m [1 mark] = 0.45 Nm [1 mark]

b anticlockwise moment = 0.45 Nm = force (exerted by muscle) × 0.03 m [1 mark]
force exerted by muscle = 0.45 Nm ÷ 0.03 m = 15 N [1 mark]

c The force is bigger because anticlockwise moment = clockwise moment (for the system to remain balanced). [1 mark] The distance from the pivot is much less. [1 mark]

7 Students should be marked on the use of good English, organization of information, spelling and grammar, and correct use of specialist scientific terms. The best answers will explain in detail how a bag of crisps appears to expand at a higher altitude. [6 marks maximum]
Examples of correct scientific points:
The bag of crisps contains air. Air molecules collide with the inside of the bag. Air molecules in the atmosphere collide with the outside of the bag. If the pressure is the same inside and outside the bag, the bag does not get bigger. Atmospheric pressure decreases with height, because gravity pulls the air molecules down. There are fewer collisions between air molecules and objects as you go higher. The air pressure inside the plane is less than the air pressure on the ground (inside the crisp packet), so the bag gets bigger.

8 a There is no turning force [1 mark] because the weight of the plank acts through the shoulder. [1 mark]

b The weight produces a moment about the new pivot. [1 mark] The person will need to exert a moment in the opposite direction, [1 mark] so the moments are equal. [1 mark] (An example of a moment in the opposite direction could be: the person pushes down on the opposite end of the plank.)

Index

Great Clarendon Street, Oxford, OX2 6DP, United Kingdom

Oxford University Press is a department of the University of Oxford.
It furthers the University's objective of excellence in research,
scholarship, and education by publishing worldwide. Oxford is a
registered trade mark of Oxford University Press in the UK and in
certain other countries.

British Library Cataloguing in Publication Data
Data available

978-1-38-203645-0

10 9 8 7 6 5 4 3 2 1

Paper used in the production of this book is a natural, recyclable
product made from wood grown in sustainable forests.

The manufacturing process conforms to the environmental regulations
of the country of origin.

Printed and bound by CPI Group (UK) Ltd, Croydon, CR0 4YY

Acknowledgements
Reviewer: Deborah Roberts

Cover illustration: Ángel Svoboda

Artwork by Q2A media

Every effort has been made to contact copyright holders of material
reproduced in this book. Any omissions will be rectified in subsequent
printings if notice is given to the publisher.

Links to third party websites are provided by Oxford in good faith
and for information only. Oxford disclaims any responsibility for the
materials contained in any third party website referenced in this work.